LEAP OVER A WALL

LEAP OVER A WALL

EARTHY SPIRITUALITY
FOR EVERYDAY CHRISTIANS

Yea, by thee I can crush a troop,
and by my God I can leap over a wall.

—2 SAMUEL 22:30

EUGENE H. PETERSON

This Billy Graham Evangelistic Association
special edition is published with permission
from HarperCollins Publishers, Inc.

HarperSanFrancisco
A Division of HarperCollins*Publishers*

Grateful acknowledgment is made to the following
for permission to reprint previously published material:

From "Why Should Not Old Men Be Mad?" by W. B. Yeats.
Reprinted with permission of Simon & Schuster from
The Poems of W. B. Yeats: A New Edition, edited by Richard J. Finneran.
Copyright 1940 by Georgie Yeats. Copyright renewed © 1968 by
Bertha Georgie Yeats, Michael Butler Yeats, and Anne Yeats.

Excerpt from "Murder in the Cathedral" by T. S. Eliot, copyright 1935 by
Harcourt Brace & Company and renewed 1963 by T. S. Eliot,
reprinted by permission of the publisher.

HarperCollins®, ▦®, and HarperSanFrancisco™
are trademarks of HarperCollins Publishers Inc.

Library of Congress Cataloging-in-Publication Data
Peterson, Eugene H.
Leap over a wall : earthy spirituality for everyday Christians /
Eugene H. Peterson.
Includes bibliographical references.
ISBN 0-913367-07-9

1. David, King of Israel.
2. Bible. O.T. 1 Samuel XVI–1 Kings II—Criticism, interpretation, etc.
3. Bible. O.T.—Biography.   I. Title.

For Leif

love words . . . love mountains

Contents

Acknowledgments
and a Note to the Reader

I have been fortunate in having lived and worked among people who have loved God's word in stories and listened to me tell those stories in a number of different ways and settings: the congregation of Christ Our King Presbyterian Church (Bel Air, Maryland), students at Regent College (Vancouver, Canada), and assorted gatherings of people in retreats and conferences, colleges and seminaries across North America. The intensity and prayer with which so many of them listened, entered into, and responded to these seminal, spirit-shaping David stories in turn yielded insights that eventually got worked into the storytelling itself.

Two persons in particular stand out: Hebrew scholar Walter E. Brown, in his careful reading of the manuscript and generous exegetical remarks that so much improved the accuracy of my writing; and artist Louise Wheatley, in making works of art from these stories, both in her textiles and in her life.

• • •

THE REVISED STANDARD VERSION (RSV) of the Scriptures has been used throughout. Exceptions are noted in the text. The Gospel epigraphs for each chapter and the Psalms that are inserted at appropriate places in the text are from *The Message: New Testament with Psalms and Proverbs* (NavPress, 1995).

LEAP OVER A WALL

STORIES

DAVID AND JESUS

1 Samuel 16 to 1 Kings 2

All Jesus did that day was tell stories—a long
storytelling afternoon. His storytelling fulfilled the
prophecy:

> *I will open my mouth and tell stories;*
> *I will bring out into the open*
> *things hidden since the world's first day.*

—MATTHEW 13:34–35

I HAD A STORYTELLING MOTHER and heard these David stories
first from her. I usually heard them at bedtime, but there were other occasions also that provided containers for story: thunderstorms in the
summer and blizzards in the winter were storytelling times. To this day,
winter and summer storms and the darkness that nudges toward sleep

are redolent with story. My mother was good with words; she was also good with *tones*. In her storytelling I not only saw whole worlds come into being, I felt them within me through the timbre of her voice.

She told stories of her parents, who had brought eleven children from Norway to the sparsely populated but promised land of Montana to begin a new life. In the first few years after their settling in, she and her sister were born, making thirteen in all. By the time I was born, her parents and some of her brothers and sisters were dead; but they never seemed dead—the stories kept them alive in me. Norwegian trolls and giants got mixed into the storytelling as well. There were times when I wasn't sure where the trolls left off and my uncles began. The whole enterprise took on a huge mythological grandeur.

Mostly, though, she told Bible stories. And among Bible stories, the David stories took pride of place—not to the exclusion of Moses and Elijah and Jesus, but something in her narrative imagination kicked in with extra energy in the David stories. The David stories formed the basic groundplan for learning about and understanding what it meant to grow up human and Christian. In those stories, the two words— *human* and *Christian*—became synonyms.

When I was older and reading the Bible for myself, I was surprised, but also a little disappointed, to find that some of the details that I loved most were extracanonical. She didn't scruple, I realized, to considerably improve the biblical version when she felt like it. But I also realized, in my adult assessment of her narrative practice, that she rarely, if ever, violated or distorted the story itself. She held the entire Story, from Genesis to Revelation, in her believing imagination, with Jesus as the central and controlling presence throughout. However many details she got wrong (or invented), she never got the Story wrong—she knew it inside and out, knew Jesus obediently, the Holy Spirit reliving these texts in her as she prayed her way through the years in our Montana valley.

In later life I realized how fortunate I had been under this tutelage, for the David stories have been used in exactly such ways throughout much of our Christian past: training the believing imagination to think *narratively*, immersing the praying imagination in *earthiness*.

THE DAVID STORY

Story is the primary way in which the revelation of God is given to us. The Holy Spirit's literary genre of choice is story. Story isn't a simple or naive form of speech from which we graduate to the more sophisticated, "higher" languages of philosophy or mathematics, leaving the stories behind for children and the less educated. From beginning to end, our Scriptures are primarily written in the form of story. The biblical story comprises other literary forms—sermons and genealogies, prayers and letters, poems and proverbs—but *story* carries them all in its capacious and organically intricate plot. Moses told stories; Jesus told stories; the four Gospel writers presented their good news in the form of stories. And the Holy Spirit weaves all this storytelling into the vast and holy literary architecture that reveals God to us as Father, Son, and Holy Spirit in the way that he chooses to make himself known. Story. To get this revelation right, we enter the story.

The David story is the most extensively narrated single story in this large story. We know more about David than any other person in Holy Scripture. As we tell and listen to the David story, we're at the same time being trained in the nature of story itself as the primary literary form for receiving God's revelation. The reason that story is so basic to us is that life itself has a narrative shape—a beginning and end, plot and characters, conflict and resolution. Life isn't an accumulation of abstractions such as love and truth, sin and salvation, atonement and holiness; life is the realization of details that all connect organically, personally, specifically: names and fingerprints, street numbers and local weather, lamb for supper and a flat tire in the rain. God reveals himself to us not in a metaphysical formulation or a cosmic fireworks display but in the kind of stories that we use to tell our children who they are and how to grow up as human beings, tell our friends who we are and what it's like to be human. Story is the most adequate way we have of accounting for our lives, noticing the obscure details that turn out to be pivotal, appreciating the subtle accents of color and form and scent that give texture to our actions and feelings, giving coherence to our meetings and relationships in work and family, finding our precise place in the neighborhood and in history. Story relishes sharp-edged, fresh-minted details; but story also discovers and reveals the substrata of meaning and purpose and design implicit in all the details. Small and large are accorded equal dignity and linked together in an easy camaraderie by means of story.

Because the David story takes up so much space in our Scriptures, giving sustained attention to one person, we find ourselves becoming accustomed to and unobtrusively trained in this skillful, revealing, dignifying storytelling. Somewhere along the way, most of us pick up bad habits of extracting from the Bible what we pretentiously call "spiritual principles," or "moral guidelines," or "theological truths," and then corseting ourselves in them in order to force a godly shape on our lives. That's a mighty uncomfortable way to go about improving our condition. And it's not the gospel way. *Story* is the gospel way. Story isn't imposed on our lives; it invites us into its life. As we enter and imaginatively participate, we find ourselves in a more spacious, freer, and more coherent world. We didn't know all this was going on! We had never noticed all this significance! If true—and the Bible is nothing if not true—story brings us into more reality, not less, expands horizons, sharpens both sight and insight. Story is the primary means we have for learning what the world is, and what it means to be a human being in it. No wonder that from the time we acquire the mere rudiments of language, we demand stories. More often than not, at least among Christians and Jews, the demand has been met by telling David stories.

DAVID AND GOD

What do these stories tell us about living this human life well, living it totally? Primarily and mostly they tell us that it means dealing with God. It means dealing with a lot of other things as well: danger and parents and enemies and friends and lovers and children and wives and pride and humiliation and rejection and siblings and sickness and death and sexuality and justice and fear and peace—to say nothing of diapers and faxes and breakfast and traffic jams and clogged drainpipes and bounced checks. But always, at the forefront and in the background of circumstances, events, and people, it's God. It's always God with whom we have to do. And the God with whom we have to do can never be dealt with in an antiseptic theological laboratory as a specialty of heaven, but only on this earth—". . . on *earth* as it is in heaven." Earth and the conditions of earth—weather, digestion, family, job, government—define the context in which we deal with God.

The David story is simultaneously earthy and godly. A common, maybe the most common, error in our quest to live well is to set up a model that we then attempt to emulate. The model shows us what we can become, a perfection to which we can aspire. But it also continuously shows us what we *aren't* yet, how far we have to go. After we try this for a while, it turns out that most of us don't have much good to say about models. They have an honored place in museums, and some of them seem to make a great deal of money posing for photographers and getting their pictures in magazines, but they don't seem to help us much in getting the hang of becoming human. The Bible is conspicuously lacking in models; what it's full of is stories—like the David story.

The David story, like most other Bible stories, presents us not with a polished ideal to which we aspire but with a rough-edged actuality in which we see humanity being formed—the *God* presence in the *earth/human* conditions. The David story immerses us in a reality that embraces the entire range of humanness, stretching from the deep interior of our souls to the farthest reach of our imaginations. No other biblical story has this range to it, showing the many dimensions of height, depth, breadth, and length of human experience as a person comes alive before God—aware of God, responsive to God. We're never more alive than when we're dealing with God. And there's a sense in which we aren't alive at all (in the uniquely human sense of "alive") until we're dealing with God. David deals with God. As an instance of humanity in himself, he isn't much. He has little wisdom to pass on to us on how to live successfully. He was an unfortunate parent and an unfaithful husband. From a purely historical point of view he was a barbaric chieftain with a talent for poetry. But David's importance isn't in his morality or his military prowess but in his experience of and witness to God. Every event in his life was a confrontation with God.[1]

We can't be human without God. That's what Christians believe. We believe that this human life is a great gift, that every part of it is designed by God and therefore means something, that every part of it is blessed by God and therefore to be enjoyed, that every part is accompanied by God and therefore workable.

We can't get away from God; he's there whether we like it or not, whether we know it or not. We can refuse to participate in God; we can act as if God weren't our designer, provider, and covenant presence. But when we refuse, we're less; our essential humanity is less. Our lives are diminished and impoverished.

And it's just this sense of *lessness* that gives us an important clue to understanding ourselves. We're aware of something we need or lack most of the time. We're not complete. We're not fully human. This sense of being unfinished is pervasive and accounts for a great deal that's distinctive in us humans. We then attempt to complete ourselves by getting more education or more money, going to another place or buying different clothes, searching out new experiences. The Christian gospel tells us that in and under and around all of these incompletions is God: God is who we need; the God-hunger, the God-thirst is the most powerful drive in us. It's far stronger than all the drives of sex, power, security, and fame put together.

And the David story is the most complete, detailed rendering of God-dimensioned humanity that we have, the common life that God uses to shape humanity to his glory. As the story develops, we see everything about us interpenetrated with God; our imaginations expand and we see what it means to live largely, aware of God's grace and beauty in every detail of which we're invited to participate in.

THE JESUS STORY

But the primary story in our storytelling Scriptures isn't David, but Jesus. Jesus is the pivotal story in God's revelation, the story that gathers all the other stories into its orbit, establishes the center, and provides the comprehensive coherence. Its foursquare centrality is articulated by four storytellers, each telling the same story, this Jesus story, but each in a distinctive way. Matthew, Mark, Luke, and John tell the story of Jesus, making clear that this is the story of God revealing himself in the person of Jesus: *God* revealing himself in a named *human being* in *our* history. In John's straightforward, no-nonsense language, "The Word was God . . . [and] became flesh and dwelt among us" (John 1:1, 14).

A surprising thing about the readers of this story is that, by and large, through the Christian centuries, we've had a harder time taking seriously the human elements of the story than the divine. It's been easier to believe that Jesus was God than that Jesus was human. For millennia, all over this planet earth, we've had gods aplenty. We're used to them. Divinity and the supernatural are old hat to us. But humanity is a mystery. We don't know what it means to be a woman, how to act like a man. And so when we're presented with a story in which God and the human come together in the same person, we make it easier for ourselves by minimizing or getting rid of the human and reading it as a purely God story. We love having gods around and telling stories about the gods, but God in a named, historical, flesh-and-blood human person who moves into our neighborhood—well, that's God too close for comfort.[2]

Jesus, revealing God to us, doesn't arrive on the scene out of the blue, unprecedented, like Athena stepping out of the head of Zeus, fully formed and in stately dignity. The revelation of Jesus Christ is foreshadowed and foretold, anticipated and prepared for, prophesied and promised throughout the nearly two thousand years of Hebrew history. St. Paul refers to this centuries-long "pregnancy" in his arresting phrase "when the time had fully come, God sent forth his Son, born of woman . . . " (Gal. 4:4). We're given a richly detailed orientation in the ways of God with us, God's word, God's act. Not just *that* God speaks and acts, but the *way* in which he speaks and acts, and the consummate unity of Word and Act. And what becomes abundantly evident in all this is that God's way is to immerse himself in history and invite men and women to freely participate in his ways. God doesn't stand outside the story and hurl thunderbolts into it. Humans are treated with immense respect in this story; they aren't just put up with but given an astonishing dignity. To put it a little differently, as our Scriptures reveal God to us as Father,

Son, and Spirit—these holy mysteries! these divine immensities!— *human* is never a term of denigration or dismissal but of honor. And in such company! But it's difficult to remain comfortable in this biblical affirmation, because *human,* for us humans, is so frequently experienced as dishonorable and wicked, flawed and foolish. Given our unhappy experience with so much of our humanity, it's hard to maintain respect for it and be patient with the human condition. It looks easier and far more attractive to specialize in something we're apt to call "spiritual," to throw all our efforts into trying to be "like gods," forgetting that that's how we got into all this trouble in the first place. But the brisk trafficking in gods and religion through the centuries—our own generation not excepted—provides no evidence that it improves competency in being human. If anything, it has a reverse effect: the more religious activity, the less human competency.

At the point that God's revelation becomes total and focused in Jesus, the Gospel writers take particular pains to make sure that we don't lose touch with the human. They insist on Jesus' real birth and real death, Jesus' eating of plain bread and speaking of plain words. But even so, it isn't easy to keep a grip on the human, for the birth was a virgin birth, the death was succeeded by a glorious resurrection, and there were a number of indisputably supernatural works that are a very natural part of the story. In the case of Jesus, human isn't *just* human.

The Evangelists' first task, of course, is to give witness that Jesus is God-with-us, "who for us and for our salvation came down from heaven."[3] And that they do. The Christian life begins at the point where Jesus is confessed as "Christ, Son of the living God" (Math 16:16). God. Supernatural. John speaks for his fellow Gospel writers when he sums up by saying, "[T]hese are written that you may believe that Jesus is the Christ, the Son of God, and that believing you may have life in his name" (John 20:31). But having gotten us to that place, to the head-realization and heart-belief that in Jesus we're dealing with the God who "made heaven and earth" and works our salvation, *then* the Evangelists must make sure we realize that our very humanity is the actual stuff that God uses in this work. The Gospel writers, having gotten us in touch with *God* in Jesus, now have to do their level best to keep us in touch with who *we* are in Jesus—our *human* selves. God doesn't take shortcuts to heaven, by-passing our troublesome humanity; and we had better not try either.

One of the unobtrusive but highly effective ways in which they do this is to keep introducing Jesus as "Son of David." That designation isn't an incidental detail of genealogy but a major item of theology—that is, it's about *God*. The David story anticipates the Jesus story. The Jesus story presupposes the David story. David. Why David? There are several strands that make up the answer, but prominent among them is David's earthiness. He's so emphatically human: David fighting, pray-ing, loving, sinning. David conditioned by the morals and assumptions of a brutal Iron Age culture. David with his eight wives. David angry; David devious; David generous; David dancing. There's nothing, ab-solutely nothing, that God can't and doesn't use to work his salvation and holiness into our lives. If we're going to get the most out of the Jesus story, we'll want first to soak our imaginations in the David story.

There was a moment, some years ago, when I realized with consid-erable astonishment that there isn't a single miracle in the David story. Not one. There's never any question but that God is at the center of the plot and always present (although usually silent and hidden) in the de-tails. But this is a story that never bypasses the ordinary, the everyday. David's humanity provides material that's worked on from the inside—quietly, insistently, hiddenly. The David story is a plunge into the earth-iness of our humanity.

As we follow Jesus and explore the life of salvation, we're frequently tempted by a variety of seductions to deny or avoid or denigrate ordi-nariness, the common way. We're incited to lust after miracle and ec-stasy, after flashy displays of the supernatural. Newcomers to this are often unaware of the thin ice they're walking on. Here's the danger: there are most emphatically miracles and ecstasy and the supernatural in the Christian life, but they're never an escape from our humanity, never a shortcut around our humanity. Generally, they're revealed from *within* our humanity. Austin Farrer once observed that none of us supposes that Jesus in the carpenter shop invoked the Holy Spirit to straighten a bent nail.[4] The entire meaning of the incarnation is that God *enters* our human condition, embraces it, comes to where we are to save us.

The David story serves to train us in the normative, in seeing, accepting, participating in the miracle hidden in the ordinary, the supernatural suffusing the natural. Thoroughly trained by David, we're not apt to impulsively discard our lifejackets and abandon daily meal preparation—supposing that this is the way to "deeper" or "higher" spiritual life—when Jesus walks on the water and feeds the five thousand.

EARTHY SPIRITUALITY

I've always had an aversion to what I call "boutique" spirituality, the "nice" religion that Henry James once criticized as "little more than cathedrals and mild social convenience."[5] I've found the David story, as so many have before me, a major means for recovering an earthy spirituality that's exuberantly holy; I then use it as a primer to the Jesus story (which is even more exuberantly holy).

This is a well-traveled road, this David story, but it hasn't been well traveled in our times. New roads to self-understanding, to life-discovery, to "spirituality" are being built by psychologists, politicians, economists, social engineers, philosophers, physicists, biologists; every expert in the country is setting up as an authority on spirituality! There are some things to be learned from many of these roadbuilders, but compared with the David/Jesus story, they're alleys and detours. And not a few of them are outright dead ends.

The streets of our cities and the pews of our churches are crowded these days with emaciated men and plastic women. "There are too many limp souls," notes R. P. Blackmur.[6] I want to keep company with the men and women who expand and deepen our capacity to live our true, God-created, Jesus-saved, Spirit-filled lives.

David attracts attention by his vigor, his energy, his wholeheartedness, his God-heartedness. In the middle of his wonderful Psalm 18 he shouts,

> *Yea, by thee I can crush a troop,*
> *And by my God I can leap over a wall!*

(Ps. 18:29)

The image of David vaulting the wall catches and holds my attention. David running, coming to a stone wall, and without hesitation leaping the wall and continuing on his way—running toward Goliath, running from Saul, pursuing God, meeting Jonathan, rounding up stray sheep, whatever, but running. And leaping. Certainly not strolling or loitering.

David's is a most exuberant story. Earthy spirituality characterizes his life and accounts for the exuberance.

Earthy: down-to-earth, dealing with everydayness, praying while doing the laundry, singing in the snarl of traffic.

Spiritual: moved and animated by the Spirit of God and therefore alive to God.

NAMES

DAVID AND SAMUEL

1 Samuel 16:1–13

*Jesus said, "God authorized and commanded me to
commission you: Go out and train everyone you meet,
far and near, in this way of life, marking them by
baptism in the threefold name: Father, Son, and Holy
Spirit."*

—MATTHEW 28:19

SAMUEL WAS AN OLD MAN with his beard down to his knees. I
learned this from my mother, from whom I first heard this story. He
was a thick, stocky man who from a distance looked like a fountain,
white hair pouring from his head.

There was an unhurried air about him, leisurely even. The kind of
relaxed leisureliness that flows from a person who knows what he's
about, who knows where he's going and what he's doing. No need for
hurry if you're confident in who you are.

He was headed for Bethlehem, a small town nearly identical with
the one we lived in, surrounded by forested hills that were ominous

with wild beasts. Three boys, out searching in the fields for Canaanite arrowheads—arrowheads were all the rage that year, and every boy in Bethlehem had his treasured collection—spotted him and ran back to town to report what they had seen. The news spread rapidly: God's prophet approaching the village! Legendary Samuel. Fierce and famous Samuel. Fear gripped every heart. What had they done wrong? Who had sinned? Samuel wasn't known for his casual, drop-in visits. His enormous reputation didn't rest on a lifetime of accumulated small talk. What terrible misdoing in Bethlehem requiring prophetic visitation had reached the ears of Samuel?

But the anxiety soon gave way to anticipation. Samuel let them know that he had come to lead them in festive worship, gather them in celebration before God. Word got around. The mood shifted from guilt to gaiety in no time. A heifer was killed and a barbecue pit prepared. Before long the entire village was caught up in something that resembled what I knew as the county fair, which arrived the first week in August and was the high point of every summer for me.

As she told the story, my mother didn't herself introduce carnival rides and kewpie dolls, cotton candy and the aroma of hot dogs into Iron Age Bethlehem, but she did nothing to interfere with my imagination. I filled in all the details required to make me fully at home in the story: calf-roping, bull-riding, the greased pig, a Ferris wheel, all my friends with their 4-H animals, cowgirls and cowboys from miles around resplendent in sequined shirts and shining boots.

• • •

AS IT TURNED OUT, there was more to Samuel's visit than a village-wide celebration as the people of God. A local farmer named Jesse and his eight sons were singled out for attention. Why Samuel was interested in Jesse and his sons wasn't made clear to the villagers, and very likely the general festivities in which everyone was caught up distracted people from noticing the prophet's interest in the Jesse family, which is exactly what they were intended to do. But *I* knew why Samuel was interested. The storyteller had confided in me; I had insider information. And it was this: Samuel was out looking for a replacement for King Saul.

Having located Jesse and his sons, Samuel proceeded to interview and examine each of them. I pictured this as taking place at the grandstand in the fairgrounds with Samuel, severe and venerable, out in the middle of the field at the judge's stand. Jesse brought his sons before Samuel one at a time, like prize farm animals on a halter. The grandstand was packed with spectators.

Eliab, the eldest son and a swaggering bully, was first. His mountainous size and rough-hewn good looks commanded attention. Samuel was impressed. (Who could *not* be impressed?) Hulking and brutish, Eliab was used to getting his own way by sheer force of muscle. He had a black mop of hair that he never bothered to brush. His nose wandered down his face looking, until it was almost too late, for a good place to stop. He dressed in bib overalls and wore hobnailed boots. He never changed his socks. It mattered little whether people liked or disliked what they saw—Eliab *dominated*. Clearly, here was a man who could get things done. Samuel, like everyone else in the community, was taken in by his appearance. But soon Samuel's God-trained prophetic eye penetrated the surface appearance to Eliab's interior. There he didn't see much to write home about. No king material within.

Abinadab, the next, was an intellectual snob. A tall, stringy beanpole, he stood before Samuel with sneering arrogance. He was the only brother who had been to college. He used big words, showing off his prestigious learning every chance he got. He had squinty eyes behind thick Coke-bottle glasses. Samuel dismissed him with a gesture.

Shammah, also called Shimea, was third. Shammah was a mincing little sophisticate in Calvin Klein jeans and alligator cowboy boots. He hated living in backwater Bethlehem. He could hardly get across the street without getting cow flop on his boots. Mingling with all these common people, with their vulgar games and coarse entertainment, was torture for him. He didn't know what Samuel was up to, but it looked as if it could be a ticket to a finer life—a life of culture and taste. But Samuel dismissed him with a shake of his head.

After the third son, the Bible quits naming.[1] It was years before I knew that, for my mother named them all. It didn't matter that the names departed substantially from Semitic sounds; they served her purposes and my imagination well enough. Ole was the fourth, then Gump, Klug, and finally Chugger. (Later in life, when I was reading the Bible for myself, I was frequently surprised by the omissions in the text. The Holy Spirit left out some of the best parts!) Proudly presented by Jesse, each stood before Samuel. As each, in turn, was rejected, tension built up—*this* son, certainly, would be chosen. Yet none was chosen.

The show was over. Jesse was pathetic in his disappointment. The seven sons were humiliated. The grandstand and bleacher crowds were starting to get restless, feeling gypped, some of them demanding their money back. They had paid a good price, after all, to see Samuel in his prophet appearance. And the performance had started off well enough as he got everyone's attention, skillfully building to a climax. And now this . . . this, *nothing*.

Samuel was bewildered. Had he missed a key element in God's message? Was he losing his prophetic edge? Did he have the right town? "This *is* Bethlehem, isn't it?" Did he have the right family? "You *are* Jesse, aren't you?"

Well—there must be another son.

• • •

AS IT TURNS OUT, and as the whole world now knows, there was another son, David. But he enters the story unnamed, dismissively referred to by his father as "the baby brother"—in Hebrew, *haqqaton*, the youngest, in effect saying: "Well, there's the baby brother, but he's out tending the sheep" (1 Sam. 16:11). If you're the youngest of seven brothers, you're probably never going to be thought of as other than the kid brother. *Haqqaton* carries undertones of insignificance, of not counting for very much—certainly not a prime candidate for prestigious work. The family runt.

His father's condescending opinion of him (shared, presumably, by his brothers) is confirmed by the job to which he's assigned—"tending the sheep." The least demanding of all jobs on the farm, the place where he could do the least damage. Baby-sitting for a neighbor or sacking groceries at the supermarket would be equivalent jobs in our economy.[2]

Because David was out of the way and mostly ignored as he tended the sheep, nobody had thought to bring him to Bethlehem that day. Yet David was chosen. Chosen and anointed. Chosen not for what anybody saw in him—not his father, his brothers, not even Samuel—but because of what God saw in him. And then chosen and anointed by God through Samuel to live to God's glory.[3]

As so often happens in things like this, the dissonance between what was done and what people expected was so great that it's unlikely that anyone in Bethlehem that day "saw" the anointing. In looking back, they would have remembered their surprise that Jesse's fine sons had been turned down for some important job, remembered that David had showed up late as usual. But those memories would have faded fast. It wouldn't have been long before the seven brothers were dominating the town again with their pushiness and David was out with his sheep, out of sight and out of mind.

But I didn't forget. Throughout my childhood, in my mother's telling of the story, I became David. I was always David. I'm *still* David. It's the intent and skill of this scriptural storyteller to turn everyone who reads or hears the story into realizing something essentially Davidic about him- or herself: "In my insignificant, sheep-keeping obscurity, I am chosen."

THE ORDINARY PERSON

It's highly significant and not sufficiently remarked that this David story, the story that provides more plot and detail, more characters and landscape than any other in Scripture to show us how to live entirely before and in response to God, features an ordinary person. David was, in our dismissive and condescending terminology, "just" a layperson. His father omitted to present him to Samuel; indeed, it probably didn't even occur to him. To his brothers he was a nonentity. Worse, as we learn from examining his genealogy, he had bad blood in his family tree, hated and despised Moabite blood.[4]

The choice of David, the runt and the shepherd, to be the anointed, to be a sign and representative of God's working presence in human life and history, is surely intended to convey a sense of inclusion to all ordinary men and women, the plain folk, the undistinguished in the eyes of their neighbors, those lacking social status and peer recognition. Which is to say, the overwhelming majority of all who have lived on this old planet earth. Election into God's purposes isn't by popular vote. Election into God's purposes isn't based on proven ability or potential promise.

Our culture holds experts and professionals in a regard that's inflated out of all proportion to reality. The corollary of this is that we regard the layperson as a near idiot, competent only when consulting with or deferring to the expert. The consequences aren't encouraging. We turn the care of our bodies over to the medical experts. Result? Continually worsening per-capita health. We turn responsibility for our learning over to the educational experts. Result? A population unable to think for itself, ignorant of most human literature and history, undefended against the cynical manipulations of advertisers and politicians. We turn responsibility for developing and repairing personal relationships over to the psychological experts. Result? Experiences of intimacy at all-time lows, emotional health alarmingly bad, friendships rare, marriages and family life in ruins. We turn responsibility for faith over to the religious experts. Result? A public Christian identity dominated by bumper-sticker labels and television celebrities that nurture in people an insatiable appetite for watching religious performance and an indiscriminate eagerness for buying junk religious artifacts. The communication and merchandising of religion is greater than ever before in human history. The experts make a lot of money from it, but laypersons, trained from infancy to defer to the experts, experience neither confidence nor competence in believing and praying, loving enemies and welcoming strangers. Put to the 1 John 4:8 test (in blunt paraphrase: "You can't know [God] if you don't love"), our so-called Christian nation rates maybe a C-minus.

So it's of considerable moment to realize that the centerfold account in Scripture of a human being living by faith comes in the shape of a layperson. David wasn't ordained to the priesthood. He wasn't called, as we say, "to the ministry." He was "just" a layperson, *haqqaton*. But there isn't a hint in the narrative that his status is evidence of inadequacy. This is humanity burgeoning and vital, bold and extravagant, skillful and inventive in love and prayer and work.

David's life is the premier biblical instance of what's sometimes called "the priesthood of all believers." Luther made a lot of it during the Reformation, but he didn't make it up. There are a variety of offices in the community of faith—prophet, priest, wise person, elder, apostle, deacon, bishop, and so on—but throughout the church, the primary emphasis is on the *people*. All the offices/jobs are servant positions for assisting and encouraging men and women to be the people of God and not merely a crowd of religious consumers. These servants are set among the people to counter the downward-slipping inertia by which people tend to congeal into a sodden, undifferentiated mush—all this while a few individuals, genetically endowed with an edge over the others in cleverness and energy, ambitiously assert themselves into positions of privilege and power. In the community of faith this "bilevelism" is unacceptable. Biblically, there's unremitting war against it. In the church the war has been intermittent, more or less, but it's still war. When Christian communities are healthy, the "little ones" aren't demeaned and dispirited into being followers and consumers but find themselves acquiring initiative and originality as their priests and pastors, deacons and bishops, friends and neighbors serve *them*.

David's ancestors, freshly rescued from a doomed life in Egypt, heard the constituting sentence: "You shall be to me a kingdom of priests" (Exod. 19:6). When that sentence struck their ears, they could only have reacted with a kind of uncomprehending astonishment. Nothing in their experience in Egypt could have prepared them for such a definition of their lives. In Egypt a few priests held all the power, controlled the rituals, and ran the affairs of the nation from the great temple complexes along the Nile. Extravagantly garbed, surrounded by fawning servants, they were a privileged and impressive upper class. In the presence of such a priest, a mere layperson could only feel a kind of disreputable inadequacy. Dwarfed by the Brobdingnagian statuary at Karnak, Abu Simbel, and Thebes—even in their ruins still staggeringly impressive three thousand years later—no one would dream of daring to carry out anything *priestly.* As well that a checkout clerk perform open-heart surgery. As well that a truck driver fly a 747.

And yet, there it was: "You shall be to me a kingdom of priests." Out in the desert with a pop-up tent for a temple, forced into a rough-and-ready equality by the austere conditions of wilderness survival, they were not to *have* priests but to *be* priests. Priests without robes, without temples, without training, without hierarchical status.[5] The first Christians were assigned the same identity. When Jesus Christ freed them from their sins, he made them, among other things, priests (1 Pet. 2:5, 9; Rev. 1:6; 5:10; 20:6).

Called something by God that no one else would dream of calling them, they were forced to figure out what, in fact, a priest is. Not how a priest dresses, not what temple he's in charge of, not what rituals he presides over, not what lore he's privy to—but "What *is* a priest, anyway?"

Put that way, the answer is obvious enough. A priest presents a person to God, or presents God to a person. A priest makes the God-connection verbal or visible. A priest represents human needs before God, sets God's word before men and women. God and humans have something to do with one another, *everything* to do with one another. A priest says and acts that reality.

The Hebrews became an entire community of people doing that for one another. Each was learning an identity that consisted of being the "image of God." Each was being trained in the rigors of a life of faith that consisted of listening to God, receiving his grace, obeying his commands, receiving his promises. Simply by being out of Egypt and on the far shore of the Red Sea, they were in a position to realize that nothing in them or about them could ever again be understood apart from the presence and action of God. That, and that alone, whether they carried through on it or not, *qualified* them to be priests.

Embarrassingly forgetful of the God who saves us, and easily distracted from the God who is with us, we need priests to remind us of God, to confront us with God. And we need a lot of them. God, knowing our need, put us in a kingdom of priests. But for the most part they're priests who don't look like priests, priests who don't take on the airs of priests, priests who don't dress like priests, priests who don't talk like priests. But they're *priests* all the same.

David is such a priest. He was never *called* a priest; all his life he was what we dismissively describe as *just* a layperson. Yet all his life those around him recognized God's rule and grace and mercy being mediated to them through his life and work. David is the basic biblical rebuke to the minimizing adjective *just*.[6]

CHET ELLINGSON

Most people who venture upon a life of faith are laypersons. Why do so many of them habitually and pliantly take a subordinate position under the certified experts in matters of faith—that is, the clergy? As a pastor myself, I've never quite gotten over either my surprise or my dismay at being treated with doggish deference by so many people. Where do all these Christians, who by definition are "new creatures in Christ" and therefore surely eager to taste and see for themselves (a universal characteristic in newborns) that the Lord is good, pick up this deprecating self-understanding? They certainly don't get it from the Bible or from the gospel. They get it from the culture, whether secular or ecclesial. They get it from leaders who love the prerogatives and power of expertise and bully people by means of their glamorous bravado into abdicating the original splendor of a new life in Christ and declining into the wretched condition of the consumer. The consumer is passivity objectified: passive in the pew, passive before the TV screen, vulnerable to every sort of exploitation and seduction, whether religious or secular.

Along with a great company of other priests and laypeople, living and dead, I have determined throughout my lifetime to do whatever I can to abolish this expert/layperson division in the Christian community. One important way I've found to do it is to get the story of David into the active and praying imaginations of the Christians with whom I live, thereby reestablishing the immediacy and primacy of the layperson in all matters of faith.

• • •

I WAS AT DINNER ONE EVENING with a few friends. It was a simple dinner—freshly baked bread, the aroma of its baking still in the room, a hearty tomato soup, and a salad artfully seasoned with herbs. All of us were Christians. Over coffee our host said, "I want everyone here to talk about a person who made a difference in your life, someone whose words or actions shaped your life in a spiritually formative way." No one had trouble remembering someone. The stories poured out. When my turn came, I told my friends about Chet Ellingson, who was important to me in my adolescent years.

Chet Ellingson was about ten years older than I, a businessman in our town and a friend to my parents. He was also a Christian, but he had only a marginal place in our church because he had been divorced; in our congregation divorce blacklisted a person from any position of influence or leadership. He often invited me to go hunting with him. On autumn mornings in the cold dark, the headlights of his Buick would signal his arrival and I would run out of the house and climb into his car. A half-hour later we would be in Pink Miller's duck blind in a marshy backwater of the Flathead River, waiting for the mallards to come in. I shivered there with my twelve-gauge Winchester, waiting, talking, feeling adult. Chet treated me as an adult before I was an adult. He accepted me into a world of responsibility and respect before I had given any evidence that I belonged there. The "Christian thing," his phrase, was implicit in our conversation but never seemed to be the explicit subject. Jesus and Spirit and Scripture were expressed in the shivering cold offhandedly. I can't remember him ever instructing me or giving me advice. There was no hint of condescension or authority. The faith was simply there, spoken and acted out in the midst of whatever else we were doing—shooting, rowing, retrieving; or, at other times, working or worshiping or meeting on the street and making small talk. I think now that he had no formulated purpose in being with me. He wasn't trying to do anything for me (and never knew what he was, in fact, doing). What he did was become a bridge on which I traveled from immaturity to maturity, on my way to becoming ". . . fully developed within and without, fully alive like Christ" (Eph. 4:13, *The Message*), although I wouldn't have been able to say it in those words at the time. He connected me with an adulthood that was virtually synonymous with "Christian." Through those confused and awkward years of adolescence, when I was with him I was, without being particularly conscious of it, an adult believer in Jesus.

When everyone around the table had contributed, I noticed that while each story had included details that were formative (and sometimes critical) in our entering or continuing the Christian life, not one them had been about a pastor or professor, missionary or evangelist. The people we characteristically slot in the front ranks of leadership in matters of acceptance and growth in the faith—the religious professionals—hadn't once been mentioned as we drank our coffee and told our stories; they probably didn't "have time" to do what Chet did. The people in our stories did exactly what leaders do—motivate, guide, instruct—but not one of them perceived him- or herself as a leader. Nor did we at the time perceive them that way. Only in retrospect did we realize the spiritually formative influence they had on us.

That dinner conversation and its stories, and others like it with their stories, continue to provoke reflection. Pastors and professors, evangelists and missionaries are by no means excluded from these stories, but I keep noticing the many casual encounters that alter my course ever so slightly, unplanned conversations that open up insights, observed attitudes and behaviors that tip the balance in me from indecision to commitment. Evidence mounts: most of what I experience and have experienced in the way of help, encouragement, and wisdom in the actual day-by-day believing and praying, loving and hoping, helping and persevering, obeying and sacrificing in the name and for the sake of Jesus comes from people who aren't considered competent to give it.

And I keep noticing the significance and spiritual force that these stories—these *lives!*— acquire when set in the context of the David story, a story that plunges us into the ordinary and saturates us in the everydayness in which the Holy Spirit is writing the story of *my, your,* salvation.

The Name

In this narration of the selection and anointing of David, his personal name is withheld until the very end (v. 13), giving it a special place of prominence. That name, David, then enters our history. It will be repeated more than six hundred times in the Old Testament and another sixty times in the New.

The personal name is the seed that germinates and grows into the personal story. In this way, story as a way of speech quietly insists that all truth is personal and relational. God deals with persons, *named* persons, not numbers or abstractions or goals or plans. Language at its best and purest turns on naming and names.[7]

David's name, not his role or position, is the final word in this initial story of his life. Our personal name is at one and the same time the most common element in our identity and the most distinctive. We all have names; but each name is exclusive to each of us. We're named, not numbered, at our birth and baptism. Naming is honoring. Naming is choosing. The unnoticed and uninvited shepherd, anointed by the prophet and by the Spirit, is now named: *David.* And the story begins.

WORK

DAVID AND SAUL

1 Samuel 16:14–23

Jesus said, "The person who trusts me will not only do
what I'm doing but even greater things, because I, on
my way to the Father, am giving you the same work to
do that I've been doing."

—JOHN 14:12

KING SAUL WAS IN RUINS. "Now the Spirit of the LORD departed from Saul, and an evil spirit from the LORD tormented him" (1 Sam. 16:14). His mind and emotions were in chaos. Saul entered the biblical story magnificent: his stature compelling, his humility endearing. Samuel wasn't exaggerating when he presented him: "Do you see him whom the LORD has chosen? There is none like him among all the people." And the people were entirely enthusiastic, shouting their approval: "Long live the king!" (1 Sam. 10:24). Everything about him was promising.

And everything began well. The honor and responsibility of being chosen as Israel's first king obviously didn't go to his head; he kept right on with his ordinary farm work. Whatever else "king" meant to Saul, it certainly didn't mean privilege; it didn't mean exemption from the chores. When the first crisis of his reign came and the call went out to deliver Jabesh-gilead in a military expedition, the people came out one and all, not a laggard among them (1 Sam. 11:7), showing that they were as willing to follow him into danger as they were to praise him at the inauguration. That first military effort, the deliverance of Jabesh-gilead from the Ammonites, was a resounding success. The defeat of the Ammonites was followed by victories right and left over the Philistines.

As matters developed, it turned out that he was not only a good general, he was also a good *person*. Following that first victory, when he was still riding high on the zealous enthusiasm of his supporters, the cry went up to purge the riffraff, the "worthless fellows" who had refused to join in the earlier acclamations of Saul's kingship (1 Sam. 10:27), but Saul, gracious and generous in his exercise of power, refused to do it.

Although Saul continued to assert superiority over enemies on every front (1 Sam. 14:47), it wasn't long before signs began to appear that all was not well. While the defeat of brutal Philistines and mean Amalekites features prominently in the storytelling, we begin to pick up indications that Saul, for all his charisma and charm, wasn't all that much interested in God. He became more and more absorbed in the work itself. The work as such didn't seem to suffer, for the campaigns against the Philistines at Michmash and against the Amalekites in the Sinai were totally and satisfyingly decisive, but in each instance Samuel confronted Saul with an act of disobedience against God that took place in the course of carrying out the work (1 Sam. 13:13 and 15:19). Neither act of disobedience appeared sinful. Neither involved immorality or injustice. Both of them made perfect sense in terms of military strategy; in fact, both acts were dictated by good military strategy.

Both acts of disobedience involved, interestingly and most significantly, worship. In the case of the Philistine disobedience, Saul offered sacrifices to the Lord in order to keep the people together and ready for battle; in the case of the Amalekite disobedience, Saul—who had been told by God through Samuel to utterly destroy the Amalekites and all that they possessed—let the people keep the best animals back for offering sacrifices to the Lord. Whether they did it or not, we don't know—

probably not. But Saul was quite ready to side with the people in letting them worship God on their terms rather than on God's terms. Even though it appeared that the worship of God motivated these actions, they weren't primarily concerned with God but were motivated by Saul's concern with the people—in the first instance, to keep them united and focused; in the second instance, to keep them happy. The people loomed large in Saul's considerations, far larger than God. Saul was, it seems, trying to do good work, and he saw bringing God in as a way to do good work, be a good king. But "bringing God in" reversed reality. Saul was treating God as a means, as a resource. And God will not be used.

Somewhere along the line Saul's God-anointed work ceased to be an expression of God's sovereignty and became Saul's responsibility for sovereignty. The prevailing political model of kingship obliterated the prophetic model. The telling detail is that worship and work became two different things, one at the service of the other. The worship was undertaken so that the work would prosper. The consequence was fatal. (The reverse arrangement, work undertaken so that worship will prosper, is equally fatal.) What we're after is a seamless world of work and worship, worship and work. Only God is sovereign. Our work is derivative from God the worker.

GOD THE WORKER

God is first presented to us in our Scriptures as a worker, a maker.[1] In the beginning, God went to work. A six-day work week concluding in worship frames the entire spirituality of creation, with God in the role of worker (Gen. 1:1–2:4). In the second creation story, man and woman are placed in the garden as workers, employed at tasks assigned by their maker (Gen. 2). Work is the primary context for our spirituality. Most children's play is practice for adult work. We play our way into adult work; our games are apprenticeships. The spiritual life begins— seriously begins—when we get a job and go to work.

Work is our Spirit-anointed participation in God's work. When Jesus stood up in the Nazareth synagogue to announce that he was going to work, and how he was going to go about it, he said, "The Spirit of the Lord is upon me because he has *anointed* me . . . " (Luke 4:18).

In our biblical texts being anointed means being given a job by God. It means employment. We're told, in effect, that there's a job to be done and that we're assigned to do it—and that we *can* do it. Anointing connects our work with God's work. Anointing is the sacramental connection linking God's work with our work. God is a worker, a maker. God does things. He *is,* of course; but he also *acts.* And it's in his acts that we know who he is.[2]

The first thing David does after he's anointed is go to work. He enters Saul's court and becomes his righthand man (1 Sam. 16:21). David's work is presented against a background of Saul's work. Saul was anointed but is no longer acting like it—not letting the anointing shape his work. David is now anointed. They're placed side by side in the same workplace.

Spirit . . . anointed. Because work originates in God's word and action and so readily and obviously expresses God, it also constitutes our chief area of temptation. When we're working well, doing good work, we're truly godlike. It isn't much of a step to thinking ourselves gods. But if we are gods, we don't need God, or at least don't need him very much. The sin of Saul took place in the midst of doing good work. Saul was ruined as a God-anointed king in the course of doing his God-appointed work. Work is a far more common source of temptation than sex. Later in the David story we'll come upon David's sexual temptation and subsequent adultery. But David's sexual sin wasn't nearly as disastrous as Saul's work sin.

THE PRIEST IN THE BUTCHER SHOP

I've always counted myself fortunate in being brought up in an environment in which work and worship were virtually indistinguishable. Work and worship were aspects of one world. The world of work was a holy place for me.

My father was a butcher and owned his own meat market. We lived in a small town, and our home was always within walking distance of my dad's store. (*Everything* in our town was in walking distance!) I can't remember a time when I wasn't part of that workplace, working in the company of my father, alongside my father. When I was very young, I didn't do any work as such. I was more or less the mascot of the place; customers would pick me up and throw me around, making jokes with me, having fun. But I was in the *place* of work, and part of it.

Our place of worship never seemed that much different from our place of work. The same kind of people. The same easygoing camaraderie. Ours was a small sectarian church of working-class people, mostly misfits. It was as if someone had taken the state of Montana, tipped it up, and let everyone who didn't fit in, wasn't nailed down in society, slide down into our little town.

I always thought of my father as a priest. He wore a white butcher's apron as he presided over the work of slaughtering heifers and pigs, dressing them out, cutting them up. He smiled easily, and the customers who came into our shop were always greeted by name. There were usually two or three other meatcutters who worked for him, and when I was young I always assumed that they were part of our family, the same as the people at church (who were always addressed as "brother" and "sister").

From the time I was four years old, my mother made me butcher's aprons that looked just like my father's. Every year she made me a new one to accommodate my growth. I always assumed that it was the same cut and design as the robe that Hannah made each year for her son Samuel as he grew up working with the priest Eli at the Shiloh sanctuary. My father was a priest in our butcher shop, and I was with him, doing priestly work. Our butcher shop was a place of blessing.

We worked hard in that place. Year after year I was taught and given tasks to do suited to my developing strength and maturity. I learned the dignity and satisfaction of work.

Ours was a storytelling church, and for a few years we had a pastor who specialized in the tabernacle, the temple, and the whole Hebrew sacrificial system. From the beginning I was an insider to exactly that sort of world of worship: I grew up experiencing the sight and sound of animals killed and offered up, the smell of fresh blood and the buzz of flies. A bull on the altar at Shiloh couldn't have looked or smelled much different than a shorthorn heifer on the butcher block in our shop on Main Street. And though we never butchered goats, and chickens were the closest thing we had to turtledoves, the rich sensuality of Hebrew worship was reproduced daily in our workplace. It never occurred to me that the world of worship was tidy and sedate.

Oddly, the only person who seemed out of place in our market was our pastor. He wasn't a regular customer, but when an evangelist or missionary would come to town, he always paid us a call. He would get my father off to the side, put his arm across his shoulders, and say in the same "spiritual" voice that he always used when he prayed, "Brother Don, the Lord has laid it on my heart that this poor servant of God hasn't been eating all that well lately and would be greatly blessed with one of your fine steaks." My dad, ever generous, always gave him two. I never heard my father complain, but I could see the other meatcutters wink and exchange knowing looks, and I was embarrassed for my pastor, who seemed so out of place in this holy place of work.

Twenty-five years later, as a pastor, I found myself dealing with men and women who didn't know how to act in the place of worship. When they entered the sanctuary, they left at least fifty percent of their vocabulary outside. They talked differently. They stiffened, ever so slightly. Not all of them, true, but enough to let me know that I had my work cut out for me, the work of speaking the word of God to them in the language of their working lives. For how were they going to hear and understand the gospel of Jesus Christ if they heard it only in "church language"? How were they ever going to get a feel for the Bethlehem manger, the Galilean fishing boats, Peter's curses, and Mary's tears, to say nothing of the Golgotha cross, if they got it only behind stained glass to organ accompaniment? And how were they ever going to realize that the adrenaline rush following Tuesday's business deal, the nausea of spousal betrayal on Wednesday, and the interminable boredom of Friday afternoon were the actual stuff in which Christ was working their salvation if they supposed that the primary place for hearing and understanding God's word was the sanctuary? The sanctuary is essential, but it isn't the primary location for the day-by-day cultivation and practice of spirituality, the Holy Spirit shaping the Christ-life in us.

I'm still engaged in that work, saying and showing—insisting!—that the world of work is the primary context for spirituality—for experiencing God, for obeying Jesus, for receiving the Spirit. And I'm not finding it any easier.

KINGWORK

God-anointed, David entered the world of work. He worked as a shepherd before he was anointed, work that provided background and metaphor for so much of the gospel. But now David's work was clearly seen as God-assigned, God-defined. All David's work now was kingwork.

After David has been presented to us as chosen and anointed, the first story about him is set in the workplace. David's earthy spirituality begins with his first job.

I want to use the word *kingwork* to represent all true work. I'm using this word in order to call attention to the essential dignity of work as such, to emphasize that our work is of a kind with God's work. All real work, genuine work, is subsumed under kingwork. I'm using the word here to distinguish true work from false work—spurious work, "work" that destroys or deceives. Just because energy is employed for a purpose doesn't qualify an action as *work*.

Work derives from and represents the sovereign God, who expresses his sovereignty as a worker: kingwork. Sovereigns work to bring order out of chaos; guard and fight for the sanctity of things and people; deliver victims from injustice and misfortune and wretchedness; grant pardon to the condemned and damned; heal sickness; by their very presence bring dignity and honor to people and land. God's sovereignty isn't abstract—it's a *working* sovereignty and is expressed in work. All of our work is intended as an extension of and participation in that sovereignty.

When the Psalmist reflects on the unique place of humans in God's creation, it's our work that's singled out for attention: "[T]hou hast made him little less than God. . . . Thou hast given him dominion over the works of thy hands; thou hast put all things under his feet" (Ps. 8:5–6). God works and we work: in the workplace we become aware of the continuities. Kingwork is elemental work, a representation of sovereignty.

In Charles Williams's novel *Shadows of Ecstasy*, an African who is being protected from mob violence by the principals in the story is discovered to be royalty—a king. The characters are aware of a sudden intrusion of the energy of royalty into a world that has lost touch with this God-anointed world of work, *kingwork,* "the making violently real of a thing that had become less than a word. For a few moments royalty— a dark alien royalty—had appeared in the room, imposed upon all of them by the mere intensity of the Zulu chieftain's own strength and conviction." But in one person, Rosamond, "the sudden consciousness of this energy and richness—believing so greatly in itself and operating so near her—had come with a shock of dismay." She wanted the house rid of his presence. She wanted everything reduced to domestic gossip and convenience, and this African could not be so reduced.[3]

Dignity is inherent in work. Royalty is inherent in work. A major and essential task of the Christian is to recover work as vocation—as holy work. Every Christian takes holy orders.[4]

A KING SERVING A KING

The story of David begins in the middle of another story. All stories do. We never get a clean start in this business of life. The tablet is already scribbled all over, smudged with ink stains, blotted with spilled coffee. Saul has made a mess of things. A royal mess. He had been given a job to do and had ruined it. David is now assigned to do well what Saul had done badly.

David was anointed by Samuel to be king, but he wasn't recognized as a king for another twenty years or so. For twenty years he was a king without looking like a king.

His first job as king was serving a bad king. Having been anointed, he entered the court of King Saul as a servant. Yet in his case being a servant wasn't the opposite of being a king. Serving, for David, wasn't *apprenticeship* for ruling. This wasn't an instance of taking the son of the president of a company (and therefore the potential president) and starting him at the lowliest job in order to train him in all the details of how the company functions from the bottom up. For David, serving was in itself ruling. The servant was simultaneously king. David in Saul's court was a king serving a king. Jesus, whom we worship as King, spent most of his life at the work of carpentry.

All true work combines these two elements of serving and ruling. Ruling is what we do; serving is the way we do it. There's true sovereignty in all good work. There's no way to exercise it rightly other than by serving.

Having a good job doesn't mean that we'll do it well. Having the right role doesn't guarantee righteousness. Saul, for example, had good work to do, yet he—as Israel's first king—failed at his job. We can't look to our jobs, our positions, for righteousness. Both Saul and David were defined by the anointing of the Spirit of God. They had equally good work to do. But having good work to do doesn't mean that we'll do good work. Saul failed at the same work that David succeeded in carrying out. Jobs are important. Things need to be done. But no job is perfectly suited for carrying out God's purposes. The key to living vocationally—that is, being "God-called," Spirit-anointed—isn't getting the right job or career but doing kingwork in whatever circumstances we find ourselves.

Why do we always want to know early on in our acquaintance with someone what his or her work is? "What do you do?" is virtually always among the repertoire of getting-acquainted questions. The reason is this: occupation, career, job can do two things—usually both at the same time. Work can reveal something essential about us—express our values, articulate our morals, act out our convictions of what it means to be a human being, created in the image of God. Conversely, work can conceal our real identity; it can be used as a front to advertise something that we want people to see in us or believe about us but that in fact we've never bothered to become within ourselves. For most of us, the two vocational elements are mixed: revealing/expressing and concealing/diverting. As we get to know someone, we want to know if that person's job is a role to hide in or behind or if it's an honest expression of character.

David's first job as king was making music, attempting to reestablish the divine order in Saul's disordered mind and emotions. Establishing order in the midst of chaos is basic to kingwork. Music is probably our most elemental experience of this essential work. Music—bringing rhythm and harmony and tunefulness into being—is at the heart of all work. Kingworkers, whatever their jobs, whistle while they work.

IMAGINATION

DAVID AND GOLIATH

1 Samuel 17

Jesus said, "The simple truth is that if you had a mere kernel of faith, a poppy seed, say, you would tell this mountain, 'Move!' and it would move. There is nothing you wouldn't be able to tackle."

—MATTHEW 17:21

MY ATTENTION IS CAUGHT and held by this wonderful but improbable scene: David on his knees at the brook; David kneeling and selecting five smooth stones, feeling each one, testing it for balance and size; David out in the middle of the Valley of Elah—in full view of two armies, Philistine and Israelite, gathered on either side of the valley— kneeling at the brook, exposed and vulnerable. He's such a slight figure, this young shepherd. He's so unprotected. The air is heavy with hostility. There isn't a man on either side of the valley who isn't hefting a spear, sharpening a sword, getting ready to kill. The Valley of Elah is a cauldron in which fear and hate and arrogance have been stirred and cooked for weeks into what's now a volatile and lethal brew. And David, seemingly oblivious to the danger, ignoring the spiked forest of spears and the glint of swords, kneels at the brook. There are buttercups sprinkled through the meadow grass. A butterfly lights on an asphodel. A bee sucks nectar from a dandelion. A riffle in the brook catches the sun and throws the light back into David's freckled and beardless face, illuminating—can this be?—the bare hint of a smile at the corners of his mouth.

The oddness and improbability of David kneeling at the brook is made even more improbable, if that's possible, by two giants, one on either side of the valley: on the Philistine side, Goliath; on the Israelite side, Saul. Saul wasn't a true giant, but his size was considerable; he stood, we're told, head and shoulders above his countrymen.

THE GREATEST CHILDREN'S STORY

The story of David and Goliath is one of the greatest of all children's stories. It's the first full-blown story about David, and the most memorable. If you know anything at all about David, you know the story of Goliath. People who've never read the Bible, people who've never so much as heard that there is a Bible, know the story of David and Goliath.

The David/Goliath story is a great children's story because it conveys an important meaning. It's not an obvious meaning, but all children must learn it if they're going to make it in the world.

But once we've learned the story and assimilated the meaning that goes with it, the story isn't over and done with. Learning stories isn't the same as learning the multiplication tables. Once we've learned that three times four equals twelve, we've learned it and that's that. It's a fact that doesn't change. The data is stored in our memory for ready access. But stories don't stay put; they grow and deepen. The meaning doesn't exactly change, but it matures. Having learned the meaning of love, for instance, we don't for a moment suppose that we've passed that course and can now go on to other things, deciding perhaps to sign up next for computer science.

No. We keep on telling stories, the same old ones, over and over and over again, in a way quite different from saying the multiplication tables over and over again. The stories keep releasing new insight in new situations. As we bring new experience and insight to the story, the story gathers that enrichment in and gives it back to us in fresh form.

And so it turns out that the David/Goliath story is as important for adults as it ever was for children. One of the great impoverishments of many adult lives is the absence of children's stories, whether read or told or listened to.

CHILDREN'S STORIES AS ADULT STORIES

I want to argue that all the great stories get their start as children's stories. That's because when we're children we're discovering the world from the ground up. We're working with the basics. And no matter how long we live, no matter how mature we become, we're never removed from the basics. Children's stories go over, inch by inch, the ground on which we spend the rest of our lives eating and sleeping, walking and running, playing and working, fighting and loving, cursing and blessing.

As we get older, as our stature elevates us inch by inch higher from the ground, we become less aware of the ground. As we acquire familiarity with the basics and become easy in negotiating them, we're less conscious of them. But we're never independent of them. This is true in every area of existence: the material basics of air and water, earth and fire; the spiritual basics of trust and love, hope and mercy; the emotional basics of fear and joy, serenity and anxiety; the mental basics of asking and telling, naming and numbering.

We never get away from the basics, but we do lose sensitivity to them. When we're new to them, experiencing them for the first time, we hear and see and feel intensely. Gradually, our perceptions dull as we become preoccupied with other things. But they're no less there, no less basic.

As children we're explorers and discoverers. Every child is a Columbus, a Marco Polo, a Galileo—and a David. The world is so wide and wonderful. There's so much to see and taste and hear. We discover rocks and animals, leaves and flowers. We wonder at various shapes, round and square, huge and small. Our fingers touch rough and smooth, dry and wet. Tongues and nostrils initiate us into sweet and sour, bland and tangy.

Parents encourage these explorations and discoveries by presenting their children with toys. Toys provide a safe, or at least safer, means of carrying out experiments on the world than wandering out into the streets and forests. Instead of sending our two-year-old down to the fire station to climb all over the fire trucks and pester the firefighters with questions, we buy a small fire truck and let him rescue people from under the dining room table. Instead of sending our three-year-old to the woods to look for bears and badgers, we buy her a few stuffed animals that will give her a feel for these creatures without the danger of her becoming a meal for them.

In the process of this exploration we learn that there's more to the world than size and shape, color and texture; there's meaning and purpose, good and bad. There's something just beneath the surface of everything, something invisible and inaudible but just as real, maybe even more real, than what we're seeing and hearing and touching. Stories are our primary means for exploring these beneath-the-surface, behind-the-scenes realities that are as present and immediate to us as anything we have access to through our five senses. Stories are as important as toys.

By means of stories we develop an imagination that can recognize and explore the tensions between good and evil, love and hate, acceptance and rejection. The world is a dangerous and fearsome place: the story of Goldilocks gets us acquainted with such dark realities. The way the people closest to us treat us isn't always the truth of our lives: the story of Cinderella opens up possibilities we hadn't guessed were there. Our first impressions of what we like and dislike are often quite wrong: Dr. Seuss's *Green Eggs and Ham* prepares us for surprising reversals on what we think we like and don't like. Clearly, the stories that tell us what the world means are as essential to our growing up as the toys that show us how the world works.

ACQUIRING A GOD-DOMINATED IMAGINATION

The theme of the David story is becoming human. What does it mean to be human, *become* human, be a real woman, a real man? What must we deal with in order to become ourselves, to grow up? In the first story we looked at, telling of Samuel's arrival at Bethlehem to select a new king from among Jesse's eight sons, we saw that it means, against all probabilities and despite the opinions of our family and friends, that we're chosen, elected by God for his purposes. The second story plunged David into a world of work in Saul's court. The place in which God's purposes are developed in our lives is a workplace in which we learn how to do kingwork. Now, in this third episode in the Davidic narrative sequence, we find ourselves faced with acquiring a God-dominated imagination and rejecting a Goliath-dominated imagination. These three stories form a base, a kind of narrative tripod, upon which the rest of the David stories will be built.

When David showed up at Ephesdammim and joined Saul's encampment in the Valley of Elah, Goliath dominated the scene. The huge giant—nearly seven feet tall,[1] twirling his twenty-five-pound spear with the careless ease of a cheerleader twirling her baton—was completely intimidating. His taunts across the valley, teasing and provoking the Israelites, each day made each man a little more of a coward. Goliath—his size, his brutality, his cruelty—centered the world. Goliath was the polestar around which everyone took his bearings.

The same debased imagination that treated Goliath as important treated David as insignificant. The men who were in awe of Goliath were contemptuous of David. Arriving with ten loaves of bread and ten bricks of cheese for his brothers in the army, David was treated by them with withering scorn. Their imaginations were so ruined by Goliath-watching that they were incapable of seeing and accepting a simple act of friendship.

The moment we permit evil to control our imaginations, dictate the way we think, and shape our responses, we at the same time become incapable of seeing the good and the true and the beautiful.

But David entered the Valley of Elah with a God-dominated, not a Goliath-dominated, imagination. He was incredulous that everyone was cowering before this infidel giant. Weren't these men enlisted in the army of the living God? God was the reality with which David had to do; giants didn't figure largely in David's understanding of the world, the *real* world.

In the Bethlehem hills and meadows, tending his father's sheep, David was immersed in the largeness and immediacy of God. He had experienced God's strength in protecting the sheep in his fights with lions and bears. He had practiced the presence of God so thoroughly that God's word, which he couldn't literally hear, was far more real to him than the lion's roar, which he could hear. He had worshiped the majesty of God so continuously that God's love, which he couldn't see, was far more real to him than the bear's ferocity, which he could see. His praying and singing, his meditation and adoration had shaped an imagination in him that set each sheep and lamb, bear and lion into something large and vast and robust: God.

His imagination was so thoroughly God-dominated that he couldn't believe what he was seeing and hearing when he walked into Ephesdammim—Goliath terror, Goliath phobia. It was an epidemic worse than cholera, everyone down with Goliath-sickness, a terrible disease of spirit that had Saul and his entire army incapacitated.

KNEELING AT THE BROOK

In my imagination I see David kneeling at the brook to select stones for his sling. The text doesn't say that he knelt, just that he "chose five smooth stones" from the brook (1 Sam. 17:50). But he must have knelt to select the stones. I see him kneeling—David kneeling at the brook, the one person that day who was spirit-healthy.

This is his first time at this brook. He had never been in the Valley of Elah before. He had never seen a giant before. He had never fought a battle. How did he know what to do? Why did he assume this particular posture, *kneeling* at the brook? How was he capable of doing something so completely unsuited to the appearance of what was required that day? Kneeling, and therefore unable to either walk or run. Kneeling, and therefore defenseless. Kneeling, and so unable to see the big picture.

Goliath is disdainful of this kneeling David. He banters mockingly, name-calling him to the other Israelites as a "stick." "Am I a dog, that you come to me with sticks?" (1 Sam. 17:43). He belches Philistine curses across the valley. Like mortars, they batter the ears of David and the Israelite army with the invective of the course pantheon of Canaanite gods, as ugly and vicious an assortment of divinities as we're ever likely to come across.

On the near side of the valley, King Saul is worried over this kneeling David. He has just tried his best to be of help by outfitting him with his own armor. He set his bronze helmet on David's head, wrapped him in his coat of mail, and handed him his sword, which David strapped around his waist. David had never been dressed like that before. And it seemed like such a good idea. Saul's armor! The king's weapons! If there was anything that would fit him out for the task ahead, it was certainly this. Was there a man in Israel who wouldn't have counted it the highest privilege to be so equipped? But when he tried to walk, he couldn't move. Weighted down under the cumbrous metal, he was reduced to a stiff and awkward waddle.

SAUL'S ARMOR

There was no question but that Saul was well intentioned. He wanted to help and was helping in the only way he knew: pile on the armor, protect yourself, get a weapon with proven effectiveness.

This is a common experience in the Valley of Elah, when an amateur ventures into a field dominated by professionals. All around us people who care about us are suddenly there helping—piling armor on us, dressing us up in equipment that's going to qualify us for the task (even though it didn't seem to be doing *them* much good). We get advice. We get instruction. We're sent off to a training workshop. We find ourselves with an armload of books. These people are truly concerned about us, and we're touched by their concern, in awe of their knowledge and experience. We listen to them and do what they tell us. And then we find that we can hardly move.

It wasn't easy to do what David did that day. David loved King Saul. He admired King Saul. He served King Saul. King Saul was splendid and powerful. King Saul loved him and was doing his best to help him.[2] But despite all that, David removed the helmet, unbelted the sword, and took off the armor. It couldn't have been easy to do that: walk away from all that proffered expertise. But to have gone to meet Goliath wearing Saul's armor would have been a disaster. Borrowed armor always is. David needed what was authentic to him.

What strikes me so forcibly in this picture is that David was both modest enough and bold enough to reject the suggestion that he do his work inauthentically (by using Saul's armor); and he was both modest enough and bold enough to use only that which he had been trained to use in his years as a shepherd (his sling and some stones). And he killed the giant.

The way we do our work is as important as the work we do. Means must be authentic, true, appropriate to our prayers and proclamations. The Quaker Isaac Pennington used to exclaim, "There is that which is near you which will guide you, O! wait for it, and be sure ye keep to it."[3]

David left Saul's armor behind and walked out into the Valley of Elah clean and spare, traveling light, delivered from an immense clutter; and he kneeled at the brook.

David at that moment, kneeling at the brook, frames something that's absolutely essential for each of us. Are we going to live this life from our knees, imaginatively and personally? Or are we going to live it conventionally and at secondhand? Are we going to live out of our God-created, Spirit-anointed, Jesus-saved being? Or are we going to toady and defer to eunuch professionals? Are we going to be shaped by our fears of Goliath or by God? Are we going to live by our admiration of Saul or by God?

A CRITICAL MOMENT

This is a critical moment not only for David but also for his unbelieving brothers—Eliab, Abinadab, Shammah, and the others—for Saul and all Israel, and for the entire people of God, which now includes us. Here's why. At that moment the religious traditions of Israel were in shambles and its spirituality in tatters. The patriarchal, exodus, and wilderness traditions had all been developed in a nomadic culture. Now God's people were settled in a world that was agrarian and urban. The recent past, in which charismatic judges had shown flashes of brilliance, had disintegrated into anarchy. The attempt, out of that chaos, to establish order again through a monarchy was already on its way to failure. While David is at the brook, Israel is at the brink of losing its identity to the Philistines.

Israel had a glorious history—Abraham and Moses, Joshua and Samuel. But history, no matter how glorious, doesn't save anyone. Every person learns the way of faith freshly or not at all. We learn to speak; we learn to walk; we learn to believe in God. And as essential as speaking and walking are, the most personal, most significant, most *human* thing we ever do is believe in God. At the same time it's the most public, the most social, the most political.

The world changes; political alliances shift; the rich and poor jockey for position; the moral fiber of society alternately strengthens and weakens. God speaks his word; God reveals his will; God chooses his people. Who's listening? Who's looking? Who's responding? At this moment in Israel not many were listening, or looking, or responding. Coming out of a century or two of moral disintegration compounded by political chaos, Israel was at the point of losing its identity as a people of God, losing touch with its history, losing hold on the theme of salvation, which provided meaning and coherence to life itself.

Meanwhile, David had been chosen to recover the health and holiness of the life of faith for and among these people. A new leadership was being formed in him, although no one knew it at the time. David wasn't yet crowned king, and it would be years before he was recognized as such. He was a marginal figure, even as any Christian—maybe especially the so-called lay Christian—is still. But his importance hinged not on his recognition but on his integrity, his faith in God.

While David knelt at the brook, the world was bounded on one side by the arrogant and bullying people of Philistia and on the other by the demoralized and anxious people of Israel. To the north of the brook the powerful but stupid giant; to the south of the brook the anointed but deeply flawed king. No one could have guessed that the young man picking stones out of the brook was doing the most significant work of the day.

Until David walked into the Valley of Elah and knelt at that brook, the only options seemed to be a bullying Might or a fearful Right. Take your choice: brutal Goliath or anxious Saul.

David kneeling, unhurried and calm, opened up another option: God, God's ways, God's salvation. How do we so easily lose sight of this, lose awareness of God? Why would any of us in our right minds exchange a God-blessed imagination capable of "seeing the invisible" for a mess of statistics? But however it happens, David kneeling at the brook leads our recovery.

David Running

Suddenly, David is no longer kneeling but running.[4] And not away from but toward the giant! David's brothers can't believe their eyes, their little brother embarrassing them in front of the whole army with his impudence. King Saul is beside himself with worry, watching this young musician to whom he has become so attached commit suicide. Goliath, lumbering in his clumsy giant steps, stops in surprise. The moment itself is so without precedent, occurs so quickly that it hardly registers in the eyes of the spectators, whether Philistine or Israelite. Two, three looping swings and one of the five smooth stones is hurled from David's sling and sinks into the Philistine's forehead. Stunned, the giant crumples to the ground and is soon dead.

The only person fully in touch with reality that day was David. The only fully human person in the Valley of Elah that day was David.

Reality is made up mostly of what we can't see. Humanness is mostly a matter of what never gets reported in the newspapers. Only a prayer-saturated imagination accounts for what made holy history that day in the Valley of Elah—the striking immersion in God-reality, the robust exhibition of David-humanity.

FRIENDSHIP

DAVID AND JONATHAN

1 Samuel 18–20

*Jesus said, "Put your life on the line for your friends.
You are my friends when you do the things I command
you."*

—JOHN 15:13B–14

IT ALWAYS COMES as something of a shock that not everyone likes
us just as we are. We enter the world, most of us anyway, cuddled and
loved, cared for and coddled. We're so *lovable!* And so loved. But it
doesn't last long. Sometimes it doesn't last much past our first change
of diapers. Sooner or later we find ourselves treated as trespassers or
rivals—the enemy.

David did. David's experience with enmity was one of the powerful
shaping influences in his life. Much of his spirituality—the way he
prayed, the way he lived—can be accounted for only by understanding
the ways he experienced and handled enmity.

Love—God's love in particular—is fundamental to the world's existence. Love is the background against which everything else is played

out. "God so loved the world that he gave . . ." is our basic text for understanding and interpreting everything that happens in and around us.

But enmity is the actual condition in which more often than not we find ourselves. We're criticized, teased, avoided, attacked, shot at, abandoned, stoned, cursed, hunted down, snubbed, stabbed in the back, treated like a doormat, and damned with faint praise. Not all of those things, and not all the time, but enough of them and often enough to realize that not everyone shares God's excellent attitude toward us.

THE ENEMY: "I WILL PIN DAVID TO THE WALL"

David's experience of enmity had its primary source in King Saul. Saul hated David and attempted repeatedly to kill him. The enmity David experienced is of a kind that always strikes us as puzzling, for it's an enmity provoked by goodness. Saul hated David because David was good.

The first murder attempt took place while David was making music for Saul. David's skill in music is what brought him to Saul's attention initially. Following on his early defections as God's king, Saul became subject to black moods, demonic visitations—evil abysses of mind and emotion. David and David's music were a healing presence at these times. And then one day instead of healing there was hate. Saul hurled his spear at David, muttering, "I will pin David to the wall" (1 Sam. 18:11). Out of the corner of his eye, David saw it coming and ducked. The spear drove into the wall, inches from David's head. Saul tried again; David ducked again.

These hot, irrational, murderous outbursts escalated into cold-blooded, carefully calculated assassination plots. Saul promised to marry his daughter Merab to David on the condition that he prove himself in battle. His plan was to expose David to such continuous danger that the Philistines would eventually kill him. When David showed up after the Philistine battles alive and ready for the wedding, Saul hastily married Merab off to another, to Adriel the Meholathite. He had never had any intention of conferring son-in-law status on David.

When Saul learned that his daughter Michal was in love with David, he used the information satanically to plot another murder attempt. He promised David that he could marry Michal if he would present him with one hundred Philistine foreskins. (Surely out of one hundred chances, David would get killed!) David, showing no sign of being offended by this outrageous demand, cheerfully went off, killed double his assigned quota, and presented the king with the obscene dowry, a sackful of two hundred Philistine foreskins. This time the marriage took place: Michal became David's wife.

But Michal's love for David only aggravated Saul's hatred of him. The king's final attempt on David's life before the young man fled the royal court for a fugitive life in the wilderness was to have been conducted by a death squad. Saul ordered his hired killers to stake out David's house and kill him first thing in the morning. Michal, having discovered the plot, helped David escape that night through a window and put a dummy in his bed with a head of goat hair. When the assassins came to get him, Michal told them that her husband was sick and couldn't see them. The killers must have been operating under some ancient code of honor by which they felt constrained not to murder a defenseless sick man; instead of barging in and making short work of him, they reported back to King Saul that David was ill in bed and couldn't come out to get murdered. Saul—and what a towering rage he must have been in by now!—ordered them to bring David to him, bed and all, and he himself would kill him. But when the men arrived, all they found in the bed was the dummy with the goat-hair wig.

• • •

DAVID WAS DOING EVERYTHING RIGHT when Saul tried to kill him. He had killed the Philistine giant, ending the impasse with Israel's enemy, and he had brought healing to Saul's tortured spirit, quieting the turbulence in the troubled king. He was just what the nation needed; he was just what the king needed. He seems to have done both kinds of work modestly and unassumingly, without showing off. For doing these good works he nearly got himself killed.

It's always disorienting to be attacked when we're doing something good—doing our very best and then suddenly and violently opposed. We don't exactly welcome punishment for our wrong actions either, but we aren't disconcerted by it. There's a moral logic to just deserts. We expect to get called on the carpet for doing wrong; we don't expect it for doing right. We echo variations on David's protest to Jonathan: "What have I done? What is my guilt? And what is my sin before your father that he seeks my life?" (1 Sam. 20:1).

Psalm 7 is the first prayer in the Psalms that gives expression to this experience of outraged innocence:

> *Yahweh! God! I am running to you for dear life;*
> *   the chase is wild.*
> *If they catch me, I'm finished:*
> *   ripped to shreds by foes fierce as lions,*
> *   dragged into the forest and left*
> *   unlooked for, unremembered.*
>
> *Yahweh, if I've done what they say—*
> *   betrayed my friends,*
> *   ripped off my enemies—*
> *If my hands are really that dirty,*
> *   let them get me, walk all over me,*
> *   leave me flat on my face in the dirt.*
>
> *Stand up, Yahweh; pit your holy fury*
> *   against my furious enemies.*
> *Wake up, God. My accusers have packed*
> *   the courtroom; it's judgment time.*
> *Take your place on the bench, reach for your gavel,*
> *   throw out the false charges against me.*
> *I'm ready, confident in your verdict:*
> *   "Innocent."*
>
> *Close the book on Evil, Yahweh,*
> *   but publish your mandate for us.*
> *You get us ready for life;*
> *   you probe for our soft spots,*
> *   you knock off our rough edges.*

And I'm feeling so fit, so safe:
    made right, kept right.
God in solemn honor does things right,
    but his nerves are sandpapered raw.
Nobody gets by with anything.
    God is already in action—
Sword honed on his whetstone,
    bow strung, arrow on the string,
Lethal weapons in hand,
    each arrow a flaming missile.

Look at that guy!
    He had sex with sin,
    he's pregnant with evil.
Oh, look! He's having
    the baby—a Lie-Baby!

See that man shoveling day after day,
    digging, then concealing, his man-trap
    down that lonely stretch of road?
Go back and look again—you'll see him in it headfirst,
    legs waving in the breeze.
That's what happens:
    mischief backfires;
    violence boomerangs.

I'm thanking God who makes things right.
I'm singing the fame of heaven-high Yahweh.

THE FRIEND: JONATHAN BOUND TO THE SOUL OF DAVID

Interwoven throughout this murderous plotting is the extraordinary friendship between David and Jonathan, Saul's son. In the middle of the craziness and madness, the meanness and hate, David experienced a most unusual love in Jonathan's friendship. In conversation and prayer, together they tried to understand Saul. But it wasn't easy.

The opportunism with which Saul had earlier treated God is reproduced in opportunism with regard to David. Just as God had become an auxiliary appendage to Saul's royal ego, to be used but not obeyed, so David was now valued only because he was useful for musical solace and military prowess. But when his attractiveness and popularity threatened Saul's supremacy, a jealous and murderous rage kicked in. More and more Saul looked at David through a lens clouded with fear and hate. All he saw through that cloudy lens was threat. And the only solution he could come up with was murder. Perhaps there were also spiritually clear moments when he saw in David the makings of the king that he himself might have become. But those moments, if there were such moments, instead of leading to repentance fueled his determination to obliterate the evidence: he would get rid of this bright goodness that exposed the spiritual rottenness that he covered with royal robes and court rituals.

Both David and Jonathan wanted what was best for King Saul. Day after day, though, the signs accumulated that Saul's intermittent rages and sporadic jealousies had settled into something determined and calculated. The two friends seemed most reluctant to come to that conclusion, giving Saul every benefit of the doubt. Finally, though, there was no more room for doubt: "Jonathan knew that his father was determined to put David to death" (1 Sam. 20:33). So Jonathan helped David escape.

• • •

JONATHAN'S FRIENDSHIP WITH DAVID brackets Saul's repeated attempts, ranging from irrational to rational, to kill David. The front bracket to the story begins with these words: "[T]he soul of Jonathan was knit to the soul of David, and Jonathan loved him as his own soul. . . . Then Jonathan made a covenant with David, because he loved him as his own soul" (1 Sam. 18:1, 3). The bulk of chapters 18 through 20 are then filled with the details of Saul's six attempts at murdering David: three times he tried to kill him with his javelin; twice he lured him into almost certain death with the Philistines by offering his daughters, first Merab and then Michal, as prizes; and once he sent in a death squad. These six failed attempts precipitate a major campaign to rid the country of David. As Jonathan enables David's escape, there's this end bracket: "Jonathan said to David, 'Go in peace, forasmuch as we have sworn both of us in the name of the LORD, saying, The LORD shall be between me and you, and between my descendants and your descendants, forever" (1 Sam. 20:42). The friendship bracketed and contained the evil. Friendship *forms*.

Friendship is a much underestimated aspect of spirituality. It's every bit as significant as prayer and fasting. Like the sacramental use of water and bread and wine, friendship takes what's common in human experience and turns it into something holy. Friendship with David complicated Jonathan's life enormously. He risked losing his father's favor and willingly sacrificed his own royal future. But neither the risk nor the loss deterred him; he became and stayed David's friend. Jonathan's friendship was essential to David's life. It's highly unlikely that David could have persisted in serving Saul without the friendship of Jonathan. Jonathan, in striking contrast to his father, discerned God in David, comprehended the danger and difficulty of his anointing, and made a covenant of friendship with him. Jonathan's friendship entered David's soul in a way that Saul's hatred never did.

• • •

JONATHAN LIVED OUT his covenantal friendship with David in hard circumstances. The friendship covenant served God's purposes in David, but Jonathan got little or no emotional reward. Jonathan never saw David again after helping him escape from Saul. Jonathan lived out his covenant of friendship in circumstances that were anti-David. For the rest of his life he served in Saul's court, fighting with his father in the Philistine wars and accompanying him, presumably, on the David hunts. But the circumstances didn't cancel out the covenant; rather, the covenant was used in the purposes of God to overcome the circumstances.

Many a covenantal friendship is lived out similarly in "Saul's court"—in marital, family, work, and cultural conditions that are hostile to a vowed intimacy. But it's the covenant, not the conditions, that carries the day.

• • •

MARTIN BUBER, a great Jewish man of God who encountered and survived much enmity in his lifetime, visited North America and was a guest at Haverford College, a Quaker school in Pennsylvania. Douglas Steere was his host when they attended a Quaker meeting. One man broke the silence of the meeting to speak of the great experience of meeting across language, racial, and religious boundaries, the wonder of being able to reach across the barriers and touch another human being, the touch turning strangers into friends. Then Buber stood up. (Everyone who talks about Buber remarks on his strong face and piercing eyes; he looked like a prophet should look.) Buber said that meeting another was a great thing, but not the greatest thing. The greatest thing any person can do for another is to confirm the deepest thing in him, in her—to take the time and have the discernment to see what's most deeply there, most fully that person, and then confirm it by recognizing and encouraging it.[1]

Each of us has contact with hundreds of people who never look beyond our surface appearance. We have dealings with hundreds of people who the moment they set eyes on us begin calculating what use we can be to them, what they can get out of us. We meet hundreds of people who take one look at us, make a snap judgment, and then slot us into a category so that they won't have to deal with us as persons. They treat us as something less than we are; and if we're in constant association with them, we *become* less.

And then someone enters our life who isn't looking for someone to use, is leisurely enough to find out what's really going on in us, is secure enough not to exploit our weaknesses or attack our strengths, recognizes our inner life and understands the difficulty of living out our inner convictions, confirms what's deepest within us. A friend.

It's a great thing to be a Jonathan. Without Jonathan, David was at risk of either abandoning his vocation and returning to the simple life of tending sheep or developing a murderous spirit of retaliation to get even with the man who was despising the best that was within him. He did neither. He accepted Jonathan's friendship and in receiving it received confirmation of Samuel's earlier anointing to kingwork and the God-dominated imagination that made it possible to live in and by God's Spirit in song and story.

Lacking confirmation by the word of a friend, our most promising beginnings fizzle. Lacking confirmation in the presence of a friend, our bravest ventures unravel. It's not unusual for any of us to begin something wonderful, and it's not unusual for any of us to do things that are quite good. But it *is* unusual to continue and to persevere. The difficulties aren't for the most part external but internal—finding the energy and vision to keep the effort going. Being good and doing good are seldom adequately rewarded: more often they get us into trouble. The world, the flesh, and the devil are in fierce opposition to the Christian way and wreck many lives that start off beautifully.

• • •

WILLIAM BUTLER YEATS wrote a meditative poem on this theme. In the persona of an old man looking back over his life and finding not a single story with "a finish worthy of the start," he remembers a young man with talent and skill in the elegant sport of fly-fishing who turns into a drunken journalist; he recalls a girl who had absorbed all the delicate spiritualities of Dante but ends up bearing children to an oafish dunce; he sketches a beautiful woman with a soaring vision of a better world, reduced to screaming angry slogans from some soapbox. And then he writes these cynical lines:

> Some think it a matter of course that chance
> Should starve good men and bad advance.[2]

Such cynicism has a patina of worldly wisdom to it. But the "wisdom" won't stand up to examination. There's no Jonathan in such a view of human life. And so, of course, no David. The Bible tells the story of our lives more truly.

The stories of survival and lasting are the ones that determine the nature and meaning of what it means to be human. And somewhere in those stories, if we look carefully enough, we find covenants of friendship that help bind beginnings and endings into the covenant purposes of God.

UNDER THE SPELL OF GOODNESS

There's a strange but true story that caps this. Some details in it elude our understanding, but the thrust of the story is clear enough. After Saul's sixth attempt on his life, David ran for protection to the prophet Samuel at Ramah, where Samuel presided over a school of prophets. I think we can imagine something on the order of a monastery of prophets, with the prophets immersed in a daily round of praying and prophesying. Saul learned of David's whereabouts and sent messengers to bring him back, but when the messengers entered the spiritual assembly, they were caught up in the prophetic ecstasies, overwhelmed by God's Spirit. A second and then a third group of messengers fared identically. Disgusted, Saul took matters into his own hands and went to Ramah. He arrived with murder on his mind, but he and his evil intent were no better able to withstand God's Spirit than his messengers had been. He was soon completely under the influence of God's Spirit and giving witness to God's presence. In the process he took off his clothes. Stripped of his royal robes, he was prostrate before Samuel a day and a night. Walter Brueggemann describes him as a "once great man, still tall but no longer great, . . . clearly not in control, shamed, now rendered powerless in a posture of submissiveness."[3] He had fallen under the spell of goodness and was rendered temporarily incapable of evil.

• • •

EVIL DOESN'T STAND A CHANCE against goodness. Persecution is futile in the presence of faithfulness. Hostility is picayune compared to friendship.

This isn't the view that's current among us. Politically and psychologically we operate from a different set of assumptions, and as a consequence we spend enormous sums of money and expend tremendous energy on defense. But if we're to live largely and freely in the context of God, we must learn what God has revealed to us.

What's revealed in this story is that massive resources of royalty are ranged against the young warrior, the raging king set against the singing shepherd, a spear pitted against a harp. And what happens? After each outbreak of violence, King Saul is weaker and more distraught; after each outbreak of violence, David is stronger and still befriended.

David, his election, vocation, and imagination confirmed by Jonathan's friendship, refuses the way of violence and embraces the way of love and service. Each episode reveals more of what he's daily becoming: singer, lover, friend. Evil doesn't diminish David; it doesn't narrow him. Bound in the covenant of Jonathan's friendship, David is protected; none of Saul's evil gets inside him. In the face of such concentrated goodness, evil is powerless to maintain itself.

· 6 ·

SANCTUARY

DAVID AND DOEG

1 Samuel 21–22

Jesus said, "I've told you these things to prepare you for rough times ahead. They are going to throw you out of the meeting places. There will even come a time when anyone who kills you will think he's doing God a favor. They will do these things because they never understood the Father. I've told you these things so that when the time comes and they start in on you, you'll be well-warned and ready for them."

—JOHN 16:1–4

DAVID IS ON THE RUN. He now knows for certain that King Saul's intent to murder him has congealed into a hard, fixed purpose. Saul's hatred is no longer a matter of black moods that will eventually pass. And his jealousy can no longer be treated as a personal matter that he can be expected to get over as David proves his loyalty. No, there's now a price on David's head. The killing of David has turned into a cause, a state policy to be implemented impersonally.

Until now life in Saul's court has been dangerous for David, but the danger has been laced with hope—hope that the king will be brought back from the dark regions of jealousy and rage, steadied and calmed and healed by sweet singing and loyal service.

So now David runs. He runs without having a chance to pack his bags, without benefit of a plan, running for his life. And where does he run? He runs to Nob, where there's a sanctuary and a priest.

AHIMELECH

A sanctuary is a holy place, and its priest—in this case, Ahimelech—is in charge of keeping it holy.

Holy is a word that we use to designate the otherness, the purity, the beauty of God. *God* is holy. We can't understand God by extrapolating from our human experience, magnifying and projecting the best that we are or can imagine, and then call that God. God isn't a human being, even the best of human beings, writ large. Because God is *other,* God is therefore also mystery. God can't be studied empirically the way we scrupulously examine evidence in a laboratory. God can't be figured out the way we logically think through the truth and falsity of language statements. God is so *other* that we can never pretend to predict what God will do, or get God under our control in any way whatever. Our only appropriate approach to God is in awe and reverence, in humble and submissive worship. Such an approach also contains elements of fear and trembling, for though we're immensely attracted to what we apprehend of God—goodness and truth and beauty—we're also apprehensive of what lies beyond our grasp, sensing that "it is a fearful thing to fall into the hands of the living God" (Heb. 10:31; also 12:25–29).[1]

Now here's the surprising thing: the holy is commonly experienced in that which is not God. Holy mountains, sacred stones, holy women and men, sacred trees, holy words, sacred song, and holy *places*— sanctuaries. In all cultures and times we have the witness of story, song, and ritual honoring this mysterious and divine otherness in things and people who are very much present, here and now. Often superstitions develop around such persons or things or places, but not always. Frequently enough there's a healthy, sane, worshipful response to what's perceived as a material and present witness to the otherness of God. Biblically, this is almost always the case. Poets and artists regularly call our attention to the holy in various and sometimes surprising places. Annie Dillard provides an exuberantly profound contemporary realization of this phenomenon in her book *Holy the Firm.*[2]

• • •

DAVID IS WELL LAUNCHED by now into a life of holiness—a life defined and initiated by God. But he's also being assaulted by its opposite. He runs to Ahimelech's sanctuary at Nob for protection, and then he finds himself immersed in holiness. A sanctuary is a place for paying attention to God, a place where the truth of God is preserved and honored, a place for remembering the events in which God has been clearly active and powerful. David arrives at the sanctuary at Nob desperate, running for his life. At the moment probably the only thing he has on his mind is saving his physical life. But in fact he needs much more; he needs help in maintaining a God-attentive life, living out the life of anointing and service and prayer that has been God-activated in him. Everything that makes him who he is has been threatened and is under attack. Saul would deny and destroy everything that makes David who he is, everything that constitutes his very humanity, everything that we would name in retrospect *Christian.*

Ahimelech seems to be a little bewildered, maybe even shaken, by David's breathless entrance into the sanctuary at Nob: "Ahimelech came to meet David trembling" (1 Sam. 21:1). Why is David in such a hurry? Why is David by himself? What's going on here?

David reassures the priest by lying to him. In a few moments he will lie to him again saying, in effect, "Everything is going to be all right; I'm on the king's business. And I will be joined soon by some young men. We need food; what do you have? Give me five loaves of bread, or whatever is here."

• • •

THIS IS PERHAPS THE PLACE to note that the story of David isn't set before us as a moral model to copy. David isn't a person whose actions we're inspired to imitate. In the company of David we don't feel inadequate because we know we could never do it that well. Just the opposite: in the company of David we find someone who does it as badly as, or worse than, we do, but who in the process doesn't quit, doesn't withdraw from God. David's isn't an *ideal* life but an *actual* life. We imaginatively enter the company of David not to improve our morals but to deepen our sense of human reality: *this* is what happens in the grand enterprise of being human. Reentering through my believing imagination the world of David, I'm more myself—free to be myself and able to find God in the middle of what's going on right now. The David stories aren't moral lessons telling me what to do or inspirational talks prodding me to set my sights higher. I once heard (or read) William James described as "a man on whom nothing was lost." David is a person on whom nothing *of God* is lost.

One of the distressing and distressingly frequent corruptions that works its way into the spiritual life is the loss of connection between who God is and who we are. We say the name *God,* we enter a sanctuary, we pray—but often the slightest tone of falsehood begins to creep in, a subtle dishonesty that gets into our speech and our action; the religious place offers an occasion to *use* God instead of submitting to him. Instead of becoming *more* before God, we become *less.* David is an antidote to this. We read David to cultivate a sense of reality for a true life, an honest life, a God-aware and God-responsive life.

• • •

DAVID ASKS FOR BREAD, but the priest has no bread, or at least no common bread. All he has is shewbread, the holy bread—called the Bread of the Presence—which in those days was placed on the altar each week as an offering to the Lord. Each Sabbath twelve loaves of wheat bread were arranged in rows on the altar. When new loaves replaced the old on the following Sabbath, the priests were permitted to eat them, but *only* the priests. It was unlawful for anybody else to consume them (Lev. 24:5–9). It was also unlikely. Week-old bread; who would want it? It's a venerable tradition in the world of religion to let the priests have it.

David would have known that such bread wasn't for a hungry man and his soldiers; nevertheless, he insisted on having it. He was on a royal mission, he said, and the men who would accompany him were consecrated for the work.

Ahimelech bent the rules and gave him the bread. Ahimelech was no literalist, fussily keeping the sanctuary inviolate. He discerned the spirit of the rules and permitted David to take the bread. The bread set apart for a solemn act of communion, something akin to our Holy Communion, was grabbed by David, ravenous for food, and wolfed down. A millennium later, Jesus, commenting on the incident, tacitly commended Ahimelech for breaking the letter and serving the spirit in the holy place (Matt. 12:1–5):

> *Since the day David's guerrillas*
> *Made field rations of the priest's Holy Bread,*
> *And in a similar field a thousand*
> *Years later Jesus' friends took grain*
> *For a trail snack, all witnesses and warriors*
> *Have shared a happy lordship,*
> *Putting their food and sabbaths to proper*
> *Use, glorifying God*
> *With holy appetites, in holy leisure.*

• • •

NEXT DAVID ASKED THE PRIEST for a weapon. He continued to lie to Ahimelech about his fugitive state: "I have brought neither my sword nor my weapons with me, because the king's business required haste" (1 Sam. 21:8). Is there anything I can use?

It happened that there was: Goliath's sword, which David himself had brought back from the Valley of Elah years earlier as a trophy of war. But it was a memorial, a museum piece in the sanctuary, preserving in the place of worship the memory of the great act of salvation in which God had used the young David to turn the tide against the

Philistine hordes. The sword was carefully kept and tended, preserved from scratches or tarnish, there to be viewed by men and women who came to pray and renew their faith and trust in God.

"There is none but that (Goliath) here," said Ahimelech. David didn't hesitate: "There is none like that; give it to me" (1 Sam. 21:9).

And with that David was on his way. He came to the holy place hungry and defenseless; he left full and equipped.

• • •

AHIMELECH AND DAVID had different ideas of what the sanctuary was for that day, but David's approach prevailed. And Ahimelech *let* it prevail. He was hesitant, not quite sure of what was going on, but he didn't stand in the way.

Is the sanctuary a place of quiet dignity where voices are lowered and good manners cultivated? Is it a place to meditate, to reflect, to remember Abraham and Moses, Peter and Paul? Yes, it is that. It's also a place to get emergency help—bread for the journey and a sword for the fight. David came to the sanctuary without food for his stomach and without a weapon in his hand. He left with a full stomach and girded for strenuous battle.

• • •

I WANT TO USE THE WORD *sanctuary* to represent all holy places and not restrict it to shrines and temples, cathedrals and chapels. A holy place is where we become aware that there's more to life than meets the eye, and that the more is "other," *Other.* God, who is beyond us, is also at hand. A sanctuary can be a garden or a park, a mountain or a desert, an automobile or a closet. Defined holy places are usually under the care of priests and pastors, but I want to leave room for exceptions: Jacob's stone pillow, Moses' burning bush, Peter's catch of fish. What I want to prevent is a kind of spirituality that turns us into aesthetes of the numinous, appreciating the fine points of liturgy and doctrine, meditating on the intricacy of roses and the rhythm of ocean waves, while escaping to quiet, secluded, protected places from the grossness of the world and messiness of family.

As I let the words and actions at Nob work themselves into my life, I realize that a sanctuary isn't only the place where my awareness of and connection with God is sharpened; it's also where I, like David, get bread and a sword, strength for the day and weapons for the fight. Both words, *bread* and *sword,* are often associated in our Scriptures with God's word. God's word is bread; God's word is a sword. These aren't fanciful associations but deeply experienced realities. When we're pushed to the boundaries of our existence, running for our very lives, without provisions and without weapons, we seek sanctuary, a holy place. And then this wonderful surprise: we discover vitality in the holiness, life-deepening energies in the holiness. We enter weakened and endangered and before we know it are strengthened and equipped to face danger.

The spirituality of sanctuary is fundamental to the Christian life. We need sanctuaries to run to in order to sustain ourselves with what is necessary to live—God and God's provisions for living in a dangerous world that's hostile to faith. Holy places are necessary for holy living.

DOEG

David wasn't the only visitor to the sanctuary at Nob that day. There was another man, sitting off to the side, watching the way David came in and lied to Ahimelech, grabbed the holy bread and the holy relic, Goliath's sword, and left.

Doeg was the man's name, Doeg the Edomite. He's described in our text as "chief of Saul's herdsmen" (1 Sam. 21:7), but recent textual studies have found evidence to redefine him as "chief of Saul's palace guard."[3] In our society that label would translate into something like "head of Saul's secret police." He, of course, would have known David well. All the time that David had been with King Saul, Doeg had also been there. He had heard David sing and play. He had seen Saul swing between doting on David and trying to kill him.

He was in the sanctuary that day for a religious ceremony of some sort. "Detained before the Lord" (1 Sam. 21:7) is the reason given in the text; he was carrying out, perhaps, some rite of penance or purification. We don't know the details of what brought him to the sanctuary, but it's obvious that it was serious religious business. He wasn't a casual tourist drop-in.

And he took meticulous note of everything David did. He heard David tell lies in the sanctuary to God's priest. He saw David take the holy bread and eat it—the bread carefully protected by Mosaic law for spiritual use only, the bread set apart from all common uses to holy use and mystery. He saw David take the famous Goliath sword—the trophy sword that schoolchildren took field trips to Nob to look at and admire, the museum sword by which pride of country was nurtured—and carry it out into the profane world. Obscure in the shadows, he observed everything David did and stored what he observed for later use. Doeg, it will turn out later, had no interest in God—he was a political man from head to toe. Though engaged in religious business, he was probably in the religious place for political gain or legitimization.

For a man like Doeg, a sanctuary isn't a place to seek an intensification of everyday life but a place to acquire a patina of self-righteousness that will give some holy polish to everyday life. A sanctuary, for someone like Doeg, isn't a place to expose weakness but a place to acquire a cover. It would have been unthinkable for Doeg to enter a holy place the way David did, breathless and disheveled, lying and grabbing—dragging the sacred elements back out into the mud of everydayness. Doeg was *proper;* religion and the things of religion were useful to him for getting ahead in career or politics. As Doeg sat in the sanctuary, it's most unlikely that he would have been thinking about God. There's nothing holy about a sanctuary to people like him.

Doeg heard David's lies, saw David take the bread and sword, and no doubt felt mighty lucky to be there that day, realizing that he had in his hands data that might be most useful in the future in putting down David and promoting his own fortunes in the court of King Saul. He returned to Saul's palace at Gibeah and waited his chance.

He didn't have long to wait. Saul got word that David had been discovered in the wilderness. He erupted in anger: Why hadn't someone told him before? Why was he the last to know where David was? He accused those in attendance on him of being in on the conspiracy against him (1 Sam. 22:6–8).

Doeg, political opportunist to the core, saw his chance to curry favor with the king and took it: he reported what he had observed at Nob—David coming for help and Ahimelech giving it to him.

Saul went into action: he arraigned Ahimelech and all the attendant priests at Nob (there were eighty-five of them) and accused them of conspiring with David against him. They protested that they were innocent, which they certainly were. (Because of David's deception, Ahimelech had had no idea that he was helping David escape.) But Saul sneered at their defense and ordered their execution.

• • •

BY NOW, KING SAUL'S IDEAS of God and religion were thoroughly twisted and completely self-serving. The task of priests wasn't to help fugitives but to protect kings. Sanctuaries weren't places for hungry and hunted men and women to get help but wayside historical shrines for preserving the memory of God and the traditions of the country. A religious priesthood that didn't make its highest loyalty the preservation of religion was dangerous to the country. But such religion isn't religion at all, but a form of power politics.

Saul's soldiers refused his order to kill the priests. They were loyal enough to their king to disobey him. They knew that a human command, even when it came with the authority of their anointed king, could never usurp God's command.

Frustrated with the insubordination of his soldiers, Saul commanded Doeg to do the work. Doeg did it, slaughtered the undefended priests, all eighty-five of them, and proceeded to massacre the entire village—women, children, and animals (1 Sam. 22:18–19). For John Calvin, Doeg is "the consummate villain."[4] We can be quite sure that Doeg, conniving and calculating, did his bloody work that day untroubled by a single question or doubt, supremely confident that he was living out his sanctuary-sanctioned identity, using what he had been given in the sanctuary to promote himself, and coolly contemptuous of the David who had dragged God into the mess of his runaway life.

David's fiery Psalm 52 is connected with this incident by its title, "When Doeg the Edomite reported to Saul, 'David's at Ahimelech's

House.'" When the massacre was reported to David, David remembered that Doeg had been at the sanctuary that day (1 Sam. 22:22) and funneled his anger, as he so often did, into prayer:

> Why do you brag of evil, Big Man?
>   God's mercy carries the day.
> You scheme catastrophe;
>   your tongue cuts razor-sharp,
>   artisan in lies.
> You love evil more than good,
>   you call black white.
> You love malicious gossip,
>   you foul-mouth.
>
> God will tear you limb from limb,
>   sweep you up and throw you out,
> Pull you up by the roots
>   from the land of life.
>
> Good people will watch and
>   worship. They'll laugh in relief:
> "Big Man bet on the wrong horse,
>   trusted in big money,
>   made his living from catastrophe."
>
> And I'm an olive tree,
>   growing green in God's house.
> I trusted in the generous mercy
>   of God then and now.
>
> I thank you always
>   that you went into action.
> And I'll stay right here,
>   your good name my hope,
>   in company with your faithful friends.

• • •

WONDERFUL THINGS HAPPEN in sanctuaries. On the run we stop at a holy place and find that there's more to life than our circumstances and feelings indicate at that moment. We perceive God in and around and beneath us. New life surges up within us. We discover a piece of our lives we had thought long gone restored to us, remember an early call of God, a place of prayer, a piece of evidence that God saves. And now, there it is again: "There is none like that; give it to me." We leave restored, revived, redeemed.

But terrible things also happen in sanctuaries. We can use a religious ritual to insulate ourselves from people we have come to despise. We can stop by a holy place to cultivate a sense of superiority, look for a way to acquire an advantage over the competition, or legitimize our hate and meanness with the authority of religion. And then we leave callous, cold, and conniving.

Every time we enter a holy place and become aware of the presence of a holy God, we leave either better or worse. If we come to separate ourselves from common people and things, we will almost certainly leave worse. We will leave, as Doeg did, ready to impose our notion of right on someone else, forcing our idea of God on another, full of indignation, crusading in a holy war. But if we enter hungry and needy, letting ourselves be vulnerable before God, bluntly, even belligerently, asking for what we need, we will almost certainly leave better. We will leave, as David did, grateful to be simply alive, amazed to know that God is with us, that the most holy sacrament is food for our most everyday needs.

· 7 ·

WILDERNESS

DAVID AT EN-GEDI

1 Samuel 23–24

At once, this same Spirit pushed Jesus out into the wild.
For forty wilderness days and nights he was tested by
Satan. Wild animals were his companions, and angels
took care of him.

—MARK 1:12–13

EN-GEDI IS A SMALL OASIS alongside the Dead Sea, the large lake of salt water at the southeastern corner of Israel. Today there's a little park for picnickers and swimmers—a cluster of palm trees, a stand where you can buy soft drinks, a bathhouse for changing and rinsing off the salt after a swim. There are usually a dozen or so swimmers—or floaters; it's hard to swim in that dense salt water. About three hundred yards to the west there's a precipitous rise of cliffs pushing up two thousand feet and topped by tableland. The plateau and cliffs are deeply grooved by erosion, making a tangle of canyons and caves. This is the wilderness of En-gedi, a vast expanse of badlands, country as harsh and inhospitable as any you're likely to find on this earth. Hyenas, lizards, and vultures are your hosts.

I spent a few hours at En-gedi a few years ago. It was a spring day; I wanted to get a feel for the country in which David had survived during the years he was a fugitive from King Saul. I climbed up into the cliffs, ducked into the caves, trying to imagine the kind of life that David eked out in that harsh environment. In a very few minutes virtually everything was different, unfamiliar, alien. Austere country. But also strangely beautiful.

An hour or so into the wilderness my perceptions began to sharpen—sights, sounds, smells. This happens in the wilderness. You see more, hear more, yes, believe more, which is why it holds such a prominent place in our traditions of spirituality.[1] No noise. Almost no people. A few animals, but they mostly stay out of sight. Yet in the solitude awareness develops of your part in this intricate and precarious web of life. A sense of holiness takes shape; the sacred surfaces.

David didn't start out in the wilderness, and he didn't end up in the wilderness. But he did spend some highly significant years in the wilderness. Everybody—at least everybody who has anything to do with God—spends time in the wilderness, so it's important to know what can take place there.

David didn't choose to enter the wilderness; he was chased there. He didn't go to the wilderness to take photographs of the wild goats and draw pictures of the exquisite wildflowers but to escape from murderous King Saul. David was in the wilderness because he was a fugitive, running for his life.

But having been chased there, David found the wilderness a place of truth, a place of beauty, and a place of love. The years that David spent in the wilderness were some of the best years of his life.

THE ESSENTIAL WILDERNESS

There's something enormously attractive about wilderness. Jack London wrote a famous book with the title *The Call of the Wild*—and it *does* call. Most of the North American continent was not so very long ago a wilderness. The First Nations' and Native American voices, ignored and nearly silent for so long, are again being heard, witnesses to the inherent sacredness of the wild, the spirituality of weather and seasons and land. Slowly the wilderness receded before loggers and miners, stockmen and ranchers, and eventually highways and pipelines and shopping malls. Acre after acre of wilderness still daily falls victim to plunder or domestication or pollution or commercialization.

A few individuals scattered here and there realized what was happening and made strenuous efforts to preserve at least pockets of wilderness.[2] John Muir, Teddy Roosevelt, and Gifford Pinchot lead the list. National and provincial parks were established, wilderness areas set apart, wildlife refuges designated. These efforts were made and continue to be made because we need access to mountains and plains, rivers and deserts that aren't *used* for anything but simply *are*. There are things that we can experience only in silence and solitude. There are essential things about being human that can be known only in the shadow of a beech tree, beside the rush of a whitewater stream, or after a long climb up a mountain. "The wilderness," writes Nancy Newhall, "holds answers to questions man's not yet learned to ask."[3]

When we're in the wilderness, we aren't in control, we have no assignment, no appointments to keep. Stay alert, stay alive—that's it. When we're in the wilderness, we commonly feel our lives simplifying and deepening. Many people, after a few days in the wilderness (sometimes after only a few hours), feel themselves to be more themselves, uncluttered and spontaneous. Very often, even though otherwise unaccustomed to it, they say the name *God*. There's something wonderfully attractive about wilderness.

> What would the world be, once bereft
> Of wet and of wildness? Let them be left,
> O let them be left, wildness and wet;
> Long live the weeds and the wilderness yet.[4]

But there's also something frightening about wilderness. The wild, while it's breathtakingly beautiful, is also dangerously unpredictable. A storm can turn an angel-caressed sky into a devil's cauldron. An animal can change in an instant from an elegant icon into a fierce killer. A mountain stream can delight the eye with a light show one moment and then, without transition, convert a slipped step into an icy drowning. The wilderness has a hundred different ways to kill us.

Always, in the wilderness, there's a tension between the beauty and the danger, between pristine simplicities and sinister threats. And because most of us can't sustain this tension for long, we live in towns and cities. We surround ourselves with water faucets and furnaces, roofs and street signs, grocery stores and police officers and firefighters. We lock our doors at night, put umbrellas over our heads when it rains, and keep our dogs on a leash.

But there are times, no matter how thoroughly we're civilized, when we're plunged into the wilderness—not a geographical wilderness but what I'm going to call a circumstantial wilderness. Everything is going along fine: we've learned the language of the country, gotten a job, decorated the house, signed up for car payments, made out a schedule that imposes some order on the chaos of time, accepted responsibilities that define our significance, heard people speak our name and determined that we're identifiable. And then suddenly we're beside ourselves: we don't know what's going on within us or in another who is important to us; feelings erupt in us that call into question what we've never questioned before. There's a radical change in our bodies, or our emotions, or our thinking, or our friends, or our job. We're out of control. We're in the wilderness.

What I want to say is this: I readily acknowledge that this circumstantial wilderness is a terrible, frightening, and dangerous place; but I also believe that it's a place of beauty. There are things to be seen, heard, and experienced in this wilderness that can be seen, heard, and experienced nowhere else. When we find ourselves in the wilderness, we do well to be frightened; we also do well to be alert, open-eyed. In the wilderness we're plunged into an awareness of danger and death; at the very same moment we're plunged, if we let ourselves be, into an awareness of the great mystery of God and the extraordinary preciousness of life.

The Three Wilderness Stories

The story of David in the wilderness of En-gedi is bracketed by two other wilderness stories: on one side the forty years that Moses led the Israelites through the Sinai wilderness; on the other the forty days that Jesus fasted in the Judean wilderness. Three great wilderness stories in our Scriptures, each influencing the others.

Wilderness stories are temptation/testing stories. Wilderness is the place of testing, the place of tempting. Wilderness is wildness. Nothing is tamed or domesticated. The accustomed supports of civilization aren't there, and life is sheer survival.

In the Moses wilderness story the people of Israel were trained to discern between idols and the living God, taught to worship; through their wilderness experience they were prepared to live totally before God. In the Jesus wilderness story our Lord learned to discern between religion that uses God and spirituality that enters into what God does, and he was thereby prepared to be our Savior, not merely our helper or adviser or entertainer. In the David wilderness story we see a young man hated and hunted like an animal, his very humanity profaned, forced to decide between a life of blasphemy and a life of prayer—and choosing prayer. In choosing prayer he entered into the practice of holiness. A very earthy holiness it was, but holiness all the same.

I'm nervous about using the words *holy* and *holiness*—nervous because the words have picked up some bad associations and I don't want to be misunderstood. *Holy* in our common usage often means "too good for this world" or "too nice to associate with someone like me." But those understandings are far off the mark. Still, there's no other word strong enough to mark what emerges in David in the wilderness years. What happens is that no matter what else David is doing, he's basically dealing with God; and the more he deals with God, the more human he becomes—the more he becomes "David." *Holy* is our best word to describe that life—the human aliveness that comes from dealing with God-Alive. We're most human when we deal with God. Any other way of life leaves us less human, less ourselves.

In the wilderness we're face to face with the basics, the Basic, with God. The confrontation is a test, a temptation. Do we deal with God or not? We take the test and become more or less. We grow up or we regress. David became more. David grew up.

And so we read these David stories of the wilderness years and look for signs of God, look for evidence of David's God-responses. It's good practice for discovering similar God-responses in the wilderness circumstances of our own lives and the lives of our friends.

KING SAUL IN THE CAVE

Fifteen stories are told out of David's wilderness years. The meeting of David and Saul in the wilderness cave near En-gedi is one of the early ones. David and a few of his men are hidden in a cave cut in the cliffs above the Dead Sea. The day is hot and the cave is cool. They're deep in the cave, resting. Suddenly there's a shadow across the mouth of the cave; they're astonished to see that it's King Saul. They didn't know that he was that close in his pursuit. Saul enters the cave but doesn't see them: fresh from the hard glare of desert sun, his eyes aren't adjusted to the darkness and don't pick out the shadowy figures in the recesses of the cave. Besides, he isn't looking for them at that moment; he has entered the cave to respond to the call of nature. He turns his back to them.

When David and his men see what's going on, they know that Saul is as good as dead, oblivious to their presence, ungirded, unarmed. The men begin to make their move, but David silently forbids them. Instead, he moves along the wall of the cave to where the king's garment has been tossed, cuts off a piece of it, and then slips back with his men. In a short while King Saul pulls on his garment, straps on his sword, and leaves. David lets him walk a healthy distance away and then goes to the mouth of the cave and calls to him. By now the king is across the canyon. David calls, "My lord the king!" (1 Sam. 24:8). Saul looks, astonished. David bows down, reverently honoring the king. And then he says, "Why do you listen to those who tell you I am your enemy? See what I have in my hand? It is the skirt of your robe. Just now, instead of cutting your robe I could as easily have cut you, *killed* you. But I will not do that. I will never do that because you are the LORD's anointed" (my paraphrase).

This is the detail in the story that catches and holds our attention: David calling Saul the Lord's anointed. "I will not put forth my hand against my lord; for he is the LORD's anointed" (1 Sam. 24:10).

In the wilderness years, as David was dealing with God, a sense of the sacred developed in him. While he was living in that austere country, his awareness of holiness, of God's beauty and presence in everything, in everyone, increased exponentially. David was above all reverent. He had an inordinate capacity for wonder. The Psalms, many of which came out of these wilderness years, are our main evidence for this. This story puts the holiness on display.

As Saul was outlined at the opening of the cave against the cobalt blue of the Dead Sea, with the red cliffs of Moab beyond, he entered the landscape—another detail of God's creation, God's blessing. David didn't see an enemy; he saw the magnificent, albeit flawed, king of God and did obeisance.

All the ingredients for a scene of coarse vulgarity are here: the king on his "throne," viewed from the backside, taking a dump. But David, though earthy, wasn't vulgar. He turned the scene into an act of generous homage, a sacred moment, a witness to an improbable and incredible reverence for life.

Some time later there's a similar scene at the hill of Hachilah in Ziph (1 Sam. 26). David penetrated Saul's camp in the middle of the night and came upon Saul fast asleep and unprotected. Again he could easily have killed him but didn't. Both times—at En-gedi and Hachilah—David's wilderness-trained eyes looked on Saul and saw not Saul the enemy but Saul the God-anointed. In the solitude and silence and emptiness of the wilderness, uncluttered and undistracted by what everyone else was saying and doing, David was able to see God's glory where no one else could see it—in Saul.

The wilderness taught David to see beauty everywhere. The wilderness was David's school in the preciousness of life; through wilderness-testing David learned to see God in places and things he would never have thought to look previously. The wilderness immersed David in beauties so profound that a cheap revenge was unthinkable. The wilderness trained David in loyalties so binding that a broken oath was impossible. The wilderness exposed David to the presence of God in the most barren piece of rock so that no thing, and certainly no man, could ever be treated with scorn or contempt.

The holiness of wilderness had entered David's soul, and now he saw holiness everywhere, even in Saul. Killing Saul would have been a desecration. A thousand years before St. Paul wrote that our bodies are temples of the Holy Spirit—holy *places*—David had discovered and experienced this fundamental truth in the unlikely body of King Saul in the wilderness of En-gedi.

"I've Run to You for Dear Life"

Simultaneously with discovering holiness, David found refuge. The books of Samuel give the story of David from the outside; the Psalms—the prayers of David—give the same story from the inside. In the word *refuge* we find the two stories intersecting

Over and over again in the Psalms we come across the word *refuge*. Beginning with the second psalm, "Blessed are all who take refuge in him," followed by the fifth, "Let all who take refuge in thee rejoice," picked up in the seventh, "O LORD my God, in thee do I take refuge," continuing in the eleventh, "In the LORD I take refuge," and on and on and on—thirty-seven times in the Psalms we find the word *refuge* (twenty-five times as a verb, twelve times as a noun). David (and the traditions flowing out of David) provides the narrative context for spiritual meaning. The wilderness was the dictionary in which David looked up the word *refuge*. The meaning he found given indicated that refuge has to do mostly with God.

A striking thing happened to this word *refuge*. Old Testament scholar J. Gamberoni has shown that it started out as a very physical word, a geographical word: a refuge is a place to run to. But in the Psalms it "lost all its physical and psychological elements associated with flight, gaining in return an exclusive reference to Yahweh in the sense of a fundamental decision for Yahweh over and above anything and anyone else, whether made once for all or actualized in the face of specific dangers and temptations."[5]

Reflecting the history of this word, in David's prayers *refuge* refers to a good experience, but what got him to refuge was a bad experience. He started out running for his life; and at some point he found the life he was running for, and the name for that life was God. "God is my refuge."

This happens all the time; it's one of the fundamental surprises in spirituality. Whatever we start out feeling or doing or thinking can lead us to God, whether directly or meanderingly. Another way to say this is that we rarely start with God. We start with the immediate data of our lives—a messy house, a balky car, a cranky spouse, a recalcitrant child (and on our good days a burst of sunrise, an ecstatic smile, a piercing insight). We start out being desperate in the wilderness of En-gedi, and before we know it we're ecstatic in the wilderness of God.

The prayer of David traditionally assigned to this story is Psalm 57.[6] While there are lines in that psalm that convey David's fugitive state at the time, its overwhelming impression is of energetic and ebullient praise of God. This means that while Saul was the occasion for David's being in the wilderness, Saul neither defined nor dominated the wilderness. The wilderness was full of God, not Saul.

> *Be good to me, God—and now!*
>   *I've run to you for dear life.*
> *I'm hiding out under your wings*
>   *until the hurricane blows over.*
> *I call out to High God,*
>   *the God who holds me together.*
> *He sends orders from heaven and saves me,*
>   *he humiliates those who kick me around.*
> *God delivers generous love,*
>   *he makes good on his word.*

I find myself in a pride of lions
    who are wild for a taste of human flesh;
Their teeth are lances and arrows,
    their tongues sharp daggers.

Soar high in the skies, O God!
    Cover the whole earth with your glory!

They booby-trapped my path;
    I thought I was dead and done for.
They dug a mantrap to catch me,
    and fell into it themselves.

I'm ready, God, so ready,
    ready from head to toe,
Ready to sing, ready to raise a tune:
    "Wake up, soul!
Wake up, harp! wake up, lute!
    Wake up you sleepyhead sun!"
I'm thanking you, Yahweh, out loud in the streets,
    singing your praises in town and country.
The deeper your love, the higher it goes;
    every cloud is a flag to your faithfulness.
Soar high in the skies, O God!
    Cover the whole earth with your glory!

Wilderness, in itself, makes nothing happen. Saul and David were both in the wilderness. Saul was running after David, obsessed with hunting him down, his life narrowed to a murderous squint. Meanwhile, David was running to God and finding himself in his God-refuge praying, wide-eyed in wonder, taking in the glory, awake and ready for God's generous love, for the God who "makes good on his word."

We can't be naive about the wilderness; it's a dangerous place. But we must never avoid the wilderness; it's a wonderful place.

BEAUTY

DAVID AND ABIGAIL

1 Samuel 25

The Word became flesh and blood,
and moved into the neighborhood.
We saw the glory with our own eyes,
the one-of-a-kind glory,
like Father, like Son.
Generous inside and out,
true from start to finish.

—JOHN 1:14

I CAN'T REMEMBER WHEN this first came to me, but for many, many years now—twenty? thirty?—I've thought of Abigail as an icon: an image that works in such a way that the beauty of the Lord pours through it, a person who lives in such a way that the beauty of the Lord streams through. *Icon* is the Greek word for *image,* but it has entered our language as a spiritually charged word—a word connoting an image that releases the light of Christ into our praying lives.[1]

Abigail on her knees in the wilderness, on her knees before David. David is rampaging, murder in his eyes, and Abigail blocks his path, kneeling before him. David has been insulted and is out to avenge the insult with four hundred men worked up into a frenzy. Abigail, solitary and beautiful, kneels in the path, stopping David in his tracks. At this moment David is full of himself and empty of God; the emptiness is visible as ugliness. Abigail recovers God for David. David is earlier described as beautiful,[2] though there's no sign of it here. But beautiful Abigail restores the beauty of God to David, his original identity.

DAVID AND HIS GOOD SAMARITANS

David found good work to do in the wilderness. He formed his men into a band of good Samaritans. In addition to the plethora of natural dangers in the wilderness, that area was also a high-crime district. Bandits frequented the wilderness, preying on travelers, ready to mug anyone who showed promise of a full wallet or salable merchandise. One of Jesus' most famous stories is about a traveler in the Judean wilderness getting robbed and beaten and then rescued by a Samaritan, the one we've known ever since as the good Samaritan. This is the kind of rescue work that David and his men appeared to have been doing in the wilderness.

It's David's good Samaritan work that occasions the encounter with Nabal, a wealthy stockman. The herdsmen who cared for Nabal's flocks were especially vulnerable to wilderness outlaws and rustlers, and David, for at least one season, provided protection. Later in the story one of the herdsmen testifies that David and his men "were a wall to us both by night and by day, all the while we were with them keeping the sheep" (1 Sam. 25:16).

What better occupation for David and his comrades during those wilderness years? "Wilderness" is a context, not an agenda. Running and hiding out from Saul hardly constituted full-time work, and so during the quiet interims when danger lessened for them, they found ways to protect others from danger. On the strength of the herdsman's remark ("They were a wall to us"), we can imagine David's company as forming a kind of unofficial neighborhood watch group and emergency ambulance service combined. As ruthless outlaws roamed the canyons and mesas, David introduced a semblance of law and order into the moral anarchy. And Nabal's herdsmen benefited.

Then sheepshearing time, which combined hard work and gala festivities, arrived. As the year's harvest of wool was gathered, banqueting tables were loaded down with food and drink. The long, hard hours of shearing the sheep now climaxed in a grand celebration.

David was in the neighborhood and sent ten of his men to ask for some food and drink from the feast tables. It was a reasonable request, and natural in the circumstances. They had been protecting these shepherds all year and no doubt living on survival rations—the wilderness wasn't plentiful in food supplies. Some of Nabal's fresh fruit and baked pastries would have been a welcome change.

But when Nabal heard the request, he acted as if he had never so much as heard of David and lumped him with the common criminals who infested the wilderness—the "many servants nowadays who are breaking away from their masters" (1 Sam. 25:10). He not only refused them food from his feast, he insulted them.

David was outraged. He determined to exact a bloody revenge. He called his men to arm themselves. They set out for Nabal's feast, where they would kill Nabal for his ingratitude, his gratuitous insult, his rudeness. Nabal's vulgarity provoked a like vulgarity in David: "So and more also do God unto the enemies of David, if I leave of all that pertain to him by the morning light any that pisseth against the wall" (1 Sam. 25:22, KJV). From that moment, Nabal was marked for death.

David lost his temper. David lost all sense of his identity as God's anointed. David lost touch with the wilderness beauty of holiness. David, who had been able to see maniacal King Saul as a temple of the Holy Spirit, now couldn't see Nabal as anything but an ugly piece of garbage that was a stench in his life. David was on the verge of becoming another Saul, out to get rid of anyone threatening his status and role.

"Bound in the Bundle of the Living"

Abigail got wind of the insult and anticipated the consequences. She took swift action to head off David's predictably angry response. She gathered together the makings of a magnificent feast, loaded everything on pack animals, and set out to intercept David. The moment she saw him, she dismounted, went to her knees, putting her face to the ground in reverence and respect, and said, "Please, please, please don't do this. This isn't an action worthy of a prince of Israel. Remember who you are. Remember God's anointing, God's mercy. Don't stoop to fighting grudge battles; your task is to fight the battles of the Lord" (my paraphrase).

And then she said this: "The life of my lord shall be bound in the bundle of the living in the care of the LORD your God; and the lives of your enemies he shall sling out as from the hollow of a sling" (1 Sam. 25:29). Rendered as poetry, it sounds like this:

> *If anyone stands in your way,*
> *if anyone tries to get you out of the way,*
> *Know this: your God-honored life is tightly bound*
> *into the bundle of God-given life;*
> *But the lives of your enemies will be hurled aside*
> *as a stone is thrown from a sling. (my translation)*

Abigail witnesses God's work in David: God's call, God's promise, God's covenant, God's word. David's life is so tangled up in God's work and revelation that there's no way he can extricate himself from it and still be himself. There's no way he can act as if God were not in him, working "according to his purpose" (Eph. 1:9). His life is formed and conditioned by the tender mercies of God, not the foolish devilries of Nabal.

Abigail witnesses God's work on behalf of David: protecting, guiding, ruling, intervening. She knows that the phrase "sling out as from the hollow of a sling" will be sure to touch David's memory and make present that long-ago day when, immersed in prayer in the Valley of Elah, he brought Goliath down with a single stone from his sling.

Abigail says, in effect, "Your task, David, is not to exact vengeance; vengeance is God's business, and you aren't God. You're out here in the wilderness to find out what God is doing and who you are before God. The wilderness isn't an experiment station in which you test yourself and find out how strong and resilient you are. It's where you discover the strength of God and God's faithful ways of working in and through your life. Nabal is a fool, but don't you also become a fool. One fool is enough in this story."

Nabal is no Goliath, but the way David chooses to respond to him will be just as significant in the continuing development of God's people.

Remarkably—improbably!—David stops, looks, and listens. Abigail, in the middle of nowhere, on her knees before David, speaks God back into his life in prayer and poetry. And David lets her speak it.

The accelerating momentum of the story is stopped and then re-versed by Abigail, marginal Abigail. Abigail is marginal because she's a woman in a man-dominated world. Abigail is marginal because she's weaponless in a sword-rattling world. Mostly, Abigail is marginal be-cause she's beautiful in a materialistic, utilitarian world.

Abigail's beauty is both inner and outer. Her lovely appearance is balanced in the text by the word "discretion" (v. 33). Abigail is as beauti-ful inwardly as she is outwardly. Abigail's beauty is a witness to the God-created, God-sustained, God-blessed life that's everywhere present but frequently obscured by willfulness and blasphemy. Abigail's beauty sur-prises David out of his sudden plunge into ugliness, and he sees and hears God again.

BEAUTY AS WITNESS

There's a long tradition in the Christian life, most developed in Eastern Orthodoxy, of honoring beauty as a witness to God and a call to prayer.[3] Beauty is never only what our senses report to us but always also a sign of what's just beyond our senses—an innerness and depth. There's more to beauty than we can account for empirically. In that *more* and *beyond* we discern God. Artists who wake up our jaded senses and help us attend to these matters are gospel evangelists. In the presence of the beautiful we intuitively respond in delight, wanting to be involved, getting near, entering in—tapping our feet, humming along, touching, kissing, meditating, contemplating, imitating, believing, praying. Painted prayers; sung prayers; danced prayers. It's the very nature of our five senses to pull us into whatever is there—scent, rhythm, texture, vision. And it's the vocation of the artist to activate our senses so that they do just that.[4] Beauty in bird and flower, in rock and cloud. Beauty in ocean and mountain, in star and sand. Beauty in storm and meadow, in laughter and play. But most exquisitely beauty in the human body with its fulfillment in the human face. Instinctively—unless our instincts are dulled by the habits and routines of sin—we recognize that there's more to beauty than what we discern with our senses, that beauty is never "skin deep" but always revelatory of goodness and truth. Beauty releases light into our awareness so that we're conscious of the beauty of the Lord. "It makes icons of us all. Each of us becomes a work of art, reflecting God's glory."[5]

Abigail's beauty puts David in touch, again, with the beauty of the Lord. He realizes who he is, what he's doing, what his life is for. In his encounters with Saul, David had seen the beauty of holiness in that hate-besmeared, evil-ravaged life: Saul, the anointed of God—though now corrupted—was a person in whom God could still be seen and honored. This recognition of the beauty of holiness in Saul happened twice: in the cave at En-gedi (chapter 24) and at the hill of Hachilah (chapter 26), the scenes framing Abigail's revelation (chapter 25). In that latter revelation David sees it in himself, through the beauty of Abigail—the beauty of holiness in *David*, in vengeance-obsessed, honor-defending, out-for-blood David: David, the anointed of God, a person in whom God was present and to be honored. In the revealing mirror of Abigail's beauty, David sees himself as God saw him. Abigail recovers for David the identity that God had given him.

FOOLS

There are fools aplenty in this world, and we're sorely provoked by them. But no sooner do we set out to set them right than we enter into the same foolish wickedness that we're determined to get rid of. David later prayed his way out of Nabal's influence. The name Nabal means fool (*nabal*). David's Psalm 14 is his last word on Nabal:

Bilious and bloated, they gas,
"God is gone."
Their words are poison gas,
fouling the air; they poison
Rivers and skies;
thistles are their cash crop.

Yahweh sticks his head out of heaven.
He looks around.
He's looking for someone not stupid—
one man, even, God-expectant,
just one God-ready woman.

He comes up empty. A string
of zeroes. Useless, unshepherded
Sheep, taking turns pretending
to be Shepherd.
The ninety and nine
follow their fellow.

Don't they know anything
all these imposters?
Don't they know
that they can't get away with this—
Treating people like a fast-food meal
over which they're too busy to pray?

Night is coming for them, and nightmares,
for God takes the side of victims.
Do you think you can mess
with the dreams of the poor?
You can't, for God
makes their dreams come true.

Is there anyone around to save Israel?
   Yes. God is around; Yahweh turns life around.
Turned-around Jacob skips rope;
   turned around Israel sings laughter.

Being against Nabal isn't spirituality. There's no spirituality in opposing a fool. We need only spend enough time on the matter to discern that Nabal, this strutting, arrogant, vulgar Calebite dog,[6] is a fool and then get on with what God is doing. Which is what David did, leaving Psalm 14 as a witness.[7]

When some Abigail or other shows up—a sudden beauty in song or face, in aspen or iris—we see ourselves in a larger, truer light. David had been living in the huge, vast world of God—God's love and redemption, prayer and holiness—and it nearly got away from him as he pursued his puny, small-minded revenge. Abigail's beauty—her double-edged beauty of character and countenance—recovered the beauty of the Lord for him. Abigail on her knees put David back on his knees.

Nabal died soon after this. David lost no time: he sent for Abigail, courted her, and married her.

• • •

THERE'S NOTHING MORE COMMON in the spiritual life than starting out right and then going wrong. We start out with enthusiasm and promise, surging with energy and purity of heart. And then somewhere along the line we're corrupted and spoiled. St. Paul coined the term *shipwrecks* to describe these episodes. The remains of these shipwrecks are everywhere to be seen in legislatures and courtrooms, athletic stadiums and concert halls, kitchens and bedrooms.

And most tragically, among Christians. Not one of us is exempt. Someone offends us, crosses us, doesn't give us what we want. Our self-importance flares up and we're off to do something about it—usually off to do something about it armed with righteous indignation. Wrapped up in ourselves, we're angry because our self-defined identity is violated. We're off to avenge hurt feelings, a bruised self-image. We'll get even, get back at them, show them a thing or two.

And then we're stopped by something beautiful—child, friend, stranger; cloud, song, fragrance: Abigail. We find ourselves presented with something quite other than what we're feeling and doing. And we suddenly realize that we are quite other than what we're feeling and doing. Wrapped up in ourselves, we had forgotten entirely about God; we now see ourselves as wrapped up in the bundle of God, with Nabal reduced to nothing more than a footnote to the text of our life.

COMPANY

DAVID AT ZIKLAG

1 Samuel 27

*Later Jesus and his disciples were at home having supper
with a collection of disreputable guests. Unlikely as it
seems, more than a few of them had become followers.
The religion scholars and Pharisees saw him keeping
this kind of company and lit into his disciples: "What
kind of example is this, acting cozy with the riffraff?"*

*Jesus, overhearing, shot back, "Who needs a doctor:
the healthy or the sick? I'm here inviting the sin-sick,
not the spiritually fit."*

—MARK 2:15–17

DAVID SPENT THE DECADE of his twenties in the wilderness as an
outlaw with a price on his head. He was chosen by God at a young age and
anointed to be king of Israel. He entered the court of King Saul and was
loved as a friend and singer. He saved his nation from the Philistine military assault and became a hero among the people. And then he was driven

from these accomplishments and admirations to survive as best he could in the wilderness. We don't have an exact chronology provided for us, but for roughly ten years David lived a fugitive life in the wilderness.

David, though young, was a veteran of wilderness living. He was forced into and tried out every wilderness available to him: the wilderness of Ziph (1 Sam. 23:5; 26:2), of Maon (1 Sam. 23:25), of En-gedi (1 Sam. 24:1), of Paran (1 Sam. 25:1). There are no clean-cut borders to these variously designated wildernesses—they all more or less run together and are contained in that vast southern emptiness of gullies and vultures called the Negev—the South. From a distance all wildernesses look the same—arid, unpeopled, harsh, cruel. But from within they acquire a distinct character. No two difficulties are the same; no suffering is quite like another; no test/temptation is an exact replica of any other. David mapped the geography of wilderness both internally and externally. David is our premier cartographer of wilderness.

None of us lives in a continuously ordered, protected, safe, confident world of accomplishment, basking in admiration. Accident or anger breaks in upon us, and we run for our lives. We run to the wilderness.

"Who will give me wings," I ask—
  "wings like a dove?"
Get me out of here on dove wings;
  I want some peace and quiet.
I want a walk in the country,
  I want a cabin in the woods.
I'm desperate for a change
  from rage and stormy weather.
(Ps. 55:6–8)

Wilderness is both a geographical fact and a spiritual metaphor. It was for Moses in the Sinai wilderness; it was for Jesus in the Judean wilderness; and it was for David in the wilderness world that he inhabited for most of ten years.

Since we can expect, sooner or later, to experience the wilderness, I think that it's important to get a feel for the country, find out what happens in this austere place, become familiar with the way God works in the wilderness. Our first impulse, nearly always, is to *escape* the wilderness. What I want to do is convert that escapist impulse into a biblically conditioned *embrace* of wilderness. By steeping our imaginations in David stories, we come to expect not only the worst but also the unexpected best in the wilderness.

A completely unexpected and most improbable "best" that occurred in David's wilderness years was the formation of a people of God—a community of the sort that we now call a church. As usual, though, we're dealing not with a generalized "best" but with something particular, something with its own personal name. Adullam to begin with, and then Ziklag.

THE CAVE OF ADULLAM

Alone and on the run from King Saul, David made an abortive attempt to find refuge with Saul's enemy, King Achish, the Philistine ruler of Gath (1 Sam. 21:10–15). But he quickly realized that having a common enemy didn't automatically make Achish his ally. He got out of there fast, narrowly escaping execution by acting like a crazy person and then holing up in the cave of Adullam. But he wasn't alone for long; he soon had a company of four hundred men gathered around him (1 Sam. 22:1–2).

This is our first notice of a people of God being formed in the wilderness—and a most unlikely people of God it was. The description begins with "his brothers and all his father's house" (1 Sam. 22:1). The early notices of David's family don't prepare us for this. When David was anointed king (chapter 16), it was only after his oldest brother, Eliab—and then one by one the rest of his brothers—had been rejected. It wasn't a day that any of them looked back on with fondness. A few years later, when David visited his brothers in Saul's army during the famous standoff with Goliath, bringing them a food package from home, he was met by Eliab's angry and contemptuous accusation that the only reason he had come was to get away from his boring job with the sheep, that he was looking for excitement by hanging around the soldiers (1 Sam. 17:28). When Eliab and the rest of the family showed up at Adullam,

David wasn't likely to have interpreted their arrival as a display of loyalty and affection. Probably they were afraid that Saul's animosity toward David would spill over onto his kin; they thought that their lives were endangered, and even though they couldn't stand David, his proximity was the safest place they could think of. But perhaps their common distress made them brothers now in a way they had never been before. Misfits all, this is the one place they did fit. Soon after their arrival David took his parents across the border to Moab and left them there for safekeeping during the wilderness years (1 Sam. 22:3–4). And although the text isn't explicit, the brothers, apparently, stayed with the company.

Perhaps Psalm 133 is a record of this time when David and his brothers find themselves on common ground:

> *How wonderful, how beautiful,*
> *   when brothers and sisters get along!*
> *It's like costly anointing oil*
> *   flowing down head and beard,*
> *Flowing down Aaron's beard,*
> *   flowing down the collar of his priestly robes.*
> *It's like the dew on Mount Hermon*
> *   flowing down the slopes of Zion.*
> *Yes, that's where Yahweh commands the blessing,*
> *   ordains eternal life.*

Those who came to him are described as "every one who was in distress, and every one who was in debt, and every one who was discontented" (1 Sam. 22:2). This is the sociological profile of David's congregation: people whose lives were characterized by debt, distress, and discontent. It isn't what we would call the cream of the crop of Israelite society. More like dregs from the barrel. Misfits all, it appears. The people who couldn't make it in regular society. Rejects. Losers. Dropouts.

These are the people David lived with for that decade of wilderness years. They foraged together, ate together, prayed together, fought together. There's nothing explicit in the text about the spirituality of David's company—nothing that says they became a community of faith and searched out the ways in which God worked his salvation in their lives—but the context demands it. We know that David prayed; I think it's safe to assume that he taught his companions to pray, surviving in hostile surroundings and realizing that God was with them, working out his sovereign purposes in them. That motley collection of unloved and unlovable people—the distressed, the debtors, the discontented— achieved a remarkable and high-spirited camaraderie, a morale explic- itly noted in the summarizing retrospective of David's company written later in 1 Chronicles 12.

The large context in which this story is placed—God working his salvation out among those who need to be saved—not only permits but requires that we see David's morally and socially ragtag band as an em- bryonic holy people of God. We must stretch our imaginations to the horizons of God's sovereignty and see that David's company, even though made *up* of the distressed, the debtors, and the discontented, was made *by* God—a people defined not by where they came from or what they did but by what God did in and for them. This seems to be the sort of people that God commonly uses to form companies of be- lievers, disciples, worshipers. Not all scholars are agreed on this, but it's probable that the word *Hebrew* wasn't in the first place an ethnic desig- nation but originally referred to a social class of despised drifters and outcasts who existed on the margins of the Middle Eastern cultures.[1] And it was these men and women, not the cultural and political sophis- ticates of Egypt and Assyria, who were elected to form the "people of God" through whom God would reveal his saving purposes.

It's important to step back a moment and take this in, for a failure to realize this is a constant source of confusion and disaffection, bewilder- ment and scandal. In no area is disappointment and disaffection in the spiritual life as frequent as in the experience (or *inexperience!*) of com- munity. We enter a church looking for God and to our dismay find our- selves surrounded by a bunch of fractious gossips. From the pulpit we hear Jesus' words read out, "Come to me, all who labor and are heavy laden, and I will give you rest. . . . [Y]ou will find rest for your souls. . . . [M]y yoke is easy, and my burden is light" (Matt. 11:28–30).

Having decided on the spot that that's exactly what we've been looking for, the very next Sunday we realize that we're being raked over the coals from the pulpit for not jumping onto the latest mission bandwagon. On a church sign we see written, "O taste and see that the Lord is good!" (Ps. 34:8), and suddenly realize that we're hungry and thirsty for righteousness—starved for it! Before we know it, we've been recruited for a committee in charge of arranging baby-sitting for the monthly potluck suppers. This happens a lot. At their exit interviews these people say, "I love God, but I hate the church."

The most common contemporary North American response to this is to try to improve the image of "church" by public relations and professional staging. When it's successful, which it often is, the results are hard to distinguish in both content and spirit from the world of sales and soap opera.

For myself—and I think I stand at the historical and biblical center on these matters—I refuse to either apologize for the church as it is or attempt to improve its image. Apologize for David's crew—the distressed, the debtors, and the malcontents at the cave of Adullam? Improve the image of Jesus eating with crooks and whores? St. Paul is more realistic: "Take a good look, friends, at who you were when you got called into this life. I don't see many of 'the brightest and the best' among you, not many influential, not many from high-society families. Isn't it obvious that God deliberately chose men and women that the culture overlooks and exploits and abuses, chose these 'nobodies' to expose the hollow pretensions of the 'somebodies'? That makes it quite clear that none of you can get by with blowing your own horn before God. Everything that we have—right thinking and right living, a clean slate and a fresh start—comes from God by way of Jesus Christ. That's why we have the saying, 'If you're going to blow a horn, blow a trumpet for God'" (1 Cor. 1:26–31, *The Message*).

It isn't always this way, but for most of us wilderness spirituality includes being in the company of people we wouldn't ordinarily choose to be with (and who wouldn't ordinarily choose to be with us!). These are not, for the most part, nice people. We'd better get used to it. David did. Jesus did. Paul did.

Achish of Gath

And now here's a surprising thing, maybe even more surprising than the makeup of David's company. David, his company of societal misfits now swelled to six hundred, takes employment with King Achish of Gath (1 Sam. 27:2), the same king he narrowly escaped from earlier as a solitary refugee. A Philistine king no less.

The Philistines had been Israel's primary enemy all through that century. David was first known among his people as champion over the Philistine giant, Goliath, and then as the scourge of Philistines.

The most popular song of the day, sung and played at folk dances, was built upon this refrain:

Where Saul killed a thousand Philistines,
David killed ten thousand!
(18:7; 29:5; MY TRANSLATION)

It was that song, as much as anything, that incited King Saul's jealousy and put David in the wilderness.

And now David, instead of killing Philistines, is cozying up to them, ingratiating himself with them. The last sixteen months of David's wilderness years are spent in the Philistine camp as an ally of the Philistines. David's despair at ever being safe from Saul's murderous campaign drives him, finally, into making common cause with his and Israel's classic enemy, the Philistines.

But David does worse. He not only joins the enemy, he double-crosses the enemy. He pretends to have turned traitor to his own people, pretends to be out marauding and looting Israelite villages on a daily basis, while in actual fact he's massacring tribes to the south, longtime enemies of Israel, bringing back the plunder—plunder identified to Achish as coming from Israelites—and sharing it with the king. Achish, of course, is pleased to have such an enterprising and loyal military associate—so pleased that he hands over the town of Ziklag to David.

What are we to make of this?

Commentators on this text commonly do one of two things: they moralize or they secularize. The moralizing approach is to criticize and condemn David for his spiritual backsliding. He knows better. He betrays his high calling as Israel's anointed. He fails to trust God to care for him, as God has cared for him so amply in the past. David loses it.[2]

The secularizing approach reads this as an admiring account of how David successfully comes to power, the outcome of incredible good luck and shrewd wit. By joining Achish, he puts himself out of reach of King Saul and simultaneously vaults his wives Abigail and Ahinoam into a higher standard of living after all those years of wilderness precariousness. And he manages to use the Philistine King Achish for his own purposes without getting caught in the deception. David is unstoppable—nothing to write home about ethically, but what a hero! And isn't all fair in love and war?

But if we read this text in its context, enter the story and let the story interpret itself to us, we realize something quite different. Even though there's no explicit reference to God and God's purposes here, what we realize is that it's in fact God's purposes that are being worked out, detail by detail. As Walter Brueggemann notes, "We are dealing with a highly self-conscious literature that observes the undercurrent of divine governance without being explicit. Yahweh is with David everywhere. . . . "[3] God's salvation, not David's shoddy morals or clever genius, is the subtext here.

David is more or less doing what he has to do: surviving as best he can under conditions that are decidedly uncongenial to what we're apt to call "the spiritual life." He doesn't stand up in indignation against Achish, confront his Philistine culture of brutality and idolatry. He doesn't get on his moral high horse and announce to Achish that the only way he can in good conscience serve him is as a noncombatant and offer his company's good Samaritan experience and expertise in his service. None of that. He lives not only on the money economy of Philistine Gath but also on the moral economy.

The storyteller doesn't say that this is the right thing to do, simply that this is what David does. And in precisely these conditions, God works out his purposes. God protects David from violating the covenant; he guards David's faithfulness to his anointing; he works out his salvation. The primary concern of the spiritual life isn't what we do for God but what God does for us.[4]

The David/Achish episode isn't a biblical license for caving in to the culture; on the contrary, we're repeatedly admonished to "come out from among them; be ye separate." We're taught in many and various ways to resist the undertow of the world's culture. It is, though, a story of what happens to us when we find ourselves overwhelmed by our culture with seemingly no way out—a story of God's hidden providence, God's behind-the-scenes efforts, doing for us what we aren't doing for ourselves.

I know scores of men and women who are living under the patronage of Achish of Gath. Many of them feel terrible about it. Many of them feel guilty but quite honestly don't know what else they can do. They have jobs with companies that do business in defiant contempt of the Kingdom of God. They're married to spouses who hate the name of Jesus. They seem to be inextricably tangled in an economic system that exploits the poor and ignores the oppressed. They're doing their best to honor parents who dishonor God in thought, word, and deed. There's hardly a Christian I know who hasn't put in time, sometimes far more than David's sixteen months, under Achish of Gath.

And what I want to say is this: God is perfectly capable of working out his purposes in our lives even when we can't lift a finger to help. Better yet, God is faithfully working out our salvation even when every time we lift a finger it seems to contribute to the wrong side, the Philistine side.

ZIKLAG

Serving Achish as he was, David asked for his own town to live in and operate from. Achish gave him Ziklag. Ziklag became David's base, his "church," if you will, for his family and his soldiers.

Moralism is death on spirituality. Moralism is the approach that puts all the emphasis on our performance. It operates out of a conviction that there's a clear-cut right that we're capable of discerning, choosing, and carrying out in every and all circumstances. It puts the entire burden of our spirituality on what we do. God is marginalized. And it crushes our spirits. There's no mercy in it.

Secularism is also death on spirituality. Secularism is the approach that the world as it is establishes the primary context for our daily living and the better we understand and accommodate ourselves to the world the better off we'll be. We can then use whatever advantages accrue to us—money, position, reputation— to "serve the Lord." It operates out of the conviction that spirituality is basically otherworldly and irrelevant regarding basic living. Spirituality is an extra that's added on to a secular base of economic savvy, career know-how, and social smarts. God is trivialized. Secularism is contemptuous of our spirit. There's no salvation in it.

Ziklag, for me, is the premier biblical location for realizing that when we get serious about the Christian life we eventually end up in a place and among people decidedly uncongenial to what we had expected. That place and people is often called a church. It's hard to get over the disappointment that God, having made an exception in my case, doesn't call nice people to repentance.[5]

The Christian life is never just my story; it's a community of stories. I learn my story in company with others. Each story affects and is affected by each of the others. Most of these others are distressed, in debt, and discontent. This complicates things enormously, but there's no getting around it. We're a company. We're looking for a central meaning to our lives. We catch a thread of the plot and begin to follow it, receiving the good news that God is gracious, receiving the sacraments of God's action in our actual lives. And then we bump into another story and are thrown off balance; distracted, we stumble. Safe, we think, in the company of God's people, we're tripped by a moralist and sent sprawling; we're seduced by a secularist and defrauded. We're in Ziklag.

Disillusioned, we go off on our own and cultivate a pure spirituality uncontaminated by religious hucksters and hypocrites. But eventually, if we're honest and reading our Bibles honestly, we find we can't do it. We can't survive in the wilderness alone. We need others, and we need a leader. And then we begin to get it: God's purposes are being worked out most profoundly when we're least aware of them. Spirituality most of the time doesn't look like spirituality, or at least what the moralists and secularists told us it was supposed to look like. Sometimes all we can see is David serving Achish of Gath and leading a company of moral and social ragamuffins in Ziklag.

Every time I move to a new community, I find a church close by and join it—committing myself to worship and work with that company of God's people. I've never been anything other than disappointed: every one turns out to be biblical, through and through: murmerers, complainers, the faithless, the inconstant, those plagued with doubt and riddled with sin, boring moralizers, glamorous secularizers.[6] Every once in a while a shaft of blazing beauty seems to break out of nowhere and illuminate these companies, and then I see what my sin-dulled eyes had missed: word of God–shaped, Holy Spirit–created lives of sacrificial humility, incredible courage, heroic virtue, holy praise, joyful suffering, constant prayer, persevering obedience. I see "Christ—for Christ plays in ten thousand places,/ Lovely in limbs, and lovely in eyes not his/ To the Father through the features of men's faces."[7]

And in Ziklag, of all places.

GENEROSITY

DAVID AT THE BROOK BESOR

1 Samuel 30

*"Master, what are you talking about? When did we
ever see you hungry and feed you, thirsty and give you a
drink? And when did we ever see you sick or in prison
and come to you?" Then the King will say, "I'm telling
you the solemn truth: Whenever you did one of these
things to someone overlooked or ignored, that was me—
you did it to me."*

—MATTHEW 25:37–40

THE BROOK BESOR marks an important episode in human history.
An event was enacted there that's definitive for people whose family tree
goes back to Jesus, a tree of life with roots in David. I've never understood why the Brook Besor doesn't rank along with other definitive
place names, such as Bethany, Galilee, Shiloh, Calvary, and Bethel. But
that portion of the David story that originates at the Brook Besor keeps
being reenacted among men and women who stay in touch with the
God of their everydayness.

Names are important. They identify particular places, specific persons. They save us from the swamps of undifferentiated generality. They protect us from the arid wastelands of abstraction. A name is a lifejacket that keeps us afloat in the ocean of anonymity. *What's your name? Where were you born? Where do you live? Who is your God?* Names locate and identify. Generalities and abstractions, useful as they are in their own way, are as useless for actual nutrition as the label on a can of refried beans, listing calories 120, sodium 570 mg, carbohydrate 28 g, protein 7 g—excellent information, but certainly not food for the hungry.

Ernest Hemingway once wrote, "I was always embarrassed by the words *sacred, glorious,* and *sacrifice,* and the expression *in vain.* Abstract words such as *glory, honor, courage,* or *hallow* were obscene beside the concrete names of villages, the numbers of roads, the names of rivers, the numbers of regiments and dates."[1]

The Brook Besor is narrative nutrition: a story that feeds an essential aspect of our God-designed humanity. In a world of disembodied advice it puts our size-seven bone-and-flesh feet on dirt and rock ground. I want to pull the Brook Besor from its undeserved obscurity and put it on our maps—*name* what we might otherwise miss because we had filed it under some category such as "care," or "charity," or "generosity."

THE WASTING OF ZIKLAG

The story begins in disaster. David and his company of six hundred men, off on a military mission with King Achish of Gath, had left their wives and children at Ziklag unprotected. A raiding band of Amalekites, persistent and longtime enemies of Israel, came down on the village, captured the women and children for slaves, looted the place, and carried off a huge booty, leaving behind them nothing but smoking rubble.

When David's men returned, they were greeted by the rubble and smoke. The six hundred were a volcano of lament that soon turned into anger (lamentation often does)—a great anger against David. He was their leader, after all, and shouldn't have left the village unprotected. The anger congealed into a plot to kill him. Grief clouded their minds; anger hardened their hearts. "David ought to be stoned," first uttered as whispered bitterness, quickly turned into a rallying cry, "Let's stone David!" (my paraphrase).

Catastrophe brings out either the best or the worst in us. At Ziklag it first brought out the worst. David had been leading these six hundred men along trails of salvation and providence through the wilderness years, bringing beauty and holiness to their notice, leading them into lives of prayer, working the slow transformation from "the distressed, the debtors, and the discontented" into a company of friends and lovers. Two steps forward, one step back—or one step forward, two steps back. Spiritual formation is a slow business. And then this Amalekite disaster wiped out not only their homes and families but every bit of slowly acquired righteousness as well.

But catastrophe brought out the best in David. In the chaos of lamentation, anger, and bitterness, with storm clouds of murder rolling in across the horizon, we come on this wonderful line: "But David strengthened himself in the LORD his God" (1 Sam. 30:6). David prayed; David worshiped; David called on his pastor, Abiathar, for counsel. David went deep within himself, met God, and found strength and direction to stride into the way of salvation. As his exterior world collapsed, he returned to the interior, rebuilt his primary identity, recovered his base. The moment of disaster freed him, immediately and amazingly, from the sixteen months of servitude under Achish, and David was dealing with God again—listening intently, obeying boldly. David and Abiathar came out from the place of quietness and counsel and prayer with a plan.

Now there was something to do, a strategy adequate to the disaster. But note the contrast. The company also had a strategy, but it was conceived in bitterness—kill David. There's an enormous amount of outrage in the world that's converted into angry plans of attack and destruction. A great deal of social action and political reform is fueled by anger; the results are nearly always worse than the conditions that provoked the action. If we're going to do something about what's wrong with the world—the spectrum of wrongs stretches from marital fights to world wars, from disobedient children to destruction of the rain forests—we have to acquire a better base to work from than our anger.

David's strategy came out of prayer and counsel. He set out to bring back the lost women and children.

THE SICK EGYPTIAN

David's six hundred men were ill-prepared to hunt down the Amalekite marauders. They had just returned from a long march back from the Philistine military front. They were fatigued. They were demoralized by the sack of Ziklag. And they weren't trusting David one bit. David's plan didn't seem at all promising.

But they went. David roused his troops to action and led them on a forced march south. Pushing hard for fifteen miles,[2] they reached the Brook Besor. Two hundred men, a third of David's company, at that point were exhausted and unable to continue. They said, in effect, "We can't go another step. We don't have the strength and we don't have the spirit. We've had it." And so they were left, left at the Brook Besor.

David and his remaining four hundred men crossed the brook and continued deeper into the desolate desert badlands. They weren't finding a trace of the Amalekites. As hour succeeded hour, it looked more and more as if they were on a wild goose chase. And then they came on a sick Egyptian, half dead.

A sick puppy of an Egyptian couldn't have hoped for much in the way of care and compassion from a bunch of tired and vengeful Israelites. But somewhere along the way some of the old good Samaritan habits and desert hospitality that David's company had practiced kicked in, and instead of being kicked aside as a bother and encumbrance, the Egyptian was tended to: they gave him water and food—figs and raisins. It turned out that he was servant to one of the Amalekite rulers, but when he became sick he was abandoned—too much trouble to care for—and left behind in the desert to die. The poor wretch had had nothing to eat or drink for three days. David cared for him, fed him, and saved his life.

David knew something about being ill-used in the wilderness and then, in the midst of hardship, being treated generously. Psalm 36 bears

all the marks of a wilderness experience, and it contains all the elements
that came together for the Egyptian:

> *The God-rebel tunes in to sedition—*
> *all ears, eager to sin.*
> *He has no regard for God,*
> *he stands insolent before him.*
> *He has smooth-talked himself*
> *into believing*
> *That his evil*
> *will never be noticed.*
> *Words gutter from his mouth,*
> *dishwater dirty.*
> *Can't remember when he*
> *did anything decent.*
> *Every time he goes to bed,*
> *he fathers another evil plot.*
> *When he's loose on the streets*
> *nobody's safe.*
> *He plays with fire*
> *and doesn't care who gets burned.*
>
> *God's love is meteoric,*
> *his love astronomic,*
> *His purpose titanic,*
> *his verdicts oceanic.*
> *Yet in his largeness*
> *nothing gets lost;*
> *Not a man, not a mouse,*
> *slips through the cracks.*
>
> *How exquisite your love, O God!*
> *How eager we are to run under your wings,*
> *To eat our fill at the banquet you spread*
> *as you fill our tankards with Eden spring water.*

> *You're a fountain of cascading light,*
>   *and you open our eyes to light.*
> *Keep on loving your friends;*
>   *do your work in welcoming hearts.*
> *Don't let the bullies kick me around,*
>   *the moral midgets slam me down.*
> *Send the upstarts sprawling*
>   *flat on their faces in the mud.*

What David experienced from God, the Egyptian experienced from David: "Not a man, not a mouse, slips through the cracks." And then eating his fill at a banquet of water and figs and raisins.

When we're living this life right, this is what happens. We pass on the experience, pass on the God-experience to the people we meet. They experience a piece of what we've experienced in God.

Saved and grateful as a recipient of David's Psalm 36 desert hospitality, the revived Egyptian told them where the Amalekites were. They had been on their way to a victory celebration when the Egyptian slave had fallen sick and been dumped. Knowing exactly where they had been headed, he guided David and his company to the place.

It was now dusk, and the party was in full swing—eating, drinking, dancing—whooping it up. Amalekites everywhere, feasting on the food and drink they had looted from Ziklag and other towns and villages in this, their latest piracy. They were far from the places they had pillaged and therefore hadn't set a guard. Carousing, they were sitting ducks for David's avengers. Soon they were dead ducks.

The recovery was absolute. Not a wife, not a child was lost. Nothing that had been stolen was missing. Not only that, but they also had the extensive Amalekite booty of flocks of sheep and herds of cattle. David and his men returned with everything and everyone in triumph. The so recently demoralized, grieving, and angry men were now ecstatic. And David, whom hours earlier they had been ready to kill, was honored and acclaimed as they gave him all the credit, shouting out, *Zeh sh'lal David, zeh sh'lal David,* "This is David's spoil!" (1 Sam. 30:20).

AT THE BROOK BESOR

That sounds like the climax to the story, but it isn't. The climax takes place back at the Brook Besor. As the ecstatically victorious four hundred return to Ziklag, they arrive at the brook where they had left the two hundred. The exhausted two hundred, the two hundred who had had to drop out in mid-pursuit, the two hundred who had been soaking their feet in the brook and feeling left out of the action while the four hundred had been risking the terrors of wilderness and Amalekites. The left-behind two hundred were now up on their feet hugging and kissing their wives and children, delighting in the success that they hadn't been able to help bring about.[3]

But there were mean-spirited men among the four hundred, who bristled at the notion of sharing the victory booty with their weaker brothers. It was enough that they get their wives and children back, but nothing else—not a single piece of Amalekite plunder, not so much as one sheep or goat or heifer.

Just then David stepped in. His intervention is the climax to the story. David intervened at the Brook Besor, and his intervention is pure gospel.[4] David ruled that everybody at the brook that day—the two hundred who had been unable to continue and had been given the undramatic, behind-the-scenes work of watching over the supplies at the brook (1 Sam. 30:24) and the four hundred who had fought for their lives— were equals and would share everything equally: "Everything we have is a gift from God; we share it with all who are saved by God" (1 Sam. 30:23–25).

The ringleaders of the "fairness" policy are called "wicked and base fellows" (1 Sam. 30:22). Strong words, it would seem, for what sounds like common sense and plain justice. Until we remember who these people are and where they are: these are the men of Ziklag with nothing in their backgrounds to be proud of, all of them picked up from a disreputable life and brought, through no merit of their own, into the net of God's providence and salvation. And the Amalekite chase itself? They had started out wanting to kill David, and only through David's prayer with Abiathar and their desert hospitality to the Egyptian had they gotten their families back.

Everything they experienced was sheer grace. How could they talk about dividing things up fairly? God was treating them with marvelous and generous grace; David would see to it that they treated one another with marvelous and generous grace.

"CARING IS THE GREATEST THING"

It's often remarked that David was a passionate man. He threw himself recklessly into whatever was there before him: song, battle, prayer, love, God. What's not as often noticed but is equally true is that he was a compassionate person. His passion was a community affair, *compassion*. He cared. He cared about others with the same passion with which he came before God.

David doesn't fit a preformed mold. When we enter the story of David, we don't find what our sociologists and psychologists call a "role model," a kind of slot into which we can slide without going through the pain of becoming human ourselves. He worked out firsthand what it meant to be alive before God in the midst of those who were concerned only with staying alive. His care for and sensitivity toward others had nothing to do with conforming to the expectations of others. He didn't bend to the cowardice that we neutralize with our phrase "peer pressure." But for all that, he cared for others. He would have nothing to do with a salvation that was for himself alone. He had no interest in a security gained at the expense of the people with whom he lived. He wasn't out to save his own soul. He was, in a word, compassionate.

"Caring is the greatest thing," said von Hugel. "Christianity taught us to care."[5] A generation later, W. H. Auden brought out his ultimatum: "We must love one another or die."[6]

But we live in an age that has replaced compassion with sentiment. Sentiment is a feeling disconnected from relationship. Sentiment is *spilled* compassion. It looks like concern; it could develop into compassion, but it never does. Sentiment is the patriotic catch in your throat as the flag goes by—a feeling that never gets connected with the patriotic honesty of paying your income tax. Sentiment is the tears that flow in a sad movie—tears that never get connected with visiting your dying friend. We feel sorry for people; we lament the pain and suffering in the world. But having felt the internal motions of pity, wept a few requisite tears of sorrow, and sent off ten dollars to a charitable appeal, we've exhausted our capacity for care. In this callous, dog-eat-dog world, how sensitive we are! We return to our homes and jobs without knowing the names of the people we've shed tears over, without visiting a single prisoner whose fate we lament, without writing one letter to the lonely over whom our hearts break. And of course we let no strangers into our double-locked homes.

One of the supreme ironies of our age is that the society that has talked and written most about the fulfillment of the self shows the least evidence of it. People obsessed with the cultivation of the self have nothing to show for it but a cult of selfishness. A few generations of economic affluence, political liberation, and religious freedom have flowered into obesity, anxiety, and meanness. Happily, there are numerous exceptions; still, the generalizations are plausible. Our world is splendidly filled with glorious things and a glorious gospel but appallingly diminished in persons who celebrate them with passion and share them with compassion. We're not the first generation to do this. Augustine looked at the world around him and acerbically observed that his parishioners were "more pained if their villa is poor than if their life is bad."[7]

One of the reasons that Christians are dispersed in the world is to recover a life for others and practice a priesthood of all believers—connect with others in an earthy, Davidic compassion so thoroughly that no expert or professional can ever again bluff us into passivity or consumerism.

David at the Brook Besor anticipates Jesus: "Are you tired? Worn out? Burned out on religion? Come to me and you'll recover your life. I'll show you how to take a real rest. Walk with me and work with me—watch how I do it. Learn the unforced rhythms of grace. I won't lay anything heavy or ill-fitting on you. Keep company with me and you'll learn to live freely and lightly" (Matt. 11:28–30, *The Message*).

• • •

I HAVE A FRIEND who sometimes signs her letters to me, "Yours at the Brook Besor." She's never explained to me what she means, and I've never asked her. What I imagine is that she sees herself as one of the two hundred at the Brook Besor, too tired to go on (she's been living for a long time in Philistine country), feeling consigned to the sidelines because of her lack of stamina, resigned to a marginal status with the people of God but inwardly assured of God's affirmation. And then hearing it again, undeserved and unexpected, the generous Davidic verdict. Brook Besor, indeed.

GRIEF

DAVID IN LAMENT

2 Samuel 1

When Jesus saw [Mary] sobbing and the Jews with her
sobbing, a deep anger welled up within him. He said,
"Where did you put him?"
"Master, come and see," they said. Now Jesus wept.
The Jews said, "Look how deeply he loved him."

—JOHN 11:33–36

THERE WERE TWO FUNERAL HOMES in my hometown, and one
newspaper. Each afternoon my Aunt Frieda retrieved the newspaper
from the lilac bushes at the side of her front porch. The paperboy delivered his papers from his bicycle. He aimed at the porch, but the momentum of the bicycle always carried the paper into the lilacs. He never
did learn to compensate for the momentum, so my Aunt Frieda had to
maneuver her considerable bulk around or into the lilacs to get the
paper. She then brought the paper into the kitchen and spread it out on
the table, open to the obituaries on the next-to-last page. Pulling out
the handkerchief she kept tucked in her bosom, she dabbed tears from

her eyes as she penciled into her calendar the scheduled times of up-coming funerals, designating the place with K or J (for the Knechtly Funeral Home or the Jackson).

My Aunt Frieda made cookies every day—far and away the best cookies of my childhood—and on my way home from school I usually made a looping detour to her kitchen; she was always generous with the first fruits from her oven, served with a cold glass of buttermilk. And so I was often there for the ritual: retrieving the paper, opening and spreading the paper, reaching for her handkerchief and dabbing her eyes with it, writing in the time and place of the funeral. It *was* a ritual—conducted daily with solemnity. I knew better than to ask questions or get in the way when it was being carried out.

From my mother I knew that my Aunt Frieda attended all those funerals, *all* of them, two a day if she was lucky. She sat in the back row at Knechtly's or Jackson's and wept quietly but copiously. She knew neither the men and women for whom she mourned nor the other mourners. She was a connoisseur of pure grief, grief uncontaminated by relationships or by other emotions. She wept and left.

By the time it occurred to me that there might be something odd about this behavior of my Aunt Frieda's, she and all the people who might have been able to provide explanation or understanding were dead. Why did she ritualize her life around grief? And how did she happen upon this method of experiencing grief without the trouble of dealing with other people? Without the confusing complication of competing emotions? There are no available answers to these questions, but the act of grieving is there, large and memorable—large as my Aunt Frieda herself, memorable as the cookies and buttermilk. And, in some strange and wonderful way, normal: grief not as something exceptional, an alien invasion interrupting normalcy, but grief incorporated into the everyday—even defining the everyday, for I never supposed my Aunt Frieda was anything other than normal, even if in adult retrospect her funeral fetishism evokes suspicions of neurosis. She loved and was faithful lifelong to her husband, raised two children to sane and moral adulthood, was a whiz at crossword puzzles, made great cookies—what more did she need to qualify as normal?

Maybe my Aunt Frieda was more or less unconsciously making up for the widespread avoidance of grief in our culture by making a specialty of it.

Maybe my Aunt Frieda was a real-life instance of the exaggerated fictional characters Flannery O'Connor was always creating—deliberately exaggerated because, O'Connor said, "to the hard of hearing you shout, and for the almost-blind you draw large and startling figures."[1]

But if my Aunt Frieda accommodated my childhood imagination to the legitimacy and pervasiveness of grief, David trained my adult spirituality in grief rightly grieved. David's mighty lament over the deaths of Saul and Jonathan draws us into the depths of a healthy human spirit as it deals honestly and prayerfully with devastating loss and all its attendant emotions.

"DAVID LAMENTED . . ."

David lamented because he cared. David lamented because he was willing and able to bring his total attention to the fact of death. Because David lamented with this lamentation recorded in 2 Samuel 1, we have access to an aspect of experience that's absolutely essential if we're going to live God-responsively, live God-abundantly.

It seems odd, even contradictory, that in order to live totally we must face death totally. But it's true. David, who lived exuberantly, also lamented fiercely. His exuberance and lamentation were aspects of the same life-orientation and commitment: life *matters*. David honored human life—the sheer fact of human life—extravagantly. The depth of the lamentation witnesses the extent of the veneration.

Seventy percent of the Psalms are laments. These laments either originate in or derive from the praying life of David. David repeatedly faced loss, disappointment, death. But he neither avoided, denied, nor soft-pedaled any of those difficulties. He faced everything and he prayed everything. David's laments are part and parcel of the craggy majesty and towering dignity of David's life.

The contrast with our contemporary culture is appalling. We have a style of print and television journalism that reports disaster endlessly and scrupulously: crime and war, famine and flood, political malfeasance and societal scandal. The one virtually foolproof way for getting noticed in our culture is to do something bad. The worse the act, the higher the profile. In the wake of whatever has gone wrong or whatever wrong has been done, commentators gossip, reporters interview, editors pontificate, pharisees moralize; then psychological analyses are conducted, political reforms initiated, and academic studies funded. *But there's not one line of lament.*

There's no lament because truth isn't taken seriously, love isn't taken seriously. Human life doesn't matter as *life*—God-given, Christ-redeemed, Spirit-blessed life. It counts only as "news." There's no dignity to any of it. It's trivialized.

". . . WITH THIS LAMENTATION"

David laments the deaths of Saul and Jonathan (2 Sam. 1:19–27). The two names store up years and years of what we would probably wrongly label unhappiness: maniacal persecution from Saul, David's malign enemy; forced separation from Jonathan, David's dear friend. Both names receive equal billing in the lamentation. Both are mourned, and in the mourning both are dignified.

> *Saul and Jonathan—beloved, beautiful!*
> *Together in life, together in death!*
> *Swifter than plummeting eagles,*
> *stronger than proud lions.*
> (MY TRANSLATION)

Saul. Saul hated David. Saul chased David. Saul defrauded David. All those wilderness years, David lived in a world sovereign with Saul's hate. Or so it seemed. Danger, hardship, loneliness, loss—all because of Saul. But there was something else going on that was more significant than Saul's hatred of David, and that was God's anointing of Saul. What God did for Saul far outweighed anything that Saul did to David. And *that* is what David chose to deal with. David chose to be influenced by and shaped under that sovereignty. God's grace in Saul's life, not Saul's

hate in David's life, is what gave content to David's prayers and decisions. Saul made life difficult for David, but he didn't destroy him. If
David had allowed Saul's hate to determine his life, he would have been
destroyed. He maybe wouldn't have been killed, but he certainly would
have been damned—reduced, cramped, and constricted by vengeance.
When he was being chased down by Saul, he prayed his distress and
anger and left it with God, Saul's sufficient judge. Saul's hate, instead of
narrowing David and reducing him, in fact provided conditions in
which he became large, expansive, and generous. Magnanimity pours
through the lament:

> *O, O, Gazelle of Israel, struck down in your prime,*
> > *the mighty warriors fallen, fallen!*
> *Don't announce it in the city of Gath,*
> > *don't post the news in the streets of Ashkelon;*
> *Don't give those coarse Philistine girls*
> > *one more excuse for a drunken party!*
>
> *No more dew or rain for you, hills of Gilboa,*
> > *and not a drop from springs and wells;*
> *For there the warriors' weapons were dragged through the mud,*
> > *Saul's shield left there to tarnish and rust.*
>
> • • • • • • • • • • •
>
> *Women of Israel, weep for Saul,*
> > *he dressed you in finest cottons and silks,*
> > *spared no expense in making you elegant.*
>
> (MY TRANSLATION)

And Jonathan. Jonathan loved David, but it was a love that David
could never sink into and enjoy. It wasn't a love he could relax and revel
in. Jonathan's commitment to his father prevented him from joining
David in exile, dogged commitment to his father taking precedence
over his devoted love of David. And David's abandonment to the sovereignty of God prevented him from recruiting Jonathan to join him in
the wilderness for emotional solace. Their friendship was based on
something more than their pleasure in one another: they had a common

love of truth, of beauty, of goodness—the cluster of transcendentals that can infuse any and all circumstances with hopeful purpose. The narrative text is sparse in detail here, so some guesswork is involved in making these assertions, but the impression stands that their friendship didn't require emotional exchanges of give-and-take; the friendship of Jonathan and David brought out the best in each through the other, and that could happen in separation as well as in presence. They didn't "need" one another emotionally. Their friendship developed out of what they both admired and gave themselves to.

C. S. Lewis, in his brilliant exposition of friendship-love, remarks that "our ancestors regarded Friendship as something that raised us almost above humanity. This love, free from instinct, free from all duties but those which love has freely assumed, almost wholly free from jealousy, and free without qualification from the need to be needed, is eminently spiritual. It is the sort of love one can imagine between angels."[2] That it's "spiritual" doesn't make it safe. Lewis makes it clear that friendship-love is subject to subtle and terrible sins. But its spiritual quality[3] does make it rare and, for those who enter into it, exquisite. David's lament over Jonathan is a primary witness to how deeply this love penetrates and preserves the soul.

> The mighty warriors, fallen, fallen,
>   in the middle of the fight!
>   Jonathan, struck down in your prime!
>
> O my dear brother Jonathan,
>   I'm crushed by your death.
> Your dear friendship was a miracle-wonder,
>   love far exceeding anything I've known
>   —or ever hope to know.

• • •

THERE ARE TWO THINGS about David's lament that invite comment and reflection. One is that somehow this lament doesn't evoke pity in us. We don't feel sorry for David in his lament. Don't we feel instead admiration? Doesn't this call out something within us that we recognize as noble? Doesn't the lament provide a vehicle of spirit that enables us to transcend self-centeredness? Lament has to do with loss; but David isn't less. *Why* is he not less?

The other striking element of the lament is that it's distilled into poetry. The lines are rhythmic. The metaphors are fresh and surprising. One line resonates with another. Verbal energy builds, accumulates, and is resolved in the resonances and repetitions.

One line is repeated three times in the lament: ". . . the mighty warriors fallen, fallen!" (*'aik naph'lu gibborim*—vv. 19, 25, 27), an exclamation of anguish, a declaration of catastrophe. The first time it's spoken over Saul as a witness to catastrophe; the second it's said of Jonathan, catastrophe compounded; but the third time, in the summary couplet, it forms a triadic chord of haunting harmonic beauty. Beauty. Lament isn't an animal wail, an inarticulate howl. Lament notices and attends, savors and delights—details, images, relationships. Pain entered into, accepted, and owned can become poetry. It's no less pain, but it's no longer ugly. Poetry is our most personal use of words; it's our way of entering experience, not just watching it happen to us, and inhabiting it as our home.

"HE SAID IT SHOULD BE TAUGHT TO THE PEOPLE"

David not only lamented with this lamentation, he ordered the people to learn it: memorize it and inhabit it as *their* experience. For loss is never merely private; it's social and political as well. Lament shapes the culture. The way we deal with loss enters into the atmosphere and makes us a people capable of nobility and beauty. Or not. Practicing the Christian life has to do, along with much else, with learning "this lamentation," and learning it well.

"He said it should be taught" (2 Sam. 1:18). Worked into our lives. Not just a piece of information but assimilated truth. Teach this lament. Teach this way of dealing with Saul's enmity and Jonathan's love. Teach one another how to take seriously these great cadences of pain, some coming from hate, some coming from love, so that we're not diminished but are deepened by them—find God in them, and beauty. Put form and rhythm and song to them. Pain isn't the worst thing. Being hated isn't the worst thing. Being separated from the one you love isn't the worst thing. Death isn't the worst thing. The worst thing is failing to deal with reality and becoming disconnected from what is actual. The worst thing is trivializing the honorable, desecrating the sacred. What I do with my grief affects the way you handle your grief; together we form a community that deals with death and other loss in the context of God's sovereignty, which is expressed finally in resurrection.

Obviously, what we must never do is get over it as soon as possible or make as little of it as we can. "Get over it" and "make little of it" are unbiblical and inhuman. Denial and distraction are the standard over-the-counter prescriptions of our culture for dealing with loss; in combination, they've virtually destroyed the spiritual health of our culture. The societal effect is widespread addiction and depression. Addiction is our most popular method of denying death. Addiction, ranging from workaholism to alcoholism, preoccupies us, *drugs* us, with the impersonal so that we lose the capacity to deal with the personal details and intimate feelings of loss.[4] Depression doesn't usually begin in outright denial but in something more like distraction; it's the cumulative result of years and years of minimizing the realities of loss and death, failure and disappointment, and it leaves us dulled and unresponsive to *all* reality. Widespread addiction. Widespread depression. Widespread inability or refusal to face pain, face rejection and frustration, endure not having what we want or getting our own way. Widespread ignorance of the stories and songs that put David's experiences of Saul's hate and Jonathan's love in a plot large enough to contain and exhibit the breathtaking and alpine beauties of divine anointing and human commitment.

That's why it's written in the Book of Jashar (2 Sam. 1:17) that we're to be taught to lament. If we're not taught to lament with this lamentation, we'll grow up believing that our immediate feelings determine our fate. We'll deny every rejection and thereby be controlled by rejection. We'll avoid every frustration and thereby be diminished by frustration. Year by year, as we deny and avoid the pains and losses, the rejections and frustrations, we'll become less and less, trivial and trivializing, empty shells with smiley faces painted on them.

I'm not suggesting Davidic lamentation as a cure to addiction and depression. By the time either of these conditions (and it's often both at once) becomes acute in a person, the way to recovery is long, arduous, and complex. But I'm bold to say that it's our most promising preventative. We don't become mature human beings by getting lucky or cleverly circumventing loss, and certainly not by avoidance and distraction. Learn to lament. Learn *this* lamentation. We're *mortals,* after all. We and everyone around are scheduled for death (*mortis*). Get used to it. Take up your cross. It prepares us and those around us for resurrection.

• • •

WE'RE NOW AT THE MIDPOINT in the David story. David's lament over Saul and Jonathan functions as a pivot: David's lament keeps everything in the first half of the story working in the second half. Lament is a bridge from life to death to life.

A failure to lament is a failure to connect. If we refuse to learn Davidic lamentation, our lives fragment into episodes and anecdotes, a succession of jerky starts and gossipy cul-de-sacs. But we're in a *story* in which everything eventually comes together, a narrative in which all the puzzling parts finally fit, about which years later we exclaim, "Oh, so *that's* what that meant!" But being in a story means that we mustn't attempt to get ahead of the plot—skip the hard parts, erase the painful parts, detour the disappointments. Lament—making the most of our loss without getting bogged down in it—is a primary way of staying *in* the story.[5] *God* is telling this story, remember. It's a large, capacious story. He doesn't look kindly on our editorial deletions. But he delights in our poetry.

12

BONEHEADS

DAVID AND THE

SONS OF ZERUIAH

2 Samuel 2–4

James and John, Zebedee's sons, came up to him.
"Teacher, we have something we want you to do for us.
. . . Arrange it so that we will be awarded the highest
places of honor in your glory. . . . "

"You've observed how godless rulers throw their
weight around," [Jesus] said, "and when people get a
little power how quickly it goes to their heads. It's not
going to be that way with you. Whoever wants to be
great must become a servant."

—MARK 10:35–37, 42–43

"THEY'RE WEARING ME OUT, these sons of Zeruiah. I know that I'm God's anointed. I know that I've been preserved against formidable odds—Goliath and Saul, Philistine wars and wilderness danger—to do this work of becoming *human,* becoming a person capable of representing God as king, of bringing God's people into lives of worship and love and obedience; but these sons of Zeruiah are wearing me out. Their vendettas, their plots, their jealousies, their anger; . . . they're wearing me out. I know that God is the one with whom I have to do, and I know that the task before me is glorious, but these sons of Zeruiah are wearing me out. They take so much time, require so much watching. It seems like I'm spending all my time putting out the fires they set, straightening out the quarrels they start. They think that they're on my side; they think that they're helping; they think that I should be grateful to them. But they don't understand *God* among us. They have no idea that we're here as God's people—not Saul's, not David's, but *God's.* They don't understand that our task isn't to take over and run things efficiently but to enter into what God is doing and give witness to that. These sons of Zeruiah are wearing me out; they're too much for me."

We can easily imagine such a monologue, or something very much like it, drumming through David's head and entering into David's prayers in his early days as king of Judah. We can imagine it because we've experienced it in our own interior conversations and prayers. After years of waiting, struggling, testing, we emerge into a position of strength, a time of fulfillment: health after long illness, marriage after long loneliness, career after long preparation, retirement after long drudgery. These are going to be the best years of our lives! And then, to our surprise and dismay, we find that the very people we counted our dearest allies are making our lives miserable. Worse yet, very often they don't *know* that they're making life difficult for us because they're doing their very best to help us. They've identified their interests with our interests and suppose that they're identical. These are the sons of Zeruiah. The problem is that they're not interested in God's interests. God is, of course, God—kind of. But not a *way* of life. They'll do things their own way.

It helps, I think, to know that this is a thoroughly biblical situation, very Davidic. When we're learning to read our lives as a gospel story, there's no place or company free of the sons of Zeruiah. It helps to know that the good news has been worked out since time began in exactly these circumstances. It helps to know that the sons of Zeruiah are accounted for in God's economy, and that however difficult they make the life of faith in Jesus, they can't destroy it.

THE NEW SITUATION

Here's the situation. Saul is dead. Jonathan is dead. David has lamented these deaths magnificently. In his lament he's at his Davidic best, believing and reverent, generous and passionate. He's also king. The long-ago act of anointing by Samuel to the kingship is now out in the open. King Saul no longer obstructs the way.

David, after a decade of being hunted down in the wilderness, living on the defensive, is now in a position of strength. He's thirty years old, and the *ruler*. The tables have turned. He's no longer running, hiding, living by his wits. He's in charge. He's operating now from a position of authority. What kind of strength will he use? How will he exercise his authority? He's learned a life of reverence and compassion and prayer in the wilderness. Will he continue? Now that he no longer has to run to the Lord for refuge, is there any need for God at all?

Not, it seems, for the sons of Zeruiah: "It's quite wonderful that God helps those who can't help themselves," they might have said, "and he certainly helped us a lot when we needed help; but now that we can help ourselves, we'll go ahead and do it—our way. And of course we'll help David—our way. It wouldn't be right, would it, to become dependent on Welfare?"

ABNER AND JOAB

At this point secondary figures, Abner and Joab, take over the story. Abner, from Saul's court in the north; Joab, from David's court in the south. The Hebrew people were made up of twelve tribes. Each tribe had a strong independent identity—Simeon, Reuben, Ephraim, Benjamin, Judah, and so on—which usually took precedence over the collective "Hebrew." When outside forces got too much for them, they put aside their differences and worked together as Hebrews, but after things quieted down they more or less reverted to their primary identity as one of the twelve tribes. The eleven northern tribes were sometimes grouped together as Israel, but the large southern tribe, Judah, maintained a stronger individual identity and kept to itself. Because of the strong Philistine threat, Saul had been able to keep them all together in a rough-hewn federation, but when David was driven into exile, his home tribe, Judah, while it didn't bolt from Saul, still remained sympathetic to David. When Saul and Jonathan were killed, this tribe, Judah, immediately crowned David king in Judah's central city, Hebron. But the other tribes went along nominally with the existing royal house in the person of Ish-bosheth, Saul's forty-year-old son and only heir.

Ish-bosheth, though, wasn't a strong leader, which gave opportunity for background rogues to assert themselves. Abner and Joab now step out of the shadows and virtually take over the story, if only briefly—Abner as commander of Saul's army, Joab as commander of David's army.

Abner is the consummate opportunist. As he establishes his kingmaker role in Israel, reducing the ineffectual Ish-bosheth to a puppet figurehead, he gradually realizes that the future is with David and works out diplomatic ways of turning over the northern tribes (Israel) to David so that he can be assured a leading place in the new government. Abner uses religious language to support his schemes. He bullies Ish-bosheth with God-talk: "God do so to Abner, and more also, if I do not accomplish for David what the LORD has sworn to him, to transfer the kingdom from the house of Saul, and set up the throne of David over Israel and over Judah . . . " (2 Sam. 3:9). He woos the elders of Israel with God-talk: "[T]he LORD has promised David, saying, 'By the hand of my servant David I will save my people Israel from the hand of the Philistines, and from the hand of all their enemies'" (2 Sam. 3:18). Abner is smooth. Abner knows how to use the name of God when it serves his purposes.

Joab, on the other hand, is the prototypical strong man. He kills first and thinks later. He's also what we would call an idealogue: he serves an idea that's right—in his case, David as God's anointed—and so there's nothing further to discuss. The idealogue says, in effect, "If you oppose the idea, I can best serve the idea by getting rid of you, by fair means or foul." The combination of temper, dogmatism, and muscle is lethal. God, for Joab, provides transcendence to violence.

The opening story of the two military commanders sets the stage. Abner and Joab meet at the pool of Gibeon, each with an army. Abner takes his place on one side of the pool, Joab on the other. They each put forward a team of twelve men to engage in a contest of arms. On signal the two teams go at it, but instead of playing a game in which one wins and the other loses, they let the game get out of hand and they all kill each other. No winners, only losers—all twenty-four dead. What started out as a game turned into a riot and ended in a massacre. Despite all the bloodletting, don't we, at least from our perspective, detect a bit of vaudevillian slapstick in the narration?

This was supposed to be sporting event, a contest to which everyone except the players was a spectator, Saturday afternoon entertainment in which people yell and cheer their side on to victory. Instead, there was a freak mutation: the players went berserk and killed each other, at which point the two armies of spectators poured out of the stands onto the field in an orgy of pursuit and murder. Abner and Joab's sporting event at the pool of Gibeon set off a fierce and bloody battle between north and south, Israel and Judah. At the end of the day the body count was Israel 360, Judah 20.

We read this and think, This is senseless—this fighting and killing. This is no way to live. Violence is a stupid way to settle differences. There's no moral cause at stake here; there's no spiritual struggle going on. These are men who are obsessed with their own preeminence, trying to establish their own power, indulging their respective and considerable vanities. Abner and Joab. Joab and Abner. In the middle of the violence Abner calls out to Joab, "Shall the sword devour for ever? Do you not know that the end will be bitter?" (2 Sam. 2:26). But his questions got no answers.

• • •

IT'S TIME TO TAKE a step back and recall the underlying plot of this story: God's salvation is being established; God's people are being formed into God's kingdom. The kingship of Saul is in the process of being replaced by the kingship of David. Saul's kingship failed because of disobedience and hubris: impatient with God and God's ways, Saul took things into his own hands, took over, became self-important, obsessively determined to kill David when it appeared that God's blessing of David compromised his own self-importance. Meanwhile, David's kingship is coming into being detail by detail, shaped in obedience and trust, patient endurance, a refusal to take things into his own hands, a disciplined honoring of God's anointing of Saul even when it made no sense to David.

And then suddenly these grand contrasts and truths are obscured in the smoke and tumult of Abner and Joab. Abner and Joab, with little or no sense of God and God's providential presence, seize power and attempt to manipulate affairs to their own interests. They make so much noise and their arrogant pride so hogs the show that the story of David is pushed, if not off the page, at least into the footnotes.

In the footnotes we still detect David at his characteristic kingwork: acting generously (with Jabesh-gilead, 2 Sam. 2:5–7), raising a family (2 Sam. 3:2–5), enacting a covenant (2 Sam. 3:12–16), writing poetry, and grieving honestly (2 Sam. 3:31–37).

But Abner and Joab interfere, interrupt, destroy. They care nothing about Kingdom, nothing about God, nothing about truth and honor. They're vulgar, petty, puffed-up militarists intent on using the stage of history (God's *salvation* history!) to make their mark and get their way. Abner and Joab. Abner in a snit. Joab in a rage. Abner taking advantage of Ish-bosheth's weakness and cannily plotting a future for himself with David. Joab taking advantage of his position with David to avenge his private grudges. Lust and deceit. Assassination and murder.

BONEHEADS

We read page after page of this kind of thing and think, What's this doing in the Bible? I don't want to read about jerks like Abner and Joab. I get enough of their kind in the newspapers and on television. I want *good* news. I want the David story. I want to read about Jesus. What the Bible needs is a good editor. Why waste good gospel ink on Abner and Joab?

Why does the Bible have this stuff in it? If God is working here, speaking here, why don't things work out better? Why don't people behave better? Why are boneheads like Joab and Abner allowed to take up so much space? If God is at the center of things, why does history get so messed up?

The answer is quite obvious, even if uncongenial. *This* is the context and company in which God chooses to work out our salvation. Abner and Joab are also in this story, and the sooner we get used to it the better. We find wonderful companions in this way of faith and discipleship, men and women of grace and beauty, loyalty and prayer: Jonathans and Abigails, Samuels and Ahimelechs. But we also find ourselves joined by Abners and Joabs under many and various aliases.

Joab and Abner aren't by common definition enemies: both, if challenged, would claim to be on David's side. Abner carefully works out diplomatic means to turn Saul's kingdom over to David. Joab simply gets rid of what he perceives as the opposition in the quickest and most efficient way he knows. But they're not fundamentally interested in God's work in David; rather, they're interested in how David can further their work. Religion is a front to their self-interest. These are the people who make it so difficult to live easily and relaxed in love and community and obedient praise.

Goliath and Doeg, Philistines and Amalekites are explicitly defined enemies; we know what they're up to. We know we can't trust them. But Abner and Joab? Because *they* think they're on our side, we also assume that they are. But that assumption gets no biblical confirmation. Abner and Joab bear watching. *Means* are important. God's work can't be done other than in God's way. Exploitation (Abner) and violence (Joab) aren't God's way.

SONS OF ZERUIAH

Zeruiah is David's sister and has three sons: Joab, Abishai, and Asahel. Even though Abner isn't blood kin to them, I count him among them in kind—a character in a God-shaped, God-plotted story who is deaf and dumb to God. Abner kills Asahel in the aftermath of the pool of Gibeon fiasco, leaving two sons of Zeruiah. He does it reluctantly, having exhausted his diplomatic options. A few years later Joab, on the pretense of conferring with Abner on matters of diplomacy, with his brother's assistance kills Abner, brutally and treacherously. Asahel has been out of the way for some years; Abner is now eliminated. The remaining sons of Zeruiah, Joab and Abishai, stay in the story to the very end, a constant, unremitting thorn in David's side.

After Joab and Abishai murder Abner, David cries out, "I am this day weak, though anointed king; these men the sons of Zeruiah are too hard for me" (2 Sam. 3:39). These two sons of Zeruiah are terrific fighting men and fiercely loyal to David's political interests. But Joab and Abishai comprehend nothing of David's spirit; they hate peace and the things that have to do with peace. They want mastery and influence and power.

> The last temptation is the greatest treason:
> To do the right deed for the wrong reason.
> The natural vigour in the venial sin
> Is the way in which our lives begin.[1]

And so they constantly sabotage David's attempts at justice and peace and love. David is leading a people into the worship of God and the pursuit of holiness. Among these people are the "sons of Zeruiah," making life difficult, daily threatening to pull the whole enterprise down as they jockey for position.

The sons of Zeruiah are in the story; there's no getting around it. We would hardly notice their inclusion if this were a secular story. We expect to find them in the *Iliad* and the *Odyssey*, in Charles Dickens and William Faulkner. But this is the Bible. And we find that there's hardly a page in the Bible that doesn't insist that we take notice of them. That's why so many people quit reading the Bible, or repudiate it: "I can't read the Bible, especially the Old Testament—too much fighting, too much brutality." But that's exactly why Christians *do* read it: we find God's purposes being worked out in the precise moral and political, social and cultural conditions that we wake up to each morning, a world of shabby morality and opportunist companions, religious violence, religious propaganda—the many, many sons of Zeruiah that are too hard for us.

13

GROWTH

DAVID AND JERUSALEM

2 Samuel 5

*Jesus said, "In a word, what I'm saying is, Grow up.
You're kingdom subjects. Now live like it. Live out your
God-created identity. Live generously and graciously
toward others, the way God lives toward you."*

—MATTHEW 5:48

IT SAT THERE squat and grotesque, a small fortress city on a rock out-cropping. It was a cheerless place. Travelers avoided it. It was virtually unassailable. To the east and south the ground fell away sharply into deep ravines, an impregnable natural defense. Anyone ascending the slope of plains from the other direction would be stopped by the sight of two huge, demonic figures—misshapen bodies, distorted faces—set on the north and west walls of the city. One was an evil parody of limping Jacob, who had been lamed in his all-night wrestle with the angel at the Brook Jabok (Gen. 32:31). The other was an equally evil of parody of blind Isaac, who in his sightless old age had been hoodwinked by his wife and son (Gen. 27:1). When anyone approached those walls, the figures would slowly begin to move—jerky, lurching movements— while at the same time huge belches sounded from deep within, then shrieks of terror. It was an evil place. People stayed clear of it.

Nobody bothered the Jebusites. They lived unvisited and unattacked for centuries. Philistines, Amalekites, and Hebrews waged war with one another in battle after battle, up and down the countryside, back and forth, but the Jebusites were exempt from it all, their demon images threatening supernatural evil to anyone who dared approach too close. Parents scared their children into obedience with stories of the Jebusite demons. Young people, gathered around summer campfires, scared each other into a huddled coziness with stories of the Jebusite demons.

Ironically, the Jebusite walled city was named Jerusalem, "City of Peace." And in fact the Jebusites lived quite peaceably, let alone by the world as a black widow spider is let alone, as a water moccasin is let alone. Nobody bothered the Jebusites. Nobody, that is, until David decided to make it his capital city. It was a perfect location for his purposes, sitting as it did on the spine connecting the northern tribes of Israel with the southern tribe of Judah, and unclaimed by either side.

David had just been made king over Israel as well as Judah, uniting the separated tribes, and he needed a center for his new government. His present base was Hebron, but that was far to the south and wouldn't attract the allegiance of the northern tribes of Israel. But if he went to the north, he would leave out the southern tier. He needed a non-Israelite, non-Judaic site. Jerusalem was just the ticket: a small, fortified city set right along the border between Israel and Judah, and never occupied or in the possession of either.

David wasn't easily intimidated by displays of evil. He had become adept at dodging the evil rages of Saul; he had survived the evil of Doeg; he had put up with the evil-minded schemes of the sons of Zeruiah for years. He wasn't now about to be put off by the evil idols of the Jebusites, these cruel parodies of his ancestors in a God-devoted life, lame Jacob and blind Isaac.

And besides, he knew something about these fearsome figures. During the years of his fugitive life in the wilderness, he had picked up bits and pieces of information regarding the reclusive Jebusites. He had good reason to suspect that those huge fixtures on the walls weren't demons at all, but mechanical forms hooked up to a neat piece of hydraulic engineering. Someone had only to move a lever and the force of water from the Spring Gihon, piped into place through an ingenious system of plumbing, would set lame Jacob and blind Isaac spookily moving, lurching, while a contrivance of bellows produced the belches and screams. He knew that it was a fraud, that there was nothing to it but pipes and pulleys, hinges and smoke. Occasional Jebusite outcasts or runaways through the years had told him enough for him to put two and two together and figure it out.

Boldly then, as everyone thought, David commanded the capture of the Jebusite stronghold of Jerusalem. His instructions were simple. First smash the waterpipe; that would disengage the demonic figures from their power source. Then tear the Jacob/Isaac figures to bits, "the lame and the blind" (2 Sam. 5:8), and throw the pieces over the wall. And that's what David's men did. They found the secret entrance to the waterpipe at the base of the ravine on the east side and destroyed the plumbing; then they tore apart the anti-Jacob and anti-Isaac cloth-and-wood statues and left them a pile of rubble. It was over almost before it had started. The Jebusites were mice, it turned out. Not a weapon was used. Not a life lost. It was the easiest victory David had ever achieved, and bloodless, preserving for that day at least Jerusalem's etymology as the City of Peace. The city was also designated as "Zion"—that term enters the biblical story for the first time here—and formed the nucleus for a rich gathering of images, symbols, promises, and visions that express God's sovereign purposes worked out on the hard, inhospitable ground of our lives. From that day on it was also known as David's City.

RABBI GERSONIDES

But this is an admittedly imaginative reconstruction of a difficult text. There are many words in the Hebrew text that elude scholarly consensus. Many inventive suggestions have been proposed by Hebrew scholars over the last hundred years to correlate all the exegetical, theological, and narrative aspects of the story.

The biblical text of 2 Samuel 5:6–8 doesn't supply the details that I've used here to reconstruct the story of David's capture of Jerusalem. I got them from a French Jew, Rabbi Gersonides (1288–1344), among the most respected and influential of intellectuals who flourished in the medieval period. It was the consensus of Jewish interpreters of the Middle Ages that "the lame and the blind" in the text were two idols, deprecating images of Jacob and Isaac. Gersonides added the imaginative speculation that these were "fearsome fighting robots that were hydraulically operated and could therefore be rendered useless by an attack on the water supply."[1]

The aspect of the text that's difficult to fit into the story as it stands in 2 Samuel is the phrase "the lame and the blind," repeated three times, and qualified at its second occurrence by the phrase ". . . who are hated by David's soul." This same David later in the story will show special consideration and affection to Mephibosheth, who was disabled from an injury that occurred when he was an infant (2 Sam. 9). And in the widening context of this story, Jesus, the Son of David, will go out of his way to include the lame and the blind in his company. In this context and under these circumstances, it seems unlikely that the words "the lame and the blind" refer to actual people or are used as metaphors of derision.

A number of scholars today interpret "the lame and the blind" as referring either to the invincibility of Jerusalem (even handicapped people could defend it) or to the determination of the inhabitants to defend the city to the last man (they would fight even though the only soldiers left were the wounded). Then the reference to David's "hate" is explained in terms of the taunt, in which he answers the Jebusites by turning their own metaphor back on them.

But the playful medieval Jewish imagination hit on something that catches at the heart of the story, and so I've been bold to use it, setting it alongside various linguistic solutions put forward by modern scholars.[2]

In Gersonides' reading of the text, David captures a new site for establishing his rule, and as he does so, he cleans it of idolatry, destroying the old debased images of Jacob maimed and Isaac blind—Jebusite inventions for turning the "fathers" of Israel into demonic expressions of evil.

A LONGER STRIDE AND A LARGER EMBRACE

In wrapping up the story of the capture of Jerusalem and its establishment as the City of David, 2 Samuel offers this wonderful phrase: "And David became greater and greater, for the LORD, the God of hosts, was with him" (2 Sam. 5:10). Another way to translate the Hebrew phrase *halok v'gadol* is that David proceeded from that moment with "a longer stride and a larger embrace."

The change at this point in David's life was radical. Suddenly he was the central figure of his nation. All his life he had been marginal; now he was central. For years he had been living furtively and defensively; now he was in a position to live royally and commandingly. That's a huge change. Would David change too? Would he change into a Middle Eastern despot? Or would he grow?[3]

The phrase "greater and greater" signals David's maturity. The David story isn't a mere accumulation of incidents, one after the other, isolated anecdotes shaped by whatever circumstances prevailed at the time. No, it's a story of *growth,* each detail of the story assimilated into the next, David more *David* now than ever. This doesn't always happen, of course—either to David or to us. In fact, it sometimes seems that it doesn't happen very often. Change can diminish us; it can cut us off from our roots; it can panic us so that we abandon our past. Why is it that so many look back on childhood and youth as the best years? Why do so many try to perpetuate the infantile and the adolescent in their bodies and dress and actions?

But change can also be a catalyst for growth. It can stimulate developing, deepening, lengthening, enlarging—our lives becoming more, not less. And that's what the narrator calls attention to in David at this moment. Not David embittered by the long hostility of Saul; not David narrowed into an obsessive paranoia against the Philistines; not David reduced to a compulsive regard for his own interests; not David lazily living off the reputation of his youthful achievements; not David sidetracked into wilderness love affairs. No. Rather, all that conflict and hostility, all those blessings and wonders, all that hate and love metabolized into a holy life, a life robust in God and prayer and obedience. He lengthened his stride; he enlarged his embrace.

He lengthened his stride. He did the unexpected when he took Jerusalem. This was avoided territory. No one else ventured into this den of superstition and ghost stories. Nobody had seen Jerusalem as a strategic site. But David did. He also saw the evil parodies of his faith and the cruel mockeries of the disabled as a blemish on the landscape of the promised land, the *holy* land. In indignation he took a giant step into Jerusalem and destroyed the caricatures of his ancestors Jacob and Isaac rigged up on the walls of Jerusalem. Instead of mincing around these abominations, David confronted them. As often happens, the very thing that reduces immaturity to neurotic timidity is exposed by maturity as Wizard-of-Oz fakery.

And David enlarged his embrace. He included more and more people under his rule and in his love. He gathered *all* God's children, not just those who had been on his side, helping him out through the difficult years. Maturity translated into generosity, into reaching out to make peace with the northern tribes. David didn't use his newly acquired strength and authority to destroy or denigrate others. He gathered and integrated and led.

When we grow, in contrast to merely change, we venture into new territory and include more people in our lives—serve more and love more. Our culture is filled with change; it's poor in growth. New things, models, developments, opportunities are announced, breathlessly, every hour. But instead of becoming ingredients in a long and wise growth, they simply replace. The previous is discarded and the immediate stuck in—until, bored by the novelty, we run after the next fad. Men and women drawn always to the new never grow up. God's way is growth, not change. *Organic* is a key image. Nothing from our past is thrown out with the garbage; it's all composted and assimilated into a growing life. And nothing—no "moral," no "principle"—is tacked on from the outside. David at thirty-seven was more than he was at seventeen— more praise, saner counsel, deeper love. More himself. More his God-given and God-glorifying humanity. A longer stride, a larger embrace.

ORGANIC SPIRITUALITY

Traveling through scenic country, we sometimes come upon a sign reading, "Roadside Vista Ahead." In anticipation we slow down. And then we're there; we pull off the highway, get out of our car, stretch—and look. We see where we've been; we see where we're headed. Take a breather. Eat a snack. Enjoy the scenery. We can't *always* be driving, watching the road closely. *Not* driving is also part of the trip—savoring what we've done, absorbing the landscape, letting the contours of the land and the colors of the horizon sink into our imaginations.

These are connective moments. We have various ways of honoring them. We honor them on and with anniversaries, birthdays, graduations, retirements, reunions, celebrations—and by pulling off at roadside vistas. Honoring them is one of the ways we have of keeping our lives coherent—keeping what we've been connected with what we're becoming. Without frequent reconnaissance we're in danger of living in spasms without coordination, without rhythm.

The "greater and greater" message of 2 Samuel 5:10 is pivotal in the David story. Up to this point we've been reading the story of the rise of David; from this point on we'll be reading the story of the reign of David. David is thirty-seven years old at the time of this transition.

For seven and a half years David has been king of a single tribe, Judah, in the village of Hebron. Two years before that he was the leader of the guerrilla band of six hundred at Ziklag. For approximately eight years before that he was a fugitive in the wilderness, hiding out from the malevolence of Saul. Before that he was a musician in Saul's court and locally famous as a killer of Philistines. In the prime of his adolescence he had met the giant Goliath in battle and slain him. He first came to our notice when, as the youngest of Jesse's eight sons, he was pulled out of the sheepfolds in the Bethlehem hills and anointed as the future king of God's people.

We're getting a feel for the kind of narrative written here—an immersion in the human condition with all its glory and hurt, promise and difficulty. But we're never left with mere humanity, mere history. The skill of the narrator keeps us alert to the presence and purposes of God being worked out in this story. We're being trained to read between the lines, for much of this story is implicit. But it's unmistakably there—David isn't *David* apart from God. None of us is. Most of what we're reading about in David is *God* in David. Spirituality, but earthy spirituality.

The David story keeps us in touch with our humanity—all of which has to do with God. There's no part of our humanity that isn't God-created and God-conditioned. The David story is a primary way in which the Holy Spirit keeps us in touch, alert and responsive to the gravity and ground of our lives in God the Father, Son, and Holy Spirit and alert to the reality of evil that would destroy or weaken our humanity.

We live in a world in which a great many lies are told about who we are and the way the world is. If we're going to live well, live *saved,* we need to know the truth about who we are and what's going on around us. The world that the flesh and the devil have spread out before us offers an incredible array of religious, psychological, cultural, and political options to choose from—most of them attractive and all of them fraudulent.

The David story is a major means for providing us a narrative context for understanding our lives, in all their complexities, as God-shaped. It's a story that comes into final form in Jesus Christ, the Son of David. But in order to take in how "final" that final form is, Christians have characteristically lived themselves into the story of David.

As we do that, one of the things we realize is that the Christian life develops organically. It *grows* from a seed that's planted in the actual soil of our muscles and brain cells, our emotions and moods, our genetic code and work schedule, the North American weather and our family history. It isn't imposed from without. It isn't monitored and regulated by a religious bureaucracy. God the Father, Son, and Holy Ghost isn't a consulting firm we bring in to give us expert advice on how to run our lives. The gospel life isn't something we learn *about* and then put together with instructions from the manufacturer; it's something we *become* as God does his work of creation and salvation in us and as we accustom ourselves to a life of belief and obedience and prayer.

The recurrent error of our technologically conditioned age is to look for what's wrong in our lives so that we can fix it, or what needs doing so that we can have something worthwhile to do. There *are* things wrong that need fixing; and there *are* jobs that need doing. But the Christian life starts at the other end—not with us but with God: What is God doing that I can respond to? How is God expressing his love and grace so that I can live appreciatively and in obedience?

This is why the David story continues to prove so useful: it doesn't show us how we *should* live but how we *do* live. And how in that living, if we keep our eyes open, stay honest, and avoid pretense, we encounter God alive, God in covenant with us, God pulling the best out of us. We find ourselves at levels of aliveness that we didn't know existed, dimensions of passion that we thought were left behind in adolescence, a willingness to venture and risk that puts electricity into the word *faith*. By taking the David story seriously, we find that we're taking our own stories seriously, realizing just how God-shaped, God-influenced, God-graced these storied lives of ours in fact are.

THE LORD IS MY SHEPHERD

The rise of David is now concluded; the reign of David begins. The words that are used at this inauguration are significant: "You shall be shepherd of my people Israel, and you shall be prince over Israel" (2 Sam. 5:2). The designation *king* is used freely enough throughout the narrative, but it's not used here: the choice of the words *shepherd* and *prince* is significant.

Prince (in Hebrew *nagid*) instead of *king*, for Israel had just experienced an abusive form of rule in King Saul. David is identified as one of them who had risen through the ranks: "Behold, we are your bone and flesh" (2 Sam. 5:1). This was not to be rule imposed from without but rule developed from within.

And *shepherd.* "In times past, when Saul was king over us, it was you that led out and brought in Israel" (2 Sam. 5:2). Keep continuity with the Bethlehem sheepfolds. Keep continuity with the wilderness austerities. The shepherd is one who lives with the flock and cares; the prince is one who emerges out of the ranks and leads. David's rule is intended to develop by nurturing the shepherd instincts and skills of his youth.

David's rule is intended to grow by conserving the community sensitivities that he cultivated through the wilderness years. As David assumes his reign as king over Israel and Judah, the leaders tell him, in effect, "Be our prince: don't change into a power-hungry king who imposes his will on the people. Be our shepherd: don't change into an ego-driven king who uses the people as fodder for his self-importance. Be our prince; be our shepherd. Maintain continuity with Bethlehem and Ziklag."

David did what they asked him to do. The person he had become he continued to be. One of the primary pieces of evidence is Psalm 23. This is the premier David psalm. David's name and life are inextricably woven into the warp and woof of this psalm. We don't argue this—it's simply recognized: the fittingness of David's life and David's prayer as they mesh in this psalm:

> *God, my shepherd!*
> > *I don't need a thing.*
> *You have bedded me down in lush meadows,*
> > *you find me quiet pools to drink from.*
> *True to your word,*
> > *you let me catch my breath*
> > *and send me in the right direction.*
>
> *Even when the way goes through*
> > *Death Valley,*
> *I'm not afraid*
> > *when you walk at my side.*
> *Your trusty shepherd's crook*
> > *makes me feel secure.*
>
> *You serve me a six-course dinner*
> > *right in front of my enemies.*
> *You revive my drooping head;*
> > *my cup brims with blessing.*
>
> *Your beauty and love chase after me*
> > *every day of my life.*
> *I'm back home in the house of God*
> > *for the rest of my life.*

It's impossible to understand a single thing about David apart from God. Every image in this psalm—which is to say, every aspect of David's life—is God-defined, God-saturated. Everything that David knows about God he experiences—enters into, embraces, takes into himself. God isn't a doctrine he talks about but a person by whom he's led and cared for. God isn't a remote abstraction that distances him from the conditions of his actual life but an intimate presence who confirms his daily life as the very stuff of salvation. What he experiences in God doesn't merely change but matures. The shepherd boy of Bethlehem becomes the shepherd king of Israel.

RELIGION

DAVID AND UZZAH

2 Samuel 6

*Jesus said, "You're tied down to the mundane; I'm in
touch with what is beyond your horizons. You live in
terms of what you see and touch. I'm living on other
terms. I told you that you were missing God in all this.
You're at a dead-end. If you won't believe I am who I
say I am, you're at the dead end of sins. You're missing
God in your lives."*

—JOHN 8:23–24

WE ARRIVE NOW at an odd episode in the David story. There are details here that none of us seems to be able to account for satisfactorily.
And yet the thrust and meaning of the story are blazingly obvious.

The Ark of the Covenant had been captured by the Philistines thirty
years earlier (1 Sam. 4–7). David hadn't yet appeared in the story then.
But now David is king. Having just established his rule in Jerusalem, he
decides to bring the Ark to his new capital, signaling that Zion is not

only the place from which David rules but also the place where God is worshiped. It's an important mission, a holy task. It isn't enough to have the king's throne in Jerusalem; it's *God's* rule that must be celebrated, and for that there must be worship of God. The Ark of the Covenant provides the focus for worship.

As the Ark is being brought up, the oxen pulling the cart stumble. The Ark slides and is about to fall to the ground. Uzzah, a priest (who, with his brother Ahio, is in charge of the transfer of the Ark), puts out his hand to prevent the Ark from tumbling off the cart. Then comes this hard sentence: "God smote him . . . and he died" (2 Sam. 6:7).

David calls off the trip. Who would dare continue after that? The project is abandoned, and everyone goes home. Three months later, David returns and completes the task, this time with extravagantly expressed celebration, "with rejoicing. And David danced before the LORD with all his might" (2 Sam. 6:14).

Sometimes I think that all religious sites should be posted with signs reading, "Beware the God." The places and occasions that people gather to attend to God are dangerous. They're glorious places and occasions, true, but they're also dangerous. Danger signs should be conspicuously placed, as they are at nuclear power stations. Religion is the death of some people. The story of Uzzah and David posts the warning and tells the glory.

Uzzah and David share the story. Uzzah died; David danced. The Ark of the Covenant was the occasion for the death and the dance, Uzzah's death and David's dance.

THE MONASTERY OF THE ARK OF THE COVENANT

A few years ago I spent a day in David country with my wife and a couple of friends. Driving a rented Subaru, we left the King Solomon Hotel in Jerusalem early one morning. Jerusalem sits on a mountainous ridge that divides Israel vertically into east and west. We drove west out of Jerusalem down the long descent through the hill country toward the Mediterranean Sea. We drove through Ein Kerem, the village in which John the Baptist is thought to have grown up, into the Judean hills through what's now called the Canada Forest. Nearly fifty years ago the Israelis launched an extensive reforestation program. People from all over the world pitched in and planted trees. The Canadians picked this area. The seedlings they planted a half-century ago are now a lovely, mature forest, mostly coniferous.

In less than an hour of driving, we saw the terrain level out into the coastal plain. We stopped at a field of grass and wildflowers in the general vicinity of the Valley of Elah, where David and Goliath fought. We leaned over a fence and wondered if this might have been the very field. We knew that if we spent the rest of the day hiking up that valley, by evening we would arrive at Adullam, where David launched his wilderness sojourn. But the day was already getting hot, and we decided to stay with our air-conditioned Subaru. In another ten minutes we passed the ruins of the old village Beth Shemesh, where the Philistines had first placed the Ark after capturing it from King Saul. A short while later we swung onto the major highway that goes from Tel Aviv to Jerusalem, circling back toward our starting place of that morning.

This modern highway follows an ancient roadway, traveled for twenty-five hundred years by pilgrims making their way to Jerusalem to worship. Pilgrims converged from three directions onto this old path: from the port at Joppa, seafarers would disembark and enter directly onto this road; those who came up the coastal plain from Egypt and places south would hit this road; and the men and women who came from Syria and points north would come down the coastal plain and turn onto this route. Travelers from west, south, and north funneled into this highway and ascended, step by step, to the place of worship, up to Jerusalem.[1]

By the time travelers set their feet on this road, they knew they were close—only fifty or so miles now. Some of these pilgrims would have been on their way for weeks, some for months. Jews scattered into all nations returned for the feasts of Passover, Weeks (Pentecost), and Booths (Tabernacles). Later they were joined by Christians, pulled by the power of sacred place and story from all over Europe, Asia, Africa, and the Americas, arriving to worship at the sites where the Word became flesh and dwelt among us.

If you started walking from the seaport town of Joppa, about noon on the second day you would enter the little village of Kiriath-Jearim (also known as Baalah), a village set on the crest of a mountain ridge. Looking east, across a wide valley, you would get your first glimpse of Jerusalem. Almost there! Kiriath-Jearim was a place for pilgrims to catch their breath and gather strength for the final leg of the journey.

There's a monastery on the site now, the Monastery of the Ark of the Covenant. A community of French nuns live there. My friends and I sat on a bench on the lawn and ate our lunch of falafel and fresh cucumbers. We looked across the long valley and saw what pilgrims always so delighted to see from Kiriath-Jearim: Jerusalem, the destination of worshiping pilgrims.

We were on the site where the Ark of the Covenant had been marooned for thirty years in the house of the priest Abinadab. We were at the place where pilgrims got their first look at Zion, the Holy City. We were at the place where David came to get the Ark of the Covenant and take it to Jerusalem, his newly established center for rule and worship. We got out our Bibles and read 2 Samuel 6. We talked of worship and of the roads we had traveled to places of worship, reflecting on the drawing power of sacred place in our lives and our deep, never-to-be-quenched thirst for worship.

LET'S WORSHIP AT GOD'S OWN FOOTSTOOL!

Then we prayed together Psalm 132, the David psalm so intimately associated with this story:

> *O God, remember David,*
> *remember all his troubles!*
> *And remember how he promised God,*
> *made a vow to the Strong God of Jacob,*
> *"I'm not going home,*
> *and I'm not going to bed,*
> *I'm not going to sleep,*
> *not even take time to rest,*

Until I find a home for God,
a house for the Strong God of Jacob."
Remember how we got the news in Ephrathah,
learned all about it at Jaar Meadows?
We shouted, "Let's go to the shrine dedication!
Let's worship at God's own footstool!"

Up, God, enjoy your new place of quiet repose,
you and your mighty covenant ark;
Get your priests all dressed up in justice;
prompt your worshipers to sing this prayer:
"Honor your servant David;
don't disdain your anointed one."

God gave David his word,
he won't go back on his promise:
"One of your sons
I will set on your throne;
If your sons stay true to my Covenant
and learn to live the way I teach them,
Their sons will continue the line—
always a son to sit on your throne.
Yes—I, God, chose Zion,
the place I wanted for my shrine;
This will always be my home;
this is what I want, and I'm here for good.
I'll shower blessings on the pilgrims who come here,
and give supper to those who arrive hungry;
I'll dress my priests in salvation clothes;
the holy people will sing their hearts out!
Oh, I'll make the place radiant for David!
I'll fill it with light for my anointed!
I'll dress his enemies in dirty rags,
but I'll make his crown sparkle with splendor."

THE ARK OF THE COVENANT

The Ark of the Covenant was a rectangular box, not quite four feet in length and a little over two feet in depth and width.[2]

It was constructed of wood and plated with gold. Its lid of solid gold was called the mercy seat. Two cherubim, angel-like figures at either end, framed the space around the central mercy seat from which God's word was honored. The Ark contained three items: the tablets of stone that Moses had delivered to the people from Sinai; a jar of manna from the wilderness years of wandering; and Aaron's rod that budded. These objects were the continuing and reminding evidence that God worked among them: commanded them (the tablets), provided for them (the manna), and saved them (the rod). The Ark provided a center, giving a hard, historical focus to the revealed character of the God whom they worshiped.

The Ark didn't have magical properties. When the Hebrews treated it (and later the Temple) that way—as a source of power or good luck— the prophets did their best to confront them and face them with the reality of a personal God, as over against an impersonal relic. Later Jeremiah and Ezekiel were especially eloquent in such confrontations. Superstition wasn't encouraged in Israel. The people were never taught that the Ark was a source of power they could plug into. The Hebrews were a *historical* people. They believed that God worked in their lives, *did* things. God wasn't a blurred glow of sentiment. God wasn't an abstract concept. God wasn't a remote legislator passing laws on gravity and adultery. God wasn't a bearded judge, austere and exacting. God was personal in history: creating, directing, saving, blessing. God entered the affairs of men and women; and when he did, he judged and saved, called to account and blessed. Most of all he loved. He entered into covenants with his people, giving them the dignity of sharing his work, living by faith and in love.

The Ark kept all this before them. That was its purpose: to hold up the evidence of the kind of God with whom they had to do. This wasn't a piece of memorabilia but a display of what was going on—what was always going on, what was still going on: God's presence and action among them worked into the material (stone and pottery and wood) of their lives. The closest thing to it in Christian practice is the sacraments, material evidence of God's action in our common lives using common materials for his work—God entering into the ordinariness (water and bread and wine) of our lives and working his saving and sanctifying purposes right there.

This is what David went to get, this Ark that had been sitting for thirty years in the village of Kiriath-Jearim in the house of the old priest Abinadab. Abinadab assigned his two priest sons, Uzzah and Ahio, to supervise delivery of the Ark to Jerusalem. In Jerusalem the Ark would recover the memories of God's long dealings with his people. In Jerusalem the Ark would provide a focus that would center the tribes of Israel and Judah on God's rule, not merely David's government.

They put the Ark on an ox-cart, Brother Ahio ahead leading the oxen, Brother Uzzah alongside. One of the oxen stepped in a rut and stumbled. The cart lurched, and the Ark began to slide off. Uzzah reflexively reached out to steady it. And he died.

UZZAH'S DEATH

Why did Uzzah die? Why did God, as the text puts it so bluntly, smite him? It's difficult to fit this episode into our picture of the God who is consistently revealed as the giver of life, patiently calling us to repentance, constantly seeking the lost, undeflected in his steadfast love for us. It doesn't sit easy with us when we come across an assertion that God kills. Judgment, certainly, but sudden death? The story of the slaying of Ananias and Sapphira in the New Testament Acts of the Apostles (chapter 5) evokes a similarly puzzled response in us. The text doesn't answer our question. We'll likely go to our graves scratching our heads over this. Sometimes the Bible raises more questions than it answers!

But when a storyteller leaves gaps in the story, there's an implicit invitation for us to fill in the blanks. We're not free to insert whatever suits our fancy—our imaginations must work within the constraints of the context—but within those constraints, our praying imaginations are given license to take a hand in entering the world of the text and participating in it.

Over the centuries, as the Christian imagination has reflected on Uzzah's death, one insight has appeared over and over: it's fatal to take charge of God. Uzzah is the person who has God in a box and officiously assumes responsibility for keeping him safe from the mud and dust of the world. Men and women who take it upon themselves to protect God from the vulgarity of sinners and the ignorance of commoners keep showing up in religious precincts.

In this imaginative context we can guess that Uzzah's reflexive act—reaching out to steady the Ark as the oxen stumbled—wasn't the mistake of a moment; it was a piece of his lifelong obsession with managing the Ark. There were Mosaic traditions that gave clear directions regarding the handling of the Ark: it wasn't to be touched by human hands but carried by Levites using poles inserted through rings attached to the Ark.[3] Uzzah ignored (defied!) the Mosaic directions and substituted the latest Philistine technological innovation—an ox-cart, of all things (see 1 Sam. 6). A well-designed ox-cart is undeniably more efficient for moving the Ark about than plodding Levites. But it's also impersonal—the replacement of consecrated persons by an efficient machine, the impersonal crowding out the personal. Uzzah is the patron saint of those who uncritically embrace technology without regard to the nature of the Holy. Uzzah was in charge (he thought) of God, and meant to stay in charge. Uzzah had God where he wanted him and intended to keep him there. The eventual consequence of this kind of life is death, for God will not be managed. God will not be put and kept in a box, whether the box is constructed of crafted wood or hewn stone or brilliant ideas or fine feelings. We don't take care of God; God takes care of us.

Holy Scripture posts Uzzah as a danger sign for us: "Beware the God." It's especially important to have such a sign posted in places designated for religious worship and learning. We enter a church or school to learn God, be trained in knowledge and obedience and prayer. And we get what we came for—truth that centers, words that command and comfort, rituals that stabilize, work that has purpose, a community of relationships that strengthen, forgiveness that frees. We find God. We change our ways. We repent and believe and follow. We rearrange our circumstances and reestablish our routines around what now gives meaning and hope. We take on responsibilities in the wonderful new world of worship and work. We advance in the ranks, and before we know it we're telling others what to do and how to do it. All this is good and right. And then we cross a line—we get bossy and cranky on behalf of God. We begin by finding in God a way to live rightly and well, and then along the way we take over God's work for him and take charge of making sure others live rightly and well. We get the idea that we're important, self-important, because we're around the Important.

Religion is a breeding ground for this kind of thing. Not infrequently these God-managing men and women work themselves into positions of leadership. Over the years the basics with which they began, the elements of reverence and awe, the spirit of love and faith, erode and shrivel. Finally there's nothing left. They're dead to God.

Uzzah is a warning. If we think and act as he did, we'll be dead men and women, soon or late. Dead in our spirits. Dead to the aliveness of God. Jesus called such people "whitewashed tombs . . . full of dead men's bones" (Matt. 23:27). Uzzah's death wasn't sudden; it was years in the making, the "dead works" accumulating like dead men's bones within him, suffocating the spirit of praise and faith and worship.

DAVID'S DANCE

And David. Why did David dance? David, dancing before the Ark, reckless and joyful. David knew something about God to which Uzzah was blind and deaf.

David had been living dangerously all his life—with lions and bears, a taunting giant and a murderous king, marauding Philistines and cunning Amalekites, in wilderness caves and wadis. And with and in God: running and hiding, praying and loving. David was never in a position to take care of God. God was Savior and Commander, Shepherd and Rock. God wasn't a sheep that David tended. He wasn't a tame God. In and under these conditions David had learned to live openly, daringly, trustingly, and exultantly before God.

David wasn't careful with God. When Uzzah died, David lost his temper with God. He saw the death; he didn't see what had led up to it.

He had no sense of the years of slow suicide that came to a conclusion beside the ox-cart. All David saw was an interruption to his parade, turning it into a funeral cortege. Angry with God, David went home in a sulk, pouting.

David's anger with God didn't get him killed. It didn't get him killed because David was as alive to God in his anger as he was earlier in his praise. Alive to God. Alive. David didn't like what had happened, but at least he was treating God as *God*. Uzzah would never have gotten angry with God; he was far too well mannered and proper. And besides, one doesn't get angry with a box.

Home in Jerusalem, David had time to think it over and in three months had assembled his marching band again and was back with harps and lyres, tambourines, castanets, and cymbals, bringing the Ark to Jerusalem in grand style.

David danced. In God, David had access to life that exceeded his capacity to measure or control. He was on the edge of mystery, of glory. And so he danced. When we're going about our work responsibly and steadily, we walk. Walking is our normal mode of locomotion. But when we're beside ourselves with love, charged with excess of meaning, shaken out of preoccupation with ourselves, we dance. David danced. If David had been merely carrying out his religious duties or conducting a political ceremony, he would have walked in solemn procession before the Ark, leading it into Jerusalem with dignity. But this was no duty. He wasn't using God to give dignity to Jerusalem, or taking pains that God be properly honored. He was worshiping, responding to the living God. He was open to the life of God flowing around and through him, the God whose ways intersected history in a manner defined by that Ark, ways of salvation and revelation and blessing.

Religion—religious sites, religious occasions—is a breeding ground for joyful openness to God. We're never wholly ourselves until we're open before God, attending to the reality of God, responding to the action of God in us, receiving the word of God for us. Worship is the strategy by which we interrupt our preoccupation with ourselves and attend to the presence of God. Worship is the time and place that we assign for deliberate attentiveness to God—not because he's confined to time and place but because our self-importance is so insidiously relentless that if we don't deliberately interrupt ourselves regularly, we have no chance of attending to him at all at other times and in other places.

But even then danger intrudes, for having set the time and place, we sometimes presume to control the time and place, presume to confine God to the time and place. Uzzah again. That's why we have all these signs posted throughout our Scriptures: "Fear God." "The fear of God is the beginning of wisdom." "Beware!"

But the warnings don't reduce us to cautious timidity before God. David is proof to the contrary. What they do is prevent us from reducing God to our specifications. What they do is prevent death by religion.

MICHAL'S MOCKERY

Michal, David's wife, saw him dancing and leaping before the Ark, having a good time with the people who had been saved and led and commanded and blessed by God. She mocked him for his behavior. He ought to be acting more like a king. He ought to do what other kings did: have the gods serve him, surround himself with pomp and circumstance, organize a religion that made him look important and *kingly*. For Michal, God had become a social amenity, a political backer. Michal was first embarrassed by and then contemptuous of David's dance. I've always liked Alexander Whyte's sentence on Michal: "Those who are deaf always despise those who dance."[4]

Michal would have been comfortable walking beside the Ark with Uzzah, stately, proper, careful. And dead.

But she mocked David dancing before the Ark, reckless, daring, careless, praising. And alive.

David didn't care. David knew that "the glory of God is a human fully alive" (Iranaeus);[5] that we don't have to be careful and cautious with God; that it's death to decorously and politely manage God; that it's life eternal to let him take care of us.

SOVEREIGN GRACE

DAVID AND NATHAN

2 Samuel 7

*"My kingdom," said Jesus, "doesn't consist of what you
see around you. If it did, my followers would fight so
that I wouldn't be handed over to the Jews. But I'm not
that kind of king, not the world's kind of king."*

Then Pilate answered, "So, are you a king or not?"

*Jesus answered, "You tell me. Because I am King, I
was born and entered the world so that I could witness
to the truth. Everyone who cares for truth, who has any
feeling for the truth, recognizes my voice."*

—JOHN 18:36–37

THE MOMENTUM IS UP. Everything has come together. David is
on his way. He has put the Philistines in their place. He has consoli-
dated the country, impressively uniting north and south, he has established the new capital city, Jerusalem, and brought up the Ark of the
Covenant in a great and festive parade, signaling that we're dealing with
far more than David here: *God* reigns. David takes his place not as a

king in the usual sense but as a witness that God is King. It doesn't take long for us to realize that we're dealing with a kingdom that transcends all politics and personalities.

Goliath is dead; Saul is dead; and David is alive, very much alive, riding a crest of popular acclaim and gratitude. Everything has come together in David. The office of king, which Saul messed up so badly, is rehabilitated by David. David is king, but he doesn't follow any of the current job descriptions of kingship. David isn't a proud, royal head of state, exercising power; he's an obedient servant, representing and reporting on the sovereignty of God. David uses his throne as a pulpit from which to preach God's rule.

> *God is King, robed and ruling,*
> *God is robed and surging with strength.*
>
> > *And yes, the world is firm, immovable,*
> > *Your throne ever firm—you're Eternal!*
>
> *Sea storms are up, God,*
> *Sea storms wild and roaring,*
> *Sea storms with thunderous breakers.*
>
> > *Stronger than wild sea storms,*
> > *Mightier than sea-storm breakers,*
> > *Mighty God rules from High Heaven.*
>
> *What you say goes—it always has.*
> *"Beauty" and "Holy" mark your palace rule,*
> *God, to the very end of time.*
>
> (Ps. 93)

David's prayers are steeped in the imagery and conviction of God's sovereign rule. God's sovereignty is the single most distinctive element in the belief system that gives coherence to the many and various prayers that through the centuries were collected and arranged under David's name in the Psalms. Three hundred years after David's time, in Jerusalem, Isaiah preached what David prayed: powerful and eloquent sermons on the text "God reigns." A thousand years later Jesus began his public ministry with the text "The kingdom of God is at hand . . ." (Mark 1:15), and he concluded that ministry in Jerusalem by definitively revealing everything that was anticipated and promised—and more—in the millennium of prayers and preaching. And when John penned his flourishing wrap-up to the entire biblical revelation, he could do no better than repeat what David had sung and prayed so much and so well:

> *Hallelujah!*
> *The Master reigns,*
>   *our God, the Sovereign-Strong!*
> (REV. 19:6, *THE MESSAGE*)

DECIDING TO BUILD GOD A "HOUSE"

But no sooner had God's sovereign rule been proclaimed by David than the clarity and accuracy of that witness was threatened. And from a most unlikely quarter—from the very David who had given the witness.

It was only six miles from Bethlehem, where David had grown up as an obscure shepherd, to Jerusalem, where he was now established as Israel's finest king; but it took twenty years or so for him to make the trip. When David arrived, after all those years of trial and uncertainty, danger and hate—arrived safe and sound, arrived with a sense of God's blessings confirmed, God's promises validated, God's judgments true—he was overwhelmingly grateful. He had a home, secure and solid—a place and center after all those homeless years in the wilderness. He had reprieve from his enemies; he could rest and catch his breath after the strenuous and seemingly endless years of fighting Philistines and escaping Saul (2 Sam. 7:1).

He quite naturally wanted to do something for God, who had done so much for him. He decided to build God a sanctuary. He himself now had a home; he would build God a home. God had blessed him with a place of honor and repose; he would bless God with a place of honor and repose.

He talked it over with his pastor, Nathan. Nathan was enthusiastic: "Go, do all that is in your heart; for the LORD is with you" (2 Sam. 7:3).

Pastors love moments like these—turning-point moments when a person moves from receiving to giving. Nathan, like most pastors, must have spent much of his life being approached by people who were after something from God and wanted his assistance in getting it. Pastors and priests and prophets are supposed to know how to go about getting things people want from God. "Nathan, pray for me. My spouse is impossible; . . . my kids won't behave; . . . my job is at a dead end; . . . my nerves are frazzled; [etc., etc., etc.]. Nathan, pray for me."

And Nathan did it. Nathan was glad to do it. Asking God for help in time of need is our basic and most honest stance before God. There isn't a single area of our lives in which we're self-sufficient. We need God. We never develop or graduate to a state in which we don't need God. I once heard Isaac Bashevis Singer, master storyteller in Yiddish, say in a radio interview, "I pray only when I am in trouble; but I am in trouble all the time so I pray all the time." Everywhere throughout the biblical revelation we're encouraged to come to God with our lists of requests. God is generous and never runs out of blessings. God delights in giving—it's what he does best: life, salvation, healing, joy, peace, love, sunshine and rain, bread and wine, laughter and tears, refuge and rest. There's no end to any of it.

A deviant strain of teaching is making its rounds these days, telling us that prayers of praise must take precedence over everything else. That's not only dishonest, it's outrageously unbiblical. Praise and thanksgiving are always appropriate, certainly. And it's certain that our final prayers will be *all* praise—heaven reverberating with our amens and hallelujahs—so practicing the scales of praise is always a good idea. But for here and now we mostly ask. Jesus *taught* us to ask. In the model prayer he gave us, Jesus trained us to ask: there are six petitions in the prayer, and not a thank-you to be found.

David was a master at asking God for what he needed. Bold and eloquent in his asking—asking for help, for refuge, for healing, for salvation, for deliverance, for forgiveness, for mercy, for the Holy Spirit. He was also wonderfully robust in praise, but the praise was all mined from this hardscrabble life of asking. Psalm 21 provides a Davidic perspective on this lifetime of asking.

Your strength, God, is the king's strength.
Helped, he's hollering Hosannas.
You gave him exactly what he wanted;
you didn't hold back.
You filled his arms with gifts;
you gave him a right royal welcome.
He wanted a good life; you gave it to him,
and then made it a long life as a bonus.
You lifted him high and bright as a cumulus cloud,
then dressed him in rainbow colors.
You pile blessings on him;
you make him glad when you smile.
Is it any wonder the king loves God?
that he's sticking with the Best?

With a fistful of enemies in one hand
and a fistful of haters in the other,
You radiate with such brilliance
that they cringe as before a furnace.
Now the furnace swallows them whole,
the fire eats them alive!
You purge the earth of their progeny,
you wipe the slate clean.
All their evil schemes, the plots they cook up,
have fizzled—every one.
You sent them packing;
they couldn't face you.

Show your strength, God, so no one can miss it.
We are out singing the good news!

Men and women in Nathan's position are used to being partners to asking God for help, and rejoicing in the help God gives. They aren't used to having someone show up offering to do something for God. It's so unusual that when it does happen, prophetic and pastoral affirmation is unqualified. It feels like such a breath of fresh air! Enthusiasm is immediate and uncritical. Nathan endorsed David's proposal wholeheartedly, unthinkingly. What was there to think about? What grounds were there for suspicion? A house for God—what could be better?

But that night God gave Nathan pause. God assessed David's proposal in quite a different light than Nathan had. It turns out that there *were* grounds for suspicion.

Nathan went back to David in the morning and withdrew the building permit. Pastors and prophets and priests also find themselves doing this quite often, and always awkwardly. Why would a prophet of God discourage well-intended work for God? In the midst of the epidemic of disobedience and sloth and inertia that prevails most of the time among God's people, why would anyone say no to an obviously God-blessed, God-ardent David? Why throw a wet blanket on a blazing fire? All that enthusiasm for God, all that energy ready to be poured into doing something great for God—and instead of affirming and guiding, saying no.

But there are times when our grand human plans to do something for God are seen, after a night of prayer, to be a huge human distraction from what God is doing for us.[1] That's what Nathan realized that night: God showed Nathan that David's building plans for God would interfere with God's building plans for David.

God's word to David through Nathan was essentially this: "You want to build me a house? Forget it—I'm going to build *you* a house. The kingdom that I'm shaping here isn't what you do for me but what I do through you. I'm doing the building here, not you. I'm not going to let you confuse things by launching a building operation of your own. If I let you fill Jerusalem with the sights and sounds of your building project—carpenters' hammers, masons' chisels, teamsters' shouts—before long everyone will be caught up in what *you* are doing, and not attentive to what *I* am doing. This is a *kingdom* that we're dealing with, and *I* am the king. I've gotten along without a so-called house for a long time now. Where did you ever come up with the idea that I need or want a house? If there's any building to be done, *I'm* doing it. I've been working with you since your shepherd days, building a kingdom—a place where salvation and justice and peace can be realized. That's why you're here: to give visibility and representation to what I'm doing, not call attention to what you're doing. We've just had one failure like that in Saul, and we're not going to have another. There will come a time when it's appropriate to build something like you have in mind—your son, in fact, will do it—but this isn't the time. First we have to get the concept of *my* sovereignty established in the people's imagination and practice, your kingship a witness to my kingship, not an obscuring of it. *That's* the house I'm building—your kingship as witness and representation of my sovereignty. First things first" (2 Sam. 7:4–17).

The message that Nathan delivers to David is dominated by a recital of what God has done, is doing, and will do. God is the first-person subject of twenty-three verbs in this message, and these verbs carry the action. David, full of what he's going to do for God, is now subjected to a comprehensive rehearsal of what God has done, is doing, and will do for and in David. What looked yesterday like a bold Davidic enterprise on behalf of God now looks picayune.

• • •

DO YOU KNOW what I think? I think that David is just about to cross over a line from being full of God to being full of himself. Outwardly, everything is the same. He isn't conscious of doing anything different, not self-aware of any shift within. But David, riding the crest of acclaim, having decisively defeated the opposition, united God's people, and captured the allegiance of all Israel and Judah, heady with success, is now going to do God a favor. The telltale clue is in his proposal to Nathan: "See now, I dwell in a house of cedar, but the ark of God dwells in a tent" (2 Sam. 7:2). Implicit in that comparison (house of cedar/tent) is the judgment that David is now housed better than God, that David has achieved a better standard of living than God, and that from David's position of strength he can now do something significant for God.

If David continues to develop along these lines, he will soon be ruined as God's king. If any of us develop a self-identity in which God and

God's action are subordinated to us and our action, our kingwork is ruined. These are the moments when we need a friend, a pastor, a prophet to step in and do for us what we're unlikely to do for ourselves. God speaks to Nathan, and Nathan speaks to David. Nathan stops him in his tracks with God's message: "No, you won't build me a house; I'll make *you* a house."

SITTING DOWN

"Then King David went in and sat before the LORD . . . " (2 Sam. 7:18). David *sat*. This may be the single most critical act that David ever did, the action that put him out of action—more critical than killing Goliath, more critical than honoring Saul (his enemy) as God's anointed, more critical than bringing the Ark to Jerusalem. More critical because what David now does in response to Nathan's pastoral/prophetic counsel will either qualify or disqualify him from the kingwork for which he has been anointed, trained, preserved, and empowered.

David is at his prime: his body hard and sinewy, his mind sharply alert, his spirit blazing in worship and obedience. David tested and mature. David invested with the trust and admiration of God's people. David grateful to God for all that he has received from God. David energetically ambitious to do something for God. David crowned and enthroned. *King* David.

Now that David is king, will he become the sort of king found in the neighboring kingdoms of Egypt and Syria, Ethiopia and Assyria? Will David become tyrannical, imposing his will on those around him? Will David become proud, asserting domination over his inferiors? Will David become cruel, depersonalizing everyone into role and function? Will David come to view the God who made him king as an adjunct to his royal office, as Saul did? Or will David refuse to take on the cultural/religious/political role of king, keep a firm grip on his humanity, and represent and give witness to God the King, the Sovereign God, God Almighty?

David sat. And he sat *before God*. By sitting down, David renounced royal initiative, abdicated kingly authority, got himself out of the driver's seat, and deliberately and reverently placed himself before God his King.

In the ancient East, virtually every time a man or woman was crowned the ceremony was assumed by the now-royal person and the general public alike to confer divinity. The person on the throne was no longer human but divine, with all the privileges of divinity. It's easy for us in the modern West to be dismissively condescending to such a mindset, but something very similar takes place in our culture when we "crown" a person as physician, lawyer, senator, pastor, chair of the board, or chief executive officer. Those of us so "crowned" find people deferring to us in odd ways—treating us not at all in the ways we were used to as we grew up bruising our elbows and skinning our knees, developing clumsily through the awkward embarrassments of adolescence, learning to do our work through many a trial and error, mistake and reprimand. And now, in our jobs and professions and roles, we get treated, if not as divine, at least as something a little more than human—elevated by authority or prestige above the common lot. But every such elevation dehumanizes. Nothing we do or have done to us lifts us out of our common humanity. The moment we notice such deference, we need to be as quick as Peter in saying, "None of that—I'm a man and only a man, no different from you" (Acts 10:26); as alert as Paul in crying out, "What do you think you're doing! We're not gods! We're human just like you, and we're here to bring you the Message . . . " (Acts 14:15, *The Message*).

David sat. An incredible feat when we begin to understand the conditions under which he did it—so full of desire for God he was, so bursting with plans for God. Stopping David in that condition was like reigning in a team of runaway horses. But Nathan stopped him. More accurately, David let himself be stopped by God.

STRATEGIC "NOT DOING"

What we don't do for God is often far more critical than what we in fact do. God is the beginning, center, and end of the world's life—of existence itself. But we're often unaware of God's action except dimly and peripherally. Especially when we're in full possession of our powers—our education complete, our careers in full swing, people admiring us

and prodding us onward—it's hard not to imagine that we're at the beginning, center, and end of the world, or at least of that part of the
world in which we're placed. At these moments we need prophetic interference; we need Nathan. We need to quit whatever we're doing and
sit down. When we sit down, the dust raised by our furious activity
settles; the noise generated by our building operations goes quiet; we
become aware of the real world. *God's* world. And what we see leaves us
breathless: it's so much larger, so much more full of energy and action
than our ego-fueled actions, so much clearer and saner than the plans
that we had projected.

Modern Christians are characteristically much afraid of being
caught out doing too little for God, let alone nothing. But there are moments, far more frequent than we suppose, when doing nothing is
precisely the gospel thing to do. Every once in a while an old heresy
reappears that distorts this pregnant and worshipfully obedient "nothing" into an ill-conceived and irresponsible "nothing doing." Wrong-
headed teachers emerge from time to time telling us that since God does
everything, we must train ourselves to do nothing, cultivating a kind of
pious sloth: the less we do for God, the more God can do for us. Others
counsel stoic resignation to whatever happens, since all that happens is
"the will of God." Still others misconceive a life of prayer and faith as
acquiescence to the inevitable. But biblical not-doing is neither sloth
nor stoicism; it's a strategy.

When David sat down before God, it was the farthest thing from
passivity or resignation; it was prayer. It was entering into the presence
of God, becoming aware of God's word, trading in his plans for God's
plans, letting his enthusiasm for being a king with the authority and
strength to do something for God be replaced with the willingness to
become a king who would represent truly the sovereignty of God the
high King.

• • •

AS DAVID SAT BEFORE GOD, he prayed (2 Sam. 7:18–29). His
prayer shows how well he had listened to God's word preached to him
by Nathan. God's message came to him in the first person: God was

subject. The message was a proclamation of God's action. The evidence that David listened shows up first in his grammar: now, instead of announcing what he'll do for God, David addresses God as the person who has done and is doing things for him. The twenty-three God-in-the-first-person verbs in Nathan's message (2 Sam. 7:4–17) bear witness to the conversion of David from one who talks about God as an impersonal object (2 Sam. 7:2) to one who addresses God in the second person—a Thou, not an It.[2] Whereas before, David was full of himself, now David is full of God. Seventeen times David refers to God by name—God, Lord God, Yahweh, God of Hosts; he uses the personal pronoun for God an additional forty-five more times.

David's prayer comes to focus in an explicit and radical reversal: "For thou, O LORD of hosts, the God of Israel, hast made this revelation to thy servant, saying, 'I will build you a house'; therefore thy servant has found courage to pray this prayer to thee" (2 Sam. 7:27). And courage it does take, immense courage, to relinquish control, to resign our so recently acquired prestigious positions, to "quit our jobs" and simply sit at Jesus' feet.

David sat down; the real action started: not David making God a house but God making David a house.

There's no danger in such inaction that we'll end up with nothing to do. David did much before he sat down, and he did much afterward: God commands and we obey; God sends and we go. The Christian life is a gloriously active life as the Holy Spirit does the work of Christ in and through us. No, there's no danger that as we sit before the Lord our legs will atrophy and we'll never be able to get up again. But there *is* great danger in getting so caught up in our God-plans that we forget all about God.

Psalm 2 holds this centerpiece of David's experience firmly in focus for us, the very experience that was confirmed and given detailed exposition in King Jesus:

> *Why the big noise, nations?*
> *Why the mean plots, peoples?*
> *Earth-leaders push for position,*
> *Demagogues and delegates meet for summit talks.*

The God-deniers, the Messiah-defiers:
"Let's get free of God!
Cast loose from Messiah!"

Heaven-throned God breaks out laughing.
At first he's amused at their presumption;
Then he gets good and angry.
Furiously, he shuts them up:
"Don't you know there's a King in Zion? A coronation banquet
Is spread for him on the holy summit."

Let me tell you what Yahweh said next.
He said, "You're my son,
And today is your birthday.
What do you want? Name it:
Nations as a present? Continents as a prize?
You can command them all to dance for you,
Or throw them out with tomorrow's trash."

So, rebel-kings, use your heads;
Upstart-judges, learn your lesson:
Worship Yahweh in adoring embrace,
Celebrate in trembling awe. Kiss Messiah!
Your very lives are in danger, you know;
His anger is about to explode,
But if you make a run for God—you won't regret it!

• • •

WALTER BRUEGGEMANN identifies this David and Nathan story as "the dramatic and theological center of the entire Samuel corpus . . . one of the most crucial texts in the Old Testament for evangelical faith."[3] A true assessment, for it's our seemingly good intentions that get us in the most grievous trouble. When we do wrong, we usually find out soon enough and repent and get back on track. But when we do good, become pleased with ourselves and receive applause and commendation from our leaders and friends, we easily lose our sense of dependence on God and our always and ever increasingly desperate need for grace, *God's* sovereign grace. The last state of that person, as Jesus so solemnly warned, is worse than the first (Luke 11:26).

LOVE

DAVID AND

MEPHIBOSHETH

2 Samuel 9

Jesus said, "Love one another. In the same way I loved
you, you love one another. This is how everyone will
recognize that you are my disciples—when they see the
love you have for each other."

—JOHN 13:34–35

MEPHIBOSHETH WAS THE SON of Jonathan, David's oldest and
best friend. Three times in the David cycle his name is brought to our
attention. Cumulatively, the three stories embed Mephibosheth in
our imaginations in such a way that by now the mere mention of the
name to those of us who have entered the David story arouses latent im-
pulses of generosity and channels them into strategies of love in the men
and women who commit themselves to live by faith in Jesus Christ.

MEPHIBOSHETH (1)

When Mephibosheth was five years old, news came to Saul's palace in Gibeon that King Saul and Prince Jonathan had just been killed by the Philistines on Mount Gilboa in the battle at Jezreel. Panic was immediate and total. The Philistines were ruthless—with Saul and his sons dead, the royal house and everyone in it were slated for destruction. There would be no mercy to anyone connected with the names Saul and Jonathan. Worse, David's guerrilla band was at large. Without Saul, whom David honored as God's anointed, and without Jonathan, with whom David had a covenant of friendship, there was nothing preventing David from coming in and cleaning house, getting rid of anyone and anything left behind in the regime that had kept him in long exile.

Not knowing what to expect except the worst, all the servants in the palace ran for their lives. Five-year-old Mephibosheth's nurse grabbed him on the run and then tripped. In the fall the boy's ankles were broken—both ankles (2 Sam. 4:4). He was carried with the troop of escaping household servants east across the Jordan River valley to the safety of the small village Lo-debar. The bones knit badly. Mephibosheth was never again able to walk well. He grew up in obscurity, lame.

Mephibosheth was the only living heir of the once-great house of Saul, but nobody knew it. Because his life would have been in danger if that information were revealed, he grew up with his royal identity suppressed, grew up with all the privileges of royalty denied him; and both conditions were aggravated by his lameness. None of this was his own fault; it had all been done to him when he was too young to have been responsible for any of it: the sudden exile, the terrible fall and permanent disability, the loss of future. Mephibosheth was a victim.

Exile communities commonly maintain a sense of identity—pride even—by remembering the former days when they had played a significant role in history, recounting the stories of their displacement and debasement. It's easy enough to imagine Mephibosheth growing up on such stories, told by the servants around late-evening fires in Lo-debar. I'm guessing that his nurse was his primary storyteller and that the stories all contributed in one way or another to a deep sense of victimization.

I'm also guessing that David's name eventually got worked into all the stories as the dark presence responsible for all the ills. It was because of David that Mephibosheth's father and grandfather had been killed by the Philistines. If it hadn't been for David, there would have been no accident and no lifelong crippling disability. It was David's fault that they were living in faceless and miserable obscurity in Lo-debar. From the age of five, Mephibosheth grew up on these embittering David stories, stories in which David was cast as scapegoat and villain. Mephibosheth was trained from the age of five to look for the cause of his misery outside himself, to find someone to blame, to avoid the reality of who he was and the limitations of his condition by fantasizing revenge on the world. And that unkind, ungenerous, uncaring world had the face of David.

MEPHIBOSHETH (2)

The second Mephibosheth story took place years later. Mephibosheth was now an adult, still cruelly handicapped because of the accident. Worse, he was badly crippled in spirit because of the embittering stories. He was living out the meaning of his name, "Seething Dishonor."[1]

And then a day came when strangers arrived in Lo-debar asking for him. They found him and told him that he was wanted in Jerusalem by King David. The summons to present himself before David could only have struck terror in him. Only one interpretation could be put on the summons: David was searching the land from top to bottom, looking for any trace of Saul's descendants, determined to eliminate any possible future challenge to his kingdom. David had suffered much from Saul's enmity; he was being most careful now that there were no hidden pockets of possible insurrection left anywhere. And Mephibosheth had been found out.

Mephibosheth was put on a donkey and taken to Jerusalem. Every step brought him nearer to his anticipated doom. The wretched tale of his victimized life would terminate now in a bloody execution.

When Mephibosheth was brought into David's presence, he almost certainly expected the worst—a judicial death sentence. Mephibosheth expected the worst because he had for many years internalized the worst. He had been beaten down so often and so thoroughly that he no longer looked others—let alone the king—in the eye, even though he had royal blood in his veins. But that blood had long since curdled: Mephibosheth perceived himself as royal scum. He felt less than human, calling himself a dead dog. He bleated in embittered terror before David. Observing his terror, David addressed him by name, "Mephibosheth," and assuaged his fear, saying, in effect, "Relax, it's going to be all right" (2 Sam. 9:6–7).

What Mephibosheth didn't know when he was brought into David's court, and could never have imagined in his wildest dreams, is that he was there to be loved. A few days earlier David had asked if there were any descendants of Saul around whom he could love in his friend Jonathan's name. There had been wars to fight and borders to establish in securing his authority as king; now he was ready to do the work of king. He began with love.

What Mephibosheth didn't know was that he was standing before a very different kind of king than the world in which he had grown up had any right to expect. The suspicious paranoia that had characterized his grandfather's reign was absent here. The maniacal jealousies that had infected Saul's court were remote here. David had accomplished a transition from the fragmented and disorderly mess left over from Saul's malign rule, and the country was feeling the effects: "So David reigned over all Israel; and David administered justice and equity to all his people" (2 Sam. 8:15). Justice and equity. That's what rulers are established by God to work for and bring about. And David was doing it. But David's reign was still young, and the news hadn't yet penetrated to the remote hamlet of Lo-debar.

Nor did Mephibosheth know that years earlier his father, Jonathan, and David had made a covenant with each other, binding themselves in loyal love. As Jonathan was helping David escape from Saul's murderous plots, David gave his solemn promise to stick by Jonathan no matter what, and to continue that same loyal love to his descendants (1 Sam. 20:14–15). In that last meeting, David and Jonathan made a covenant that would extend their love beyond the present circumstances. Jonathan's last words to David cemented the conditions of the covenant: "Go in peace, forasmuch as we have sworn both of us in the name of the LORD, saying, 'The LORD shall be between me and you, and between my descendants and your descendants, for ever'" (1 Sam. 20:42). Here was the descendent. Mephibosheth didn't know it, but he was the target that very day of David's promised love, David's covenanted love. The exquisite and determined love that Jonathan had given David was now given by David to Jonathan's son, Mephibosheth.

David emerges into prominence here as a lover. His kingly rule was already marked by justice and fairness. There is, though, an element without which those qualities aren't complete, and that element is love. The Hebrew word *chesed*, narrowly translated as "love," is a large word. No single word in our language is adequate to translate it, so we revert to the use of adjectives to bring out the distinctive quality and broad reach of this love: steadfast love, loyal love, covenantal love. What we're after is an understanding that retains the affection and desire and intimacy that commonly go with love, as we sometimes experience it as parents and children, "lovers" and friends, but amalgamated now with the stability, dependability, unswerving commitment, and steady reliability that we so commonly find wanting in ourselves and others. *Chesed* is often used in the biblical revelation to designate God's love. But we humans, who have been created in the image of God, are also capable of loving this way, even though we never seem to get very good at it. *Chesed* is love without regard to shifting circumstances, hormones, emotional states, and personal convenience. This is the kind of love with which "God so loved the world. . . ." This is the kind of love to which we aspire when we take marriage vows to love "in sickness and health, till death do us part." All our scriptural witnesses, seconded by an impressive array of outside observers, agree that venturing and practicing this kind of love is an absolutely necessary (even if very, very difficult) condition of life lived on anything other than a biological level.[2]

This is the kind of love with which David loved Mephibosheth that day. Mephibosheth had never, or at least not for a long time, been loved like this.

• • •

THIS SCENE CONSTITUTES another of the critical, defining moments in David's life, and it holds before us another of the elements
apart from which we can't be human beings in any authentic or sacred
sense. David is now in a position of deciding how to exercise whatever
gifts he has been given, whatever energy he has. The question is this:
What will he choose as the navigational means for his life—power or
love? Will he manipulate and manage so that he can be in control? Or
will he be open and generous so that he can love?

He answers that question as he looks for a way to keep his love-
loyal covenant with Jonathan. He answers that question as he brings
Mephibosheth before him and decides whether to execute him as a
threat to his power or honor him by keeping his covenant of love.

When David asks if there's anyone left of Saul's family ("the house of
Saul") whom he can love in Jonathan's name, he's asking, in effect, "Is
there anyone left in the enemy camp whom I can love?" David isn't
looking for a replacement for the exquisite love that he and Jonathan
enjoyed for too short a time. He's looking for an *enemy* to love.

From a place of security, David exercises his power by looking for
ways to love. At the time that they made their covenant, neither Jonathan
nor David knew which of them would end up king of Israel. What they
promised was that *whatever* happened, love—not power—would charac-
terize their relationship; love, not vengeance; love, not convenience.

• • •

DAVID'S FIRST WORD to Mephibosheth is the young man's name.
Mephibosheth is recognized as a person. He isn't a nameless exile.
He isn't a category of victim. He has a name, and David knows it—
Mephibosheth. If there was any shame or dishonor associated with this
name through the years, as we have conjectured—a name that he was
called rather than a name by which he was addressed—it's wiped clean
of ignominy as David addresses him in loyal love. The name is used
seven times in this story of their first meeting, without a hint of oppro-
brium or denigration in the usage. From now on Mephibosheth will be

defined by covenant, not etymology. He'll get his identity not from a lexicon but from love.

Mephibosheth. A personal name. We can't love in general. We can't love by categories. We can't love by decree or legislation. We can love only a named person who has a past, a present, and a future. *Mephibosheth.*

The nature of love is clarified in David's words of reassurance: "Do not fear" (2 Sam. 9:7). We come across this phrase frequently in the biblical revelation. It's frequent for a reason: there's much to fear in life. We constantly meet up with people who have more power than we have. How will they use that power, that authority? Will they diminish us, exploit us, use us, get rid of us? We learn to be cautious, put up defenses.

And then we come before God, a God of power and mystery. How will he treat us? Will he punish us, destroy us, take away our freedom? Based on our experience, any of that is certainly possible, maybe even probable. That's why we need so much reassurance: "Relax. It's going to be all right." The phrase is often on the lips of angels, the emissaries of God's good news. It was often on the lips of Jesus, who regularly brought frightened and bewildered men and women into the very presence of God. Here it's on David's lips.

Mephibosheth had every reason to be deathly afraid of David at that moment, as we've seen. He had no reason to think that David wasn't out to get rid of him, the last vestige of Saul's family. But then he was disarmed and prepared for love by the gospel words "Fear not."

David put content into the word *love* when he turned over to Mephibosheth all the lands of his grandfather Saul so that he would have an independent income; assigned Ziba, who had once been servant to Saul, to manage the farms and take care of his affairs; and brought Mephibosheth into his household as one of the family. This is the way love *looks,* not *feels*—generous, extravagant, uncalculating. The love that germinated in a covenant became mature in the search for a long-lost heir, the restoration of confiscated lands, and daily hospitality at the royal table. This love wasn't greeting-card sentiment; it had the substance of the good earth beneath it and the regularity of three square meals a day to reinforce it.

MEPHIBOSHETH (3)

The third Mephibosheth story took place years later during the Absalom rebellion (2 Sam. 16–19). Mephibosheth had been living a long time as an honored member of the family in David's house, eating his meals there, treated as one of the king's sons. He lived in a house of love. He was the recipient of love.

We would like to know whether he himself learned to love. Was Mephibosheth changed? Were the acids of bitterness flushed from his being? Was he able to recover a sense of dignity and royal pride? Did the new routines and episodes of love replace his old nurse's poisoning stories?

Or did Mephibosheth hang on to his victim identity? While outwardly accepting David's hospitality, did he secretly suspect David of bringing him into his household to keep an eye on him, to make sure that he didn't become the center of discontent around which old Saul loyalists could gather? Or did he believe he was being used as a "poster child" to advertise to the general population David's kindness? Was David's behavior seen as a cynical public relations ploy to replace the old image of David the Philistine-killer with a gentler, kinder face?

Any of these responses to David's love is conceivable, and the narrative doesn't make it absolutely clear which is true. The ambiguity is intentional, for we mustn't suppose that there are any guarantees that a generous act of love will be rewarded by loyal gratitude. Not all, not even most, love is requited. We need to be realistic about what's involved in living out covenantal love. It's a risky business. We can be taken advantage of; we can be betrayed. Jesus was and is. David may have been.

• • •

TAKING THE MEASURE of David's love, we return to Mephibosheth and reflect on the ways in which he may have responded to David's love. Did he love in return, rejoicing in his place in the family, delighted to find himself blessed through David's honoring of the covenant with his father? Or did Mephibosheth continue to harbor his old resentments, sourly interpreting David's love in twisted ways that reinforced and documented his wretched fate as a victim? Under the cover of David's hospitality, did he spend his days bitterly fantasizing some incredible reversal of fortunes in which he, the legitimate heir to Saul's throne, would be snatched from this benign imprisonment and crowned in glory?

There are two stories in the text to support, respectively, both of these possibilities. The first story is told by Ziba, the former servant of Saul who is now responsible for the care of Mephibosheth. Ziba's story is an accusation of betrayal. The second story is from the lips of Mephibosheth himself and is a declaration of loyal love.

The two stories are told in the larger context of David's flight from and then return to Jerusalem at the time of Absalom's rebellion. The Absalom revolt is civil war: Absalom unseats his father from the throne and takes over the kingship. All the odds are against David. He escapes from Jerusalem in disgrace, cursed and maligned, with a few faithful followers. Ziba tells David his version of the story on the night of the escape (2 Sam. 16:1–4). In the war that follows, Absalom is killed. David then returns to Jerusalem, celebrated and blessed in a triumphal parade. Mephibosheth gives David his version in the course of the triumphal reentry (2 Sam. 19:24–30).

Ziba joins David on the flight out of Jerusalem; and when he's asked the whereabouts of his master, he answers that Mephibosheth deliberately stayed behind in Jerusalem, believing that in the confusion and anarchy he had a good chance of being made king. Ziba says, in effect, "Mephibosheth has betrayed you; he's a traitor: he saw a chance at becoming king and grabbed for it. But *I'm* on your side; I'm with you through thick and thin." David, without asking questions, accepts Ziba's story as true and on the spot decrees that all of Mephibosheth's land is now Ziba's.

Days later, on the return to Jerusalem following Absalom's defeat, David hears a very different story. Mephibosheth tells David that he had been all ready to join him that night in his flight from Jerusalem, but Ziba had betrayed him, leaving him behind, stranded without a mount (and, of course, unable to get about on foot). Mephibosheth's appearance corroborates his story: he's obviously been in mourning during David's absence, beard ragged and clothes looking as if they've been slept in. He certainly doesn't look as if he's spent the last few days vainly anticipating a personal coronation.

So who's telling the truth, Ziba or Mephibosheth? Most readers of the story side with Mephibosheth, but there's a deliberate withholding of a verdict by the narrator in order to give emphasis to David's response.[3]

David believed Ziba's accusation when he first heard it. As he now listens to Mephibosheth, he knows that both stories can't be true. Here the narrative takes us into new territory: David doesn't *care* who's telling the truth. There's no cross-examination here, no calling in of witnesses. He accepts both men back into his city, back into his household. His love is large enough, expansive enough to handle faithlessness, fecklessness, lies, and hypocrisy.

This is the characteristic Davidic note, the anticipation of gospel. David first sought out Mephibosheth from a position of strength. He used his strength to love generously, *covenantally.* Uncorrupted by power, love flowed unimpeded. David treated Mephibosheth with the love with which God had saved him.

In this second act of love to Mephibosheth he's fatigued from battle, having barely survived the worst rejection and betrayal of his life, grieving the terrible death of his son, abandoned by many of his trusted friends. And now Mephibosheth stands before him with Ziba's accusation of betrayal (2 Sam. 16:3) hanging over his head. There's been so much treachery in the past few days, so many faithless. Is Mephibosheth one more who has betrayed his love? If David has been betrayed by his own son, why wouldn't Mephibosheth, with a legitimate claim to the throne, also betray him?

It doesn't matter to David. He doesn't have to know. He takes Mephibosheth's story (2 Sam. 19:26–28) at face value and keeps faith with him. He persists in his love of Mephibosheth. David in weakness, his kingdom in fragments about him, is as strong as ever in love. This is love with covenant steel in it to keep it steady, persistent, committed.

• • •

I'VE ALWAYS LOVED THIS STORY. I love it because I need it. I need to keep company with this David, who in the thick of everything else—administering a new government, dealing with fractious insubordinates and rebellious children, facing a gamut of trials and temptations—determines to love an unpromising stranger, and to persist in that love no matter what.

And I love this story of David and Mephibosheth because I continue to catch glimpses of it and hear echoes of it in stories in which I have a part. The gospel miracle is that human beings like us from time to time evade the temptations of power and the brittleness of success and actually manage to vulnerably love another person who has all the potential of turning on us and rejecting us. Every time such love is ventured, another piece of the gospel is proclaimed, and the Kingdom of God is made credible.

• 17 •

SIN

DAVID AND BATHSHEBA

2 Samuel 11–12

Jesus said, "Does no one condemn you?"
"No one, Master."
"Neither do I," said Jesus. "Go on your way. From
now on, don't sin."

—JOHN 8:11

TWO NAMES ARE UNFORGETTABLY LINKED with David. People who are otherwise illiterate in the Scriptures know these names. One name is the giant Goliath; the other is the woman Bathsheba. The physical forms attached to the names could hardly be more different: Goliath—an ugly, cruel giant; Bathsheba—a beautiful, gentle woman. Goliath, an evil tyrant; Bathsheba, an innocent victim. But different as Goliath and Bathsheba are in character, appearance, and spirit, there's a similarity in their relation to David. Both bring him into a field of testing, a place of encounter that reveals David's heart.

The giant and the woman enter David's life at opposite ends. The story of David and Goliath occurs early, when David is young,

181

unknown, and untested. The story of David and Bathsheba occurs in David's mature years, when he's in his prime, having passed through hard testings and in the testings been shown to be a loyal friend, a courageous leader, a wise king.

In the encounter with Goliath, David is revealed to be a person of prayer. He's far more impressed with the invisible God than with the visible giant. David is shown to be, even in his youth, well practiced in the life of prayer, a life that works from the inside out, from the inner motions of belief and trust and petition toward the outward actions of obedience and justice and love.

In the encounter with Bathsheba, David recovers his identity as a person of prayer. But this story is more complex, for this time around David is no longer fresh and innocent; he's been scarred in many a battle, is experienced in failure and disappointment. God is no less a part of his life, but the life itself is now multilayered, carrying in it tangled and intermingled complexities of guilt and grace.

David Sins

It's spring. David's army has gone, according to the custom of the times, to raid some neighboring tribes, plundering their towns and bringing back loot. But David stays behind. He's by now well established as king and doesn't need to prove himself in battle. And besides, these aren't important wars being fought. But in his withdrawal from frontline participation with his people in battle, we see a shadow withdrawing from the page. Is staying at home symptomatic of an anemia of soul? Is he pulling back from *life*—life robust in energetic prayer and daring faith in God? We don't have to wait long for an answer.

One afternoon, while walking on the palace roof, positioned so that he can see into the courtyards of nearby houses, he sees a woman bathing. She's extraordinarily beautiful. He sends for her, takes her to his bed, and then discards her, sending her home. Her name is Bathsheba. Her husband, Uriah, is off fighting in the army. A month or so later Bathsheba learns that she's pregnant and sends word to David, "I am with child" (2 Sam. 11:5). David, good at dealing with problems, handles this one by sending for Uriah and giving him a month's leave. He expects him to go immediately to his wife and the marital bed so that he'll think he's responsible for the pregnancy. But Uriah is a loyal soldier and doesn't feel good about enjoying his wife while his fellow soldiers are roughing it out on the battlefield. So he sleeps on the porch of David's palace. David solves this complication to his strategy by sending him back to the army camp with a letter to Joab, the general, instructing Joab to place Uriah in the thick of the fighting where he'll almost certainly be killed. Joab, relishing such intrigues, carries out the instructions. Uriah is killed in the next day's battle. Word comes back to David reporting the death. After the time of mourning is complete, David sends for Bathsheba and marries her.

We aren't prepared for such a David. What begins as a lustful whim develops into an enormous sex-and-murder crime. How does such sin happen? As with most sins, gradually and unobtrusively.

The narrator skillfully draws us into an understanding of what's going on with the subtle repetition of a seemingly amoral word: *send*. We gradually realize that in this context it's not a morally neutral word at all; it signals the impersonal exercise of power. By following the use of this verb, we can trace David's descent from love and obedience into calculation and cruelty. Verb by verb, we watch David remove himself from compassionate listening and personal intimacy with others to a position outside and above others, giving orders, exercising power.

The passage begins with the curt phrase "David *sent* Joab" (2 Sam. 11:1); it picks up momentum when "David *sent*" to inquire about Bathsheba (2 Sam. 11:3); the plot thickens when "David *sent*" and got Bathsheba (2 Sam. 11:4). That these "sendings" constitute a ruthless exercise of power becomes clear in the cluster of *send*s in 2 Samuel 11:6: "So David *sent* word to Joab, '*Send* me Uriah the Hittite.' And Joab *sent* Uriah to David." After he had accomplished his cover-up, "David *sent*" for Bathsheba again and married her (2 Sam. 11:27).

Two other occurrences of the word *send* in this story subtly prepare us for the truth that David, for all his exercise of depersonalized royal power, wasn't nearly as in control as he supposed: Bathsheba "*sent* and told David, 'I am with child'" (2 Sam. 11:5); Joab "*sent* and told David all the news about the fighting" (2 Sam. 11:18), letting him know through the messenger that he understood exactly what David was up to. The operations of Bathsheba's fertile womb and Joab's sly and shifty mind eluded David's control.

In the final, and decisive, use of *send* in this story, God's sovereignty comes into play: "And the LORD *sent* Nathan to David" (2 Sam. 12:1). And that's the end of David's detour into "playing god" with people's lives. God and only God is truly sovereign.[1]

• • •

SUCH IS THE STORY. It's a story that's been repeated, with variations, over and over and over through the centuries. Sin stories, after a while, tend to sound pretty much alike: virtually all sins ring changes on the theme of wanting to be gods ourselves, taking charge of our own lives, asserting control over the lives of others. Since there are only a finite number of ways to do this, no one of us reading this story has any difficulty finding himself or herself in it. Nor does finding ourselves in this story, whether in fact or imagination, surprise us. We're sinners. The precise details of our sin may not correspond to David's, but the presence and recurrence of sin does. The moment we recognize our common sin bond with David, we're ready for the real surprise here—the gospel story that develops out of the sin story.

NATHAN PREACHES

The story takes a gospel turn when David's pastor, Nathan, shows up and preaches him a sermon. At the moment David has no idea that he's listening to a sermon, for he isn't sitting in a pew and Nathan isn't standing in a pulpit. There's no explicit reference to God in the sermon, and there's no altar call. Nathan is good at this. He stalks his prey. He tells an artless, simple story about a rich man with large flocks of sheep who needs a lamb for a dinner he's giving. But instead of taking a lamb from his own flocks, he cruelly and arrogantly takes the pet lamb of a poor man living down the street. He kills the lamb and serves it up to his guests. David, drawn into the story, is outraged at this callous cruelty and, as a righteous judge, passes a death sentence on the rich man. Then Nathan pounces: "You are the man" (2 Sam. 12:7).

This is the gospel focus: *you* are the man; *you* are the woman. The gospel is never about somebody else; it's always about you, about me. The gospel is never a truth in general; it's always a truth in specific. The gospel is never a commentary on ideas or culture or conditions; it's always about actual persons, actual pain, actual trouble, actual sin: you, me; who you are and what you've done; who I am and what I've done.

It's both easy and common to lose this focus, to let the gospel blur into generalized pronouncements, boozy cosmic opinions, religious indignation. That's what David is doing in this story, listening to his pastor preach a sermon about somebody else and getting all worked up about this someone else's sin, this someone else's plight. That kind of religious response is worthless: it's the religion of the college dormitory bull session, the TV spectacular, the talk-show gossip. It's the religion of moral judgmentalism, self-righteous finger-pointing, the religion of accusation and blame.

With each additional word in Nathan's sermon, David becomes more religious—feeling sorry for the poor man who lost his pet lamb, seething with indignation over the rich man who stole the lamb. Pitying and judging are religious sentiments that can be indulged endlessly, making us feel vastly superior to everyone around us, but they're incapable of making a particle of difference in our lives. David, pitying and judging, becoming more religious by the minute, absorbed in a huge blur of moral sentimentality.

And then the sudden, clear gospel focus: you are the one—*you*.

This is what preachers are for, to bring us into focus in the story. The art of preaching is to somehow or other get around our third-person defenses and compel a second-person recognition, which enables a first-person response. Nathan is a master of the art.

David is now in gospel focus. Addressed personally, he answers personally: "I have sinned against the Lord" (2 Sam. 12:13). He abandons the generalities of religion. He quits giving out opinions on other people's lives, good or bad, realizes his position before God—a sinner! A person in trouble, a person who needs help, a human being who needs God.

FELIX CULPA

One of the frequently misunderstood features of the gospel by out-siders—maybe *the* most frequently misunderstood—is this: that a con-fession of sin isn't a groveling admission that I'm a terrible person; it doesn't require what's sometimes described as "beating yourself up." In-siders to the gospel know that the sentence "I have sinned against the Lord" is a sentence full of hope. It's full of hope because it's a sentence full of God.

The Latin phrase *felix culpa,* usually attributed to Augustine, puts the hope in a slogan: "O happy sin!" Only when I recognize and con-fess my sin am I in a position to recognize and respond to the God who saves me from my sin. If I'm ignorant of or indifferent to my sin, I'm ignorant of or indifferent to the great and central good news: "Jesus saves!"[2]

In the Christian life our primary task isn't to *avoid* sin, which is im-possible anyway, but to *recognize* sin. The fact is that we're sinners. But there's an enormous amount of self-deception in sin. When this is com-bined with devil-deception, the task of recognition is compounded.

We don't want to face sin because we don't want to lose our god-illusions, we're afraid that if we're not the gods of our lives and actions we're nothing. But stories like this set us free from such sin-fears. When sin is discovered in us, our guilty fears often produce a sense of condem-nation. But if we stay with the story—the God story, the David story, the Jesus story—before long the condemnation gives way, whether slowly or suddenly, to the surprised realization of grace, mercy, and for-giveness. We think that if our sin is taken away, we'll become less. What happens is that we become more.

So we're trained to become sin-watchers, after the analogy of bird-watchers: we go looking for sin with a certain sense of anticipation and delight, for each discovery of sin brings us to the brink of grace. Our ap-proach to sin, then, is characterized not by warnings and threats but by encouragements to honesty, invitations to come out in the open and greet the "sun of righteousness" who rises "with healing in its wings" (Mal. 4:4). This is in stark and gospel contrast to the overcast weather of depressing moralism that keeps so many indoors, huddled in denial or guilt. *Felix culpa,* indeed!

The basic, fundamental condition of our humanity is God. We're created by God. We're redeemed by God. We're blessed by God. We're provided for by God. We're loved by God. Sin is the denial or ignorance or avoidance of that basic condition. Sin is the word we use to designate the perverseness of will by which we attempt being our own gods, or making for ourselves other gods. Sin isn't essentially a moral term, designating items of wrongdoing; it's a spiritual term, designating our God-avoidance and our god-pretensions.

That we sin so frequently is a puzzle, for our lives are always diminished in the process. But our capacity for sin is no puzzle: it's required by the nature of love and freedom, the twin aspects of our humanity in which we become what we were created to be. A coerced love is hardly love. An enforced freedom is no freedom. If God is serious about creating us to experience his love and to love freely, to experience his freedom and to freely love, then there must be the capacity to *not* love, to *not* be free. When we exercise those options negatively, regardless of the forms in which those acts come to expression, we're sinners.

This is the condition that David's pastor, Nathan, brings into focus through his sermon: God has receded into the background, and David has stepped up front and center. The more David, the less God. The less David is paying attention to God, the more he's acting as if he were God, acting like a god in relation to Bathsheba, pulling her into the orbit of his will so that she's dependent upon him; acting like a god in relation to Uriah and giving the commands that determine his fate.

The subtlety of sin is that it doesn't feel like sin when we're doing it; it feels godlike, it feels religious, it feels fulfilling and satisfying—a replay of the episode in Eden when the tempter said, "Ye shall not die . . . ye shall be as gods" (Gen. 3:4–5, KJV). David didn't feel like a sinner when he sent for Bathsheba; he felt like a lover—and what can be better than that? David didn't feel like a sinner when he sent for Uriah; he felt like a king—and what can be better than that? Somewhere along the line he had withdrawn from the life of worship: adoration of God had receded, and obsession with self had moved in.

DAVID PRAYS

When Nathan—*sent* by God!—walked into the room that day, he re-covered for David an awareness of God. Simultaneously, he aroused David's sense of sin with his parable-sermon, and David's still-tender heart was roused. And in that double awareness of God and sin, David prayed the prayer that we call Psalm 51:

> *Generous in love—God, give grace!*
> *Huge in mercy—wipe out my bad record.*
> *Scrub away my guilt,*
> *Soak out my sins in your laundry.*
> *I know how bad I've been;*
> *my sins are staring me down.*
>
> *You're the One I've violated, and you've seen*
> *it all, seen the full extent of my evil.*
> *You have all the facts before you;*
> *whatever you decide about me is fair.*
> *I've been out of step with you for a long time,*
> *in the wrong since before I was born.*
> *What you're after is truth from the inside out.*
> *Enter me, then; conceive a new, true life.*
>
> *Soak me in your laundry and I'll come out clean,*
> *scrub me and I'll have a snow-white life.*
> *Tune me in to foot-tapping songs,*
> *set these once-broken bones to dancing.*
> *Don't look too close for blemishes,*
> *give me a clean bill of health.*
> *God, make a fresh start in me,*
> *shape a Genesis week from the chaos of my life.*
> *Don't throw me out with the trash,*
> *or fail to breathe holiness in me.*
> *Bring me back from gray exile,*
> *put a fresh wind in my sails!*
> *Give me a job teaching rebels your ways*
> *so the lost can find their way home.*

Commute my death sentence, God, my salvation God,
  and I'll sing anthems to your life-giving ways.
Unbutton my lips, dear God;
  I'll let loose with your praise.

Going through the motions doesn't please you,
  a flawless performance is nothing to you.
I learned God-worship
  when my pride was shattered.
Heart-shattered lives ready for love
  don't for a moment escape God's notice.

Make Zion the place you delight in,
  repair Jerusalem's broken-down walls.
Then you'll get real worship from us,
  acts of worship small and large,
Including all the bulls
  they can heave onto your altar!

Under the power of Nathan's preached word, David saw his sin, and saw that previous to the sins that surfaced in the adultery with Bathsheba and the murder of Uriah was his violation of God. Bathsheba had been greatly wronged—exploited and demeaned. Uriah had been shamefully treated—deceived and then killed. Moral consequences from those wrongs—pain and suffering, death and lamentation—would follow hard upon David for the rest of his life. But before those wrongs came Sin—sin against God by setting himself at the center, displacing God.

David's moving Psalm 51 is the eloquent rehearsal of his God-recovery. In and through this prayer we find ourselves in a place spacious with freedom and resonant with love. When we find ourselves before God—honestly, adoringly, believingly before God—we find our true humanity. We're not less but more; we're not demeaned but dignified; we're not condemned but saved.

David's sin, enormous as it was, was wildly outdone by God's grace. David's sin cannot, must not, be minimized, but it's minuscule compared to God's salvation from it. It's always a mistake to concentrate attention on our sins; it's God's work on our sins that's the main event.

Our sins aren't that interesting; it's God's work that's interesting. There's nothing glamorous about sin, and it's the devil's work to make it look otherwise. Sin is diminishing, dehumanizing, and soon dull. After it's been recognized and confessed, the less said about it the better. Psalm 51 does it right: there are only four different words used to name the sin, so it's out in the open where it can be faced. These four sin-words are sufficient to adequately map the entire country of sin. But the central action is carried by nineteen different verbs used to invoke or declare God's action of forgiveness and restoration.[3] We have a finite number of ways to sin; God has an infinite number of ways to forgive. After observing the human condition for a few years, we find that in regard to sin we're mostly watching reruns. After a while we find that people pretty much do the same old thing generation after generation. Sinning doesn't take much imagination. But forgiveness and salvation? That's a different story: every time it happens, it's fresh, original, catching us by surprise. Sin isn't creative work, and the more we're around it, the duller it seems. Salvation, in contrast, is "new every morning" (Lam. 3:23).

> And though the last lights off the black West went
>   Oh, morning, at the brown brink eastward springs—
> Because the Holy Ghost over the bent
>   World broods with warm breast and with ah! bright wings.[4]

JESUS

There's a remarkable verbal resonance to this story of David standing before Nathan in that of Jesus standing before Pilate. They're both passion stories—David's passion for Bathsheba; Jesus' passion for us. Pilate says of Jesus, "Behold the man" (John 19:5), echoing what Nathan says to David, "You are the man."

These two sentences are alike in that they focus on a person at the vortex of the action. You, David, are the one; this Jesus is the one—the human being in whom the actions of God are being worked out. It's not through an idea or cause or law or dream or vision or organization that we come to our senses, get our feet on the ground of reality, but in *person*—who I am, who Jesus is.

The sentences are also unlike. Nathan's sentence brings David, and therefore us, to the brink of God. David realizes who he is not in himself but before God. It's God with whom he has to do. The grammar renders him personal before God: honest, open, receptive. As participants in the story, we're enabled to be ourselves, our personal selves, before God. Pilate's sentence, in contrast, brings Jesus to the brink of who *we* are, revealing that it's me, you, with whom God has to do. God is personal before us: honest, open, receptive. This personal God is facing and taking care of my personal sin, making *me* right with God.

This is the hard-to-believe but impossible-to-refute good news: that the place of sin is a place not of accusation or condemnation but of salvation. The gospel comes into focus here not in an accusation but as recognition and invitation. Recognition: I'm the one whose sense of sin arouses a sense of God. Invitation: Jesus is the one who presents God to me—I didn't know God was that close, that kindly, that inviting!—and brings me into personal relationship with him in love and salvation. I'm the one who needs God more than anything—more than pleasure with Bathsheba, more than control over Uriah. God. And Jesus is the one who brings the God I need to me.

SUFFERING

DAVID AND ABSALOM

2 Samuel 16–18

At noon the sky became extremely dark. The darkness
lasted three hours. At three o'clock, Jesus groaned out of
the depths, crying loudly, Eloi, Eloi, lama sabachthani?
which means, "My God, my God, why have you
abandoned me?"

—MARK 15:33–34

O my son Absalom,
*   my son, my son Absalom!*
Would I had died instead of you,
*   O Absalom, my son, my son!*
(2 SAM. 18:33)

These have got to be among the saddest, most heart-rending words
ever spoken—words wrenched out of David's gut when the report was
brought to him that his son had been murdered in the forest of
Ephraim. David was no stranger to death, no stranger to tears, no

stranger to murder, no stranger to disappointment, no stranger to sin. But no event combined all of these elements with such intensity, yes, ferocity, as did the matter of Absalom.

It was a bitter cup to drink. Would he drink it? This David who had experienced so many blessings, had entered into such exuberant joys, who gave us words that we use still to express the generosity of God in our lives—"My cup runneth over"—and characteristically lifted what he called "the cup of salvation" to toast God's goodness and blessing in the world and in his life . . . would he drink this cup? Would he take in the full measure of rejection, alienation, and rebellion and experience it in the depths of his being? At this moment, with David immersed in the experience of betrayal and ruin, we can almost hear the words spoken a thousand years later by Jesus: "Remove this cup from me; nevertheless not my will, but thine, be done" (Luke 22:42).

The cup was *not* removed. David, like our Lord after him, drank it to the last drop, emptied the cup. He tasted the bitterness, took in the full reality of sin-sourced suffering. It's hard to rank events, but this might very well be the most integrated human/divine thing David ever did—face, taste, and experience to the depths this complex tangle of love and hate, righteousness and sin, good and evil that came to a head in Absalom. "O my son Absalom, my son, my son Absalom! Would I had died instead of you, O Absalom, my son, my son!"

A FOCUS ON SUFFERING

I want to go over some old ground here, repeating what seems—in our culture, anyway—to need frequent repeating: entering into a life of faith, living a Davidic life, following Jesus, centering our life in the worship of God doesn't exempt us from suffering. Christians get cancer in the same proportion as non-Christians. Believers are involved in as many automobile accidents as nonbelievers. When you hit your thumb with a hammer, it hurts just as much after you've accepted Christ as your Lord and Savior as it did before.

I don't take any particular pleasure in writing this. I would feel better if I could promise that being a Christian gave us a distinct edge over the competition. Some of the most prominent and well-paid religious leaders in North America are following that line these days—giving people tips on how to be successful in marriage and business, assuring congregations that if they'll sign up and give a little more money they'll experience prosperity. They design books and lectures and sermons to sell lottery tickets on a jackpot of the supernatural.

But we didn't so learn the faith from our true and holy Scriptures and our wise and holy ancestors. Matthew, Mark, Luke, and John don't give us marketing or motivational techniques for improving our standard of living. David isn't an advertisement for a trouble-free life. What our Scriptures and evangelical traditions insist on is accuracy and reality—what God reveals as the truth about our lives and his salvation work among us. Accuracy and reality right now require a focus on David's suffering in relation to Absalom.

SUFFERING'S HISTORY

Suffering has a history, and it helps to know it. The difficulties that come into our lives aren't arbitrary intrusions; they're elements in a complex web of interconnecting sins and mercies. This doesn't mean that we can diagram lines of causation or responsibility in suffering. What we need to know is that suffering is neither an impersonal fate nor a cut-and-dried moral punishment. We're implicated in a world of sin, sometimes ours and sometimes others', and therefore in a world of suffering.

David's lament over Absalom had its immediate source in the rape of Absalom's beautiful sister, Tamar, eleven years earlier. Amnon, who was half-brother to Absalom and Tamar, was infatuated with Tamar; and after a period of pining and planning, he raped her. When Absalom learned of the rape, he was outraged and determined to avenge his sister's honor. But he didn't simply lose his temper: he plotted coolly and carefully. When the plot was in place, he brutally murdered Amnon (2 Sam. 13:1–29).

Even though Absalom knew that he was David's favorite son, he knew he couldn't trust that affection to overlook his crime. Murder is, after all, murder, even if in a good cause. So Absalom went across the Jordan into exile to Geshur, the country of his wife's family (2 Sam. 13:37–39).

After three years in exile he was allowed to come home (2 Sam. 14:1–23). At this turn in the story, David made a major contribution to his own later suffering: David refused to see Absalom (2 Sam. 14:24, 28). His pardon of Absalom was impersonal. His forgiveness was a judicial act, not a fatherly embrace. He let Absalom return to his own city and gave him a place to live, but he didn't greet him by name, wouldn't permit him in his presence—not so much as a look. David held on to his bitterness over Amnon's murder. It wasn't unmitigated bitterness, for we're also told that David was comforted over Amnon's death and longed for Absalom (2 Sam. 13:39). David's stance was probably a result of mixed political pressures and personal feelings, but whatever the ingredients, the result Absalom experienced was rejection by his father.

Sin fed on sin. The rape of Tamar fed into the murder of Amnon, which fed into the hardheartedness of David. Absalom responded to Amnon's sin by sinning. Then David responded to Absalom's sin by sinning. Absalom got rid of Amnon by killing him. Then David got rid of Absalom by shunning him. David lost his son Amnon because of the sin of Absalom. David lost his son Absalom by his own sin.

Absalom stewed in banishment. He was home, but he wasn't home. This was no life, just to be permitted to exist. He wanted acceptance, a personal word of forgiveness. He wanted his father's love. He needed more than food and drink for survival; he required grace and mercy in order to live. At first he was simply glad to be back, but gradually he came to realize that he needed far more than a piece of royal legislation in his favor; he needed a father.

I pause and reflect how differently this story would have turned out if David had anticipated the story Jesus told about the father whose son went into a far country, lived a life of self-indulgence, and returned having disgraced his father's house. Even though the son had done a terrible thing, the father never quit looking for him, looking for a way to forgive him, restore him to full sonship. When he did come, finally, the father ran to greet and embrace him, welcoming him home with a huge ban-quiet (Luke 15:11–32). What if David had been that father? What if Absalom had been allowed to sit with his father, tell the story of his affection for Tamar, his anger at Amnon, and the purgatory of his exile? The father would once more have had a son; the son would once again have had a father.

But David didn't do that. David turned hard on Absalom. He had, it's true, good reasons, and he no doubt thought that what he was doing was good for Absalom—punishing him until he felt the full weight of responsibility and pain for the murder. But whatever line David used to rationalize his position, underneath it there was a refusal to forgive, a withholding of grace, a denial of mercy.

This is the third monumental sin of David's life, the most inexcusable, and the one for which he paid the most. The adultery with Bathsheba was the affair of a passionate moment. The murder of Uriah was a royal reflex to avoid detection. But the rejection of Absalom was a steady, determined refusal to share with his son what God had so abundantly shared with him. Day by day he hardened in this denial of love. This was sin with a blueprint. This was sin that required long-term commitment, comprehensive strategy. Jerusalem was a small city: scrupulous care was necessary to avoid seeing or being seen by Absalom.

Absalom gave up hope of intimacy with his father and determined to take things into his own hands. He planned to do what had been done to him. If his father would exclude him from his presence, he would go him one better, turn the tables and exclude his father—and not only from his presence but from the kingdom itself. He returned to his old ways of plotting, brooding, vengeance. He felt the wrong of his father as he had felt the wrong of his sister's rape. He planned his revenge. When the moment was ripe, he took it (2 Sam. 15:1–12).

For four years he worked his plan, planting seeds of dissension against King David and working up a following among the people. When he was confident that he had the people on his side, he revolted: he proclaimed himself king, took over Jerusalem and the royal palace, and set out to assassinate his father, King David. David fled for his life into the wilderness. *Back* into the wilderness in which earlier he had spent so many hard years (2 Sam. 15:13–23).

DAVID IN RECOVERY

Back in the wilderness, where so much of David's character had been formed, we now see him recovering that which is, well, so *characteristically* David. Hardship brings out the best in David. Suffering can, if we let it, make us better instead of worse.

I'm going to speculate a little at this juncture in the story. I'm going to guess that during the years of his flinty rejection of Absalom, David was paying less and less attention to God, his prayers thinned down to a trickle. He was more taken up with law and order in his government than with justice and mercy in the Kingdom of God. As he refused intimacy with Absalom, he forfeited intimacy with God. As David was less and less a father, he became less and less human. As he carried out his kingly duties in self-righteous rectitude, he slipped into a godlike role before the people. As he became less compassionate with those around him, he became less passionate with the God within him.

Then he was catapulted from throne into wilderness exile. Stripped of the trappings of kingly role and palace routines, he was now just himself. He found that he had friends still. And he realized, in John Henry Newman's poignant phrase, what "I have loved long since, and lost awhile"[1]—he recovered his Davidic life.

Suffering doesn't always, or easily, make us better. It often makes us worse. It could have made David worse. He could have become defiant and bitter and lonely. But he didn't. He became again what we now look back on as characteristically David: humble, prayerful, and compassionate. There's a story that frames each of these recoveries.

• • •

IN SUFFERING, David recovered humility. He got back in touch with himself—his basic, elemental self. He recovered humility when Shimei cursed him (2 Sam. 16:5–14). As David was leaving Jerusalem, fleeing for his life during Absalom's coup, Shimei walked along a ridge above the road David was taking, throwing rocks and yelling curses. It's not difficult to imagine the language; something like: "Get out of town, you worthless old man. Murderer! Dirty old man. Murderer!" Then he threw more rocks, hurled more curses. The curses must have hurt more than the rocks: "Corrupt and stupid king! Killer!"

Abishai, one of David's captains, said, "Let me go over and take off his head—nobody is going to talk to my king this way." But David restrained him. David said, "Shimei is right; he is telling the truth about me. He is preaching God's word to me this night. God commanded him to curse me. Shimei is only a mouthpiece for God's curses. Let him alone—his sermon of curses is God's word preached to me."

The kerygmatic curses brought David to himself. He realized what he had become—all the wrongs he had committed, all the people he had failed. He could have taken a defensive and vengeful posture, but he didn't. He faced the truth about himself that he was no better than anyone else. He faced the truth that his basic identify wasn't "king" but "sinner" and that he could live only by God's mercy. Shimei's curses peeled all the royal veneer off David and exposed his soul. He let Shimei's curses be the word of God to him—kerygmatic Shimei.[2] He let the suffering bring him into the presence of the God of mercy and grace and love.

• • •

IN SUFFERING, David recovered prayer. He got in personal touch again with his personal God. David recovered prayer when he learned that Ahithophel had betrayed him.

From all appearances, Ahithophel wasn't a bad man. He did a terrible thing, but he wasn't a terrible person. Ahithophel's reputation as a wise man was, no doubt, honestly acquired. As a trusted adviser to David, he was a reliable and sage companion. When David was in a quandary, he talked to Ahithophel and things became clear again. Ahithophel was the kind of person who evokes trust and respect and honor—a person who has no illusions about life, who's able to look at all the evidence and deal with it without distorting or diminishing or denying what's there.

David counted himself fortunate to have Ahithophel. Our text tells us that "in those days the counsel which Ahithophel gave was as if one consulted the oracle of God; so was all the counsel of Ahithophel esteemed" (2 Sam. 16:23). Ahithophel was always there, there to provide breathing room, praying room. So many times David must have gone to Ahithophel confused and uncertain, and left after an hour or so knowing exactly what he must do to live wisely to the glory of God. And then, after all those years of trusted friendship, after all those conversations drenched in wisdom, at the exact moment when David needed him most, Ahithophel betrayed David.

In the light of what happened, all the probabilities are that through the years, because Ahithophel was so reliable ("as if one consulted the oracle of God") and so conveniently at hand, David bit by bit quit consulting God and was satisfied with consulting Ahithophel. It was easier than praying.

Ahithophel betrayed David that night because he thought the future of the kingdom was with Absalom. All the smart money that night was on Absalom, and Ahithophel was nothing if not smart. It turns out that at heart Ahithophel was an opportunist. Beneath that suave, sage reputation, Ahithophel had always been looking out for himself. When David was the best bet, he bet on David. Of *course* he served David faithfully and well all those years—David was the brightest star on the horizon. But the moment it appeared that the star was in eclipse, Ahithophel went for what looked like the next sure thing: good-looking, ambitious, charismatic Absalom. Despite Ahithophel's gleaming public image, it turned out that there was no character to the man, no moral substance, no spiritual muscle. He was a hollow man, pasted together with scraps of slogans and graffiti. Now that political fortunes had changed suddenly in the wind of Absalom's rebellion, he set his sails to catch the new winds of power.[3]

The news of the betrayal was reported to David: "Ahithophel is among the conspirators with Absalom" (2 Sam. 15:31). No single piece of information could have been more devastating. Ahithophel, with his counsel and reputation, was worth more to Absalom than a thousand soldiers. When word got around town that Ahithophel had joined Absalom, support of Absalom was assured.

David's Ahithophel prayer, Psalm 55, reveals his shocked rage:

This isn't the neighborhood bully
  mocking me; I could take that.
This isn't a foreign devil spitting
  invective; I could tune that out.
It's you! We grew up together!
  You! My best friend!
Those long hours of leisure as we walked
  arm in arm, God a third to our conversation.
(VV. 12–14)

. . . [T]his my best friend, betrayed his best friends,
  his life betrayed his word.
All my life I've been charmed by his speech,
  never dreaming he'd turn on me.
His words that were music to my ears
  turned to daggers in my heart.
(VV. 20–21)

David was on his knees again, recovering the life of prayer that had been integral to his life: "O LORD, I pray thee, turn the counsel of Ahithophel into foolishness" (2 Sam. 15:31).

David praying. David's life a prayer, dealing with God centrally and comprehensively. Suffering doesn't always do this. Suffering for some becomes an occasion for abandoning God and looking every other which way for help. But suffering can provide the stimulus for recovering a life of prayer. Psalm 3 has traditionally been associated with this night of suffering and prayer fleeing from Absalom:

Yahweh! Look! Enemies past counting!
  Enemies sprouting like mushrooms,
Mobs of them all around me, roaring their mockery:
  "Hah! No help for him from God!"

But you, Yahweh, shield me on all sides;
You ground my feet, you lift my head high;
With all my might I shout up to Yahweh,
His answers thunder from the holy mountain.

I stretch myself out. I sleep.
Then I'm up again—rested, tall and steady.
Fearless before the enemy mobs
Coming at me from all sides.

Up, Yahweh! My God, help me!
Slap their faces,
First this cheek, then the other,
Your fist hard in their teeth!

Real help comes from Yahweh.
Your blessing clothes your people!

• • •

AND IN SUFFERING, David recovered compassion—he got in touch with his long-estranged son Absalom. He recovered his extraordinary capacity to love.

Several days had now passed since Absalom's coup and David's flight. A civil war was raging in the country east of the Jordan River. The armies were joined, and David's old military skills were brought out of storage and put to use. He mustered troops and deployed them in thirds. He planned to be in the frontlines, inciting courage, building morale, giving commands. But his military officers urged him to stay behind: "You are worth ten thousand of us," they said; "it is better that you send us help from the city" (2 Sam. 18:3). David accepted their counsel, but he gave them strict and clearly articulated orders regarding Absalom. They were *not* to kill him: "Deal gently for my sake with the young man Absalom" (2 Sam. 18:5).

We come to these words in the story and we're startled. Are we hearing rightly? How did a sentence like that get shaped in David's mouth? David had just been catapulted from a comfortable and honored throne into a harsh and austere wilderness. Only days before he had received one of the biggest shocks of his life: he learned that Absalom for years had been undermining David's rule and David had been oblivious to it. Absalom had been plotting this for a long time, plotting to take over as king and kill his father. And any moment, in that unforgiving wilderness, Absalom's plot might have succeeded. King David was being hunted down by his son just as years before he had been hunted down by Saul. But he had been young during those early years of exile; now he was no longer young—and it was his own son who had turned the country against him and was trying his best to kill him.

As we listen to David ordering his men—"Deal gently for my sake with the young man Absalom"—we know that David's recovery is almost complete. Deep changes were taking place in David as he descended from the heights of Jerusalem down the "Jericho Road" into the wilderness of the Jordan. He was descending the road that a thousand years later Jesus ascended to suffer and die. The topographical parallel is full of suggestiveness to the meditative Christian mind: "The road that goes down is the same road that comes up" (Heraclitus). David had already recovered his sense of who he was, his true self, through the preaching of Shimei; he had recovered his sense of who God was for him, his life of prayer, through the treachery of Ahithophel; and now he recovered his life of compassion, his life of love, through the rejection and scorn of Absalom. The worst rejection of his life precipitated the most wonderful love—love for Absalom.

But David's general, Joab, didn't share his compassion and later in the day killed Absalom. Riding a mule, Absalom was caught in the branches of a tree by his magnificent head of hair (of which he was inordinately proud); he was left hanging when the mule walked on. The first man to find him, respecting David's command, reported to Joab. But Joab, not inhibited for a moment by what he almost certainly construed as a sentimental command, stabbed Absalom viciously. His ten armor-bearers then moved in for the kill and slashed away mercilessly, killing Absalom off with vehemence (18:9–15).

But there was nothing sentimental about David's command; it issued out of a deeply realized recovery of who he was and who God is. It came not from simpering emotions but from rock-hard convictions regarding humility and prayer: the earthiness of David and the livingness of God. Only when David was truly in touch with himself and truly in touch with God was he able to be in touch with Absalom and able again to love.

Loving Absalom that day was one of the most magnificent things David ever did. The fruit of humility and prayer, it gave expression to the Son of David's best and most difficult command, also given in the proximity of his betrayer: "Love one another" (John 3:34–35).

When the report of Absalom's death came to David, he wept. So far had his suffering moved him from the years of hard-hearted rejection to this heartbreaking lament:

> O my son Absalom,
>   my son, my son Absalom!
> Would I had died instead of you,
>   O Absalom, my son, my son!

• • •

IN THIS LAMENT, at the farthest descent from Jerusalem, deep in the wilderness forest of Ephraim, David's story most clearly anticipates and most nearly approximates the gospel story, the story of Jesus that now extends into our stories. Passion stories. Stories of suffering—but suffering that neither diminishes nor destroys us but makes us more human, praying and loving.

THEOLOGY

DAVID AND GOD

2 Samuel 22

Jesus said, "I came so they can have real and eternal
life, more and better life than they ever dreamed of."

—JOHN 10:10

AS THE DAVID STORY gathers to a conclusion, the voice shifts: the story that's been told *about* David now has David stepping forward and speaking—no singing—in his own voice.

Following the practice of generations of David storytellers, I've inserted prayers at certain places in the narration where they struck me as appropriate, giving inner content to the outward events. Now the original storyteller does it, and the prayer that's placed in the story at this valedictory time in David's life is Psalm 18 (placed in the narrative as 2 Samuel 22).[1]

Psalm 18 is a most exuberant prayer. Nothing David prayed gathers more of his life together in one place than does this psalm. One of the Christian church's early pastors, Irenaeus, once said that "the glory of

God is a fully alive human being."[2] David fits the description. Near the center of the psalm David shouts, "By my God I can leap over a wall" (v. 30). It's a praying shout that I like very much—my choice for an epitaph on David's tombstone.

"GOD IS BEDROCK UNDER MY FEET"

> *I love you, God—*
> > *you make me strong.*
> *God is bedrock under my feet,*
> > *the castle in which I live,*
> > *my rescuing knight.*
> *My God—the high crag*
> > *where I run for dear life,*
> > *hiding behind the boulders,*
> > *safe in the granite hideout.*
>
> *I sing to God, the Praise-Lofty,*
> > *and find myself safe and saved.*
>
> *The hangman's noose was tight at my throat;*
> > *devil waters rushed over me.*
> *Hell's ropes cinched me tight;*
> > *death traps barred every exit.*
>
> *A hostile world! I call to God,*
> > *I cry to God to help me.*
> *From his palace he hears my call;*
> > *my cry brings me right into his presence—*
> > *a private audience!*
>
> (VV. 1–7)

The single most characteristic thing about David is God. David believed in God, thought about God, imagined God, addressed God, prayed to God. The largest part of David's existence wasn't David but God.

The evidence for David's pervasive, saturated awareness of God is in his profusion of metaphors: bedrock, castle, knight, crag, boulders, hideout. David was immersed in God. Every visibility revealed for him an invisibility. David named God by metaphor. There's an organic interconnectedness in the comprehensive totality of creation, visible and invisible, "heavens and earth," by means of which everything seen and heard, tasted, touched and experienced, if only followed far enough and deep enough, brings us into the presence of God. Even rocks. *Rock* was one of David's most frequent metaphors for God—arguably his favorite, for he worked many inventive variations on it. But a rock is the furthest thing possible from God. Is there anything lower on the scale of creation than a rock? Yet the extreme unlikeness provoked in David an awareness of likeness. David noticed what was everywhere around him; and the more he noticed, the more he noticed *God.* David was a theologian—a God-noticer, a God-namer—of the best kind, noticing and naming God in the immediacy of revelation and experience.

And virtually everything David noticed and named about God, he prayed. Nothing in or about God was left on the shelf to be considered at a later time or to be brought up for discussion when there was leisure for it. God was personal and present and required *response:* "I love you. . . . I live in you. . . . I run for dear life to you. . . . I sing to you. . . . I cry for help to you." An extraordinarily wide and various range of experience is represented by these praying verbs, but they're identical in their personal immediacy. David knew nothing of God that he didn't pray.

In long retrospect over the Jewish and Christian centuries, it's no exaggeration to say that anything we know about God that's not prayed soon turns bad. The name of God without prayer to God is the stuff of blasphemy. The truth about God without love for God quickly becomes oppression. So-called theologians, whether amateur or professional, who don't pray are in league with the devil. Indeed, the devil can be defined as that species of theologian who knows everything about God but will have nothing to do with him.

David prayed. David prayed the metaphors, prayed the experience, prayed the revelation. Everything that happened to him through prayer became God's salvation within him.

"THE HIGH GOD GAVE A GREAT SHOUT"

Earth wobbles and lurches;
    huge mountains shake like leaves,
Quake like aspen leaves
    because of his rage.
His nostrils flare, bellowing smoke;
    his mouth spits fire.
Tongues of fire dart in and out;
    he lowers the sky.
He steps down;
    under his feet an abyss opens up.
He's riding a winged creature,
    swift on wind-wings.
Now he's wrapped himself
    in a trenchcoat of black-cloud darkness.
But his cloud-brightness bursts through,
    spraying hailstones and fireballs.
Then God thundered out of heaven;
    the High God gave a great shout,
    spraying hailstones and fireballs.
God shoots his arrows—pandemonium!
    He hurls his lightnings—a rout!
The secret sources of ocean are exposed,
    the hidden depths of earth lie uncovered
The moment you roar in protest,
    let loose your hurricane anger.

But me he caught—reached all the way
    from sky to sea; he pulled me out
Of that ocean of hate, that enemy chaos,
    the void in which I was drowning.
They hit me when I was down,
    but God stuck by me.
He stood me up on a wide-open field;
    I stood there saved—surprised to be loved!

(VV. 8–20)

We aren't many lines into this psalm before we recognize the revelational substratum upon which it's being built: this is God's people being rescued from Egypt and worshiping at Sinai, God's Red Sea salvation of his people from Egyptian slavery and his making covenant with them at Sinai. We've read the stories in Exodus, but where does David come up with all these details? We've never read *those* in Exodus. Clearly, David doesn't merely quote the Moses passages; he doesn't simply reference them in order to ground himself in authority; he *imagines* the scenes of the split-asunder sea and the thunder-rocked mountain. He enters the stories not to look for information but in order to become a participant. But he isn't making things up; he's making himself "at home" in the story.

David characteristically uses words magnificently. He uses words to sing and to pray. He uses words to mint reality, fresh and shining. David is a poet—which is to say, he uses words to *make* something, not just talk about something.

God doesn't reveal reality so that we can stand around and look at it as spectators but so that we can enter it and become at home in it. Language is a primary way in which we come to be "at home." As we learn language, we're finding out not so much what's there but where we are; we're learning the neighborhood and finding the words that connect us with what and who is there. Imagination supplies the connections, the continuities, the relationships. Imagination fills in the blanks, reads between the lines. All of us are poets to begin with: we *make* sense of the world with words; we *make* our way with words; we *make* present with words what was absent; we *make* known with words what was unknown. Make, make, make . . . with words. Poets.

Poetry and prayer are natural allies. It's no accident that they're so fused in the person of David. And the millennial consensus that David is so much the archetypal *human* is in no small part a result of this fusion. For prayer is practiced from the perception that the reality of God is immediate and personal; and poetry is the use of language most immediate and personal. The recovery of poetry in our lives goes hand in hand with the recovery of prayer. The fact that David is a poet is as significant in recovering our true humanity as the fact that David prays.[3]

David's prayer and poetry come together in his realization that he himself is included in the revelation: "But me he caught. . . . He stood me up on a wide open field; I stood there saved!" God's action in the past doesn't remain in the past; it becomes present. David is in on it. There's no gap between Moses and David. By faith and in prayer they're contemporaries. Nothing in this gospel life is mere history or mere doctrine; it's all present and available for *living:*

> *Open your mouth and taste, open your eyes and see—*
> > *how good God is.*
> *Blessed are you who run to him.*
>
> (Ps. 34:8)

"GOD REWROTE THE TEXT OF MY LIFE"

And then comes an abrupt change of mood and rhythm in the psalm: reflective, ruminative, meditative. Out of context, this change would mislead us entirely, for there's a tone now of mature and achieved assurance, even arrival, that could easily slip into complacency or be interpreted as self-righteousness. But held firmly between David's participation in God's glorious revelation, which begins the prayer (vv. 1–20), and David's exuberant witness to God's salvation, which concludes it (vv. 21–51), this section can't be misused as a text for a self-congratulating piety.

> *God made my life complete*
> > *when I placed all the pieces before him.*
> *When I got my act together,*
> > *he gave me a fresh start.*
> *Now I'm alert to God's ways;*
> > *I don't take God for granted.*
> *Every day I review the ways he works;*
> > *I try not to miss a trick.*
> *I feel put back together,*
> > *and I'm watching my step.*
> *God rewrote the text of my life*
> > *when I opened the book of my heart to his eyes.*
>
> (VV. 21–25)

For there *are* things we do that make a difference. Character develops, decisions are made, habits are nurtured, attention is trained, commandments are obeyed, and sins are confessed. These aren't the largest part of the Christian life—*who God is* and *what God does* make up by far the largest component—but they're part of it. With the God-context firmly and thoroughly established, we're allowed a glimpse into the dailiness of David's life.

And then, in an even further departure from the Davidic style, these gnomic lines of distilled wisdom:

> *The good people taste your goodness,*
> *The whole people taste your health,*
> *The true people taste your truth,*
> *The bad ones can't figure you out.*
> *You take the side of the down-and-out,*
> *But the stuck-up you take down a peg.*
> (VV. 26–28)

Why does this seem so out of place? Why is it such a surprise to find it here, embedded deep within David's prayer? Simply because it sounds so un-Davidic. David's life is characterized by God's mercy, God's grace, God's love. There's no moral or spiritual symmetry between David and God; it's totally lopsided on the side of God. Unknown David is named and known. Unequipped David is triumphant. Undefended David finds refuge. Undeserving David is forgiven. Unworthy David recovers his kingship.

The David story is a gospel story, God doing for David what David could never do for himself. A sinner saved. It's a story that gets completed in the Jesus story, which features God seeking the sick, the rejected, and the lost.

That's why these morally balanced, wisely observed couplets don't seem to belong here. They seem true enough; not many would argue with them. But there's nothing uniquely Davidic about them, and certainly nothing uniquely Christian about them. It wouldn't surprise us to come across these lines in an old Babylonian or Egyptian archive; it does surprise us to find them in the middle of David's prayer.

But these sentences *are* here, and so we have to ask why. Well, they're here because they describe at least one dimension of the world in which we live—a *moral* world in which the way we live affects (and is affected by) who we are. How we behave and how we think matters. God's grace doesn't exempt us from living in common courtesy. God's initiative doesn't relieve us of the responsibility of getting out of bed in the morning. A bad person doesn't see the same tree that a good person sees. A bad life incapacitates us for real life. There's a vast accumulation of aphorism and insight from every century and civilization that articulates this moral truth. Moral wisdom is no less true for not being at the heart of our humanity. The heart of our humanity is God. But moral appendages, like fingers and toes, can't be dismissed because they're not the heart. And so David's prayer also includes within it this witness to the richly textured moral wisdom common to humankind.

"You Armed Me Well for This Fight"

The reflective interlude is soon over and David is at it again, the somersaulting, cartwheeling exuberance that prays from the center of God's action in his life:

> *Suddenly, God, you floodlight my life;*
>   *I'm blazing with glory, God's glory!*
> *I smash the bands of marauders,*
>   *I vault the highest fences.*
> *What a God! His road*
>   *stretches straight and smooth.*
> *Every God-direction is road-tested.*
>   *Everyone who runs toward him*
> *Makes it.*
>
> *Is there any god like God?*
>   *Are we not at bedrock?*
> *Is not this the God who armed me,*
>   *then aimed me in the right direction?*

Now I run like a deer;
  I'm king of the mountain.
He shows me how to fight;
  I can bend a bronze bow!
You protect me with salvation-armor;
  you hold me up with a firm hand,
  caress me with your gentle ways.
You cleared the ground under me
  so my footing was firm.
When I chased my enemies I caught them;
  I didn't let go till they were dead men.
I nailed them; they were down for good;
  then I walked all over them.
You armed me well for this fight,
  you smashed the upstarts.
You made my enemies turn tail,
  and I wiped out the haters.
They cried "uncle"
  but Uncle didn't come;
They yelled for God
  and got no for an answer.
I ground them to dust; they gusted in the wind.
  I threw them out, like garbage in the gutter.

You rescued me from a squabbling people;
  you made me a leader of nations.
People I'd never heard of served me;
  the moment they got wind of me they listened.
The foreign devils gave up; they came
  on their bellies, crawling from their hideouts.

(VV. 29–46)

David's prayer now becomes a witness to how God has equipped him to do God's work, his kingwork. David in action. David infused with the energy of God, doing the work of God. For one of the supreme glories of the human condition is to be able to work, to go into action. The life of God's Spirit in David enables David's work.

That seems obvious enough. David doesn't withdraw from human society so that he can be alone with God. David does carefully plan and manage his life, however, so that he's not contaminated or frazzled or distracted by the world of work. As he reviews and reflects on his life, and then expresses that life in prayer, he doesn't highlight the times of retreat in the mountains or at lakesides or beside forest streams; rather, he highlights his highly energetic and active life of work. Work isn't a distraction from God but a working out of God in the world.

But when we look at the actual work that David does, we're shocked: David's primary work is war. Most of the work that David exults in doing because God makes it possible for him to do it has to do with killing people. His work world features weapons and fighting.

Throughout the portions of the David story that we've looked at so far this has been quite evident, but there's always been something else more interesting or more important on which to focus our attention—whether prayer, beauty, friendship, suffering, or grace. But the background condition in which virtually everything Davidic takes place is war—war in which David himself is an active participant. How do we handle this paradox: that this quintessentially human life is given to us in the middle of absolutely dehumanizing conditions and that David is a willing—yes, enthusiastic—participant in the dehumanizing, the killing?

We won't get an accurate sense of how the Christian life works if we fail to assess the conditions, or avoid facing the conditions. Conditions: weather, soil, money, racial feelings and class rivalries, tribal traditions and social customs, technology and sex, the kinds of music played and the way language is used and the sorts of stories told. The conditions, for most of us, become assumptions. We absorb these conditions with our mother's milk and rarely, if ever, think about them. Sometimes the conditions are favorable, sometimes unfavorable to being formed in the image of God, but always they're *there*. We don't become Christians in a social or cultural or political vacuum.

Charles Williams, in a brilliant exposition of the coming into being of the Christian community, writes that Jesus was born under three conditions: Roman power, Greek culture, and human sin. Williams convincingly insists that the Holy Spirit, which gave exposition to the life of Jesus in the shifting conditions of the centuries of the church's life, is *always* at work in conditions.[4] It's not that the conditions limit the Spirit's work; instead, our Lord the Spirit chooses to work within the limits. By working within these limits, the Spirit doesn't baptize the conditions—not many Christians look on first-century Palestine, for example, as a golden age. What we understand here is twofold: there are virtually no conditions that preclude the Spirit's work, and the Spirit never works apart from the conditions. God can use any conditions at hand in the making of his Kingdom.

The conditions out of which David's life is lived and narrated are made up in large part of Philistine culture and Canaanite morality—which is to say, violence and sex. The Philistine beer mugs and Canaanite fertility goddesses that archaeologists dig up from old ruins symbolize the two cultures. I can't imagine a more uncongenial time or more unlikely conditions for living a convincingly articulated life to the glory of God—unless, perhaps, ". . . under Pontius Pilate."

And yet, here it is: David—born, living, and dying in Iron Age violence and sex, not exempt from their influence but not confined to them either—in quite incredible ways transcending them so that it's possible, and common, for us to read the story and hardly notice the conditions. But we *must* notice, for we live under conditions that are equally, and similarly, unfavorable. The cultural embodiments of violence and sex, war and promiscuity don't seem to have changed that much. And because they're *human* conditions, they're the only conditions in which a holy life can be lived.

"MY FREE AND FREEING GOD, TOWERING!"

Live, God! Blessings from my Rock,
my free and freeing God, towering!

This God set things right for me
   and shut up the people who talked back.
He rescued me from enemy anger,
   he pulled me from the grip of upstarts,
He saved me from the bullies.

That's why I'm thanking you, God,
   all over the world.
That's why I'm singing songs
   that rhyme your name.
God's king takes the trophy;
   God's chosen is beloved,
I mean David and all his children—
   always.

(VV. 47–51)

There wasn't much of life left unexplored or unattended by David. And always—or at least eventually—the largest part of life for him was God. If we're not adoring, believing, and obeying, we miss out on most of what's right before our eyes. Ignoring or denying God doesn't first of all make us bad; it makes us small—puny and stringy, like the sculptures Giacometti gave to the twentieth century to show what a century of godlessness had done to men and women.

David's, in contrast, was a God-affirming and God-affirmed life, large and expansive—what Jesus named "more and better life than they ever dreamed of" (John 10:10) and what St. Paul called "the immensity of this glorious way of life [God] has for Christians, oh, the utter extravagance of his work in us who trust him" (Eph. 1:19, *The Message*).

David with all his rough edges. He never got around to loving his enemies the way his descendant Jesus would do it; his morals and manners left a lot to be desired. These aren't narrated as blemishes, however, but as conditions that we share. They aren't narrated to legitimize bad behavior but are set down as proof that we don't first become good and then get God. First we get God—and then, over a patient lifetime, we're trained in God's ways.

DEATH

DAVID AND ABISHAG

1 Kings 1–2

Jesus said, "Listen carefully: Unless a grain of wheat is buried in the ground, dead to the world, it is never any more than a grain of wheat. But if it is buried, it sprouts and reproduces itself many times over. In the same way, anyone who holds on to life just as it is destroys that life. But if you let it go, reckless in your love, you'll have it forever, real and eternal."

—JOHN 12:24–25

AND NOW DAVID DIES. No life is complete until there's a death. Death sets limits. To be human is to die. By dying, we attest to our humanity. Death doesn't so much terminate our humanity as prove it.

The original temptation is to try to be like God (Gen. 3:5). The original warning is that if we try it, we'll die (Gen. 3:3). We all try it, and we all die. The death protects and guarantees our humanity. Our attempt to be more than human or other than human (which is the common mark of sin) results in our becoming less than human. In that regard it's death that prevents our complete dehumanization.

And so learning how to live necessarily involves a good deal of meditation on and consideration of death. If we don't give our full attention to death, but spend our lives avoiding the subject and obscuring it with euphemisms, we diminish our lives. Denial of death is avoidance of life.[1] It's significant that in telling us the story of Jesus—a story that has more life in it than any other—the four Gospel Evangelists provide us with far more details about Jesus' dying and death than any other aspect of his life.

DAVID'S DEATH

Forty years before his own death David responded to the deaths of Saul and Jonathan magnificently. When they died on Mount Gilboa in battle with the Philistines, David honored and memorialized their deaths with a most exquisite lament. Death became an occasion for reverence and a witness of his love. David used words to make death large, give it dignity, charge it with a sacred beauty. Men and women who know how to live, as David did, don't avoid facing death.

But when David died, no one at all lamented him, let alone magnificently. He died in the middle of a family squabble, with no hint of either tribute or eulogy. Instead of dying in peace, with his children and wives gathered around him expressing love and gratitude, he was embroiled in a mare's nest of intrigue and deceit. And it wasn't only what others were doing; David himself contributed his share to the general messiness of the occasion. His "last words" were graceless and harsh— he ordered his old enemy, Shimei, whom he had so generously pardoned in years past, to be executed: "[B]ring his gray head down with blood to Sheol" (1 Kings 2:9).

ABISHAG THE SHUNAMMITE

Except for Abishag. Abishag is the one bright spot in the darkness and chaos surrounding David's deathbed. Abishag, in contrast to everyone else at this time, is present only to serve, content only to serve. She has no ambitions to fulfill, nothing she's scheming to get from David. Her only qualifications are nonfunctional: her beauty and her youth.

It's common nowadays to be condescending in regard to Abishag, interpreting her introduction into the story as a desperate attempt by David's loyal servants to restore the aging king's vigor. David is seventy years old; his circulation is sluggish, and the servants can't keep him warm through the night. His interest in life is flagging badly; nothing and no one holds his attention for very long. By bringing a beautiful virgin to be his nurse, serving him and sleeping with him, they hope to infuse David with energy, both royal and sexual. Sexual potency and royal power are seen as linked: if the king is sexually impotent, the country and culture will become spiritually slack and listless.[2] Abishag is thus reduced to a sexual function with political ramifications.

I don't for a moment dispute that these considerations may be present in the story, but I object to the reduction of Abishag to a function. In the story as it's given to us, she's something far more: a witness to the sanctity of death, a sacred presence to David in his dying—and as such a quiet rebuke to the others in the story who respond to David's death as either a problem to be solved, an opportunity to be seized, or a difficulty to be negotiated. We have no record of anything she says, but her very nonspeaking provides the perspective by which we notice each of these other responses for what they are—namely, dehumanizing responses to death.

These three responses continue to be common among us. One of the hardest things about dying is having to deal with people who don't know how to behave in the presence of death, who lose all sense of what it means to be a human being with limits, who under the provocations of death forget how to live and love, who flee from the mystery of death and in so doing desert the dying person. If death doesn't teach us how to live as humans (instead of attempting to be gods), it can only be feared or denied for as long as possible. But if it becomes a way to face limits and define the humanity proper to us, both death and each individual's dying can be accepted and even embraced.

As David is dying, he's deserted in turn by his servants, by his son Adonijah, and by his wife Bathsheba. Yet through each desertion, Abishag remains quietly and beautifully there.

The Servants: "Let a Young Maiden Be Sought"

The servants treat David's death as a problem to be solved. Theirs is perhaps the most understandable of the responses (and the most frequently repeated). Their assignment is to serve the king, and they interpret that assignment now as getting him out of his deathbed and acting again like his old self. They do everything they know how to do, which in this case is piling on more and more blankets. Not the most sophisticated medical treatment, perhaps, but it's the state of the art for them, and they do it.

When that doesn't work, they go looking for a miracle cure. Maybe they've heard anecdotes of beautiful virgins bringing dying old men to life again. Or perhaps some old fertility myths of the Canaanites gave them the idea. At any rate, "beautiful virgin" became their medical treatment of choice, and they went looking. The search turned up Abishag from the village of Shunem in the Jezreel valley.[3] But this treatment also failed: "[T]he king did not know her sexually" (1 Kings 1:4, NRSV).

Twice now the servants have failed to cure David from dying. Each failure turns David into more of a problem that they must deal with. And the more death is dealt with by them as a problem, the more David is a problem. The more problem, the less person. Frustrating. Depersonalizing. The more we deal with death as a problem, the more we—as onlookers—can be useful and "alive," spend our energy and money searching, buying, commanding. Thus involved, we never have to look the dying person in the eyes, wipe her tears, listen to his confession, honor this life, just as it is. The only difference between David's servants and so many of us is that we have more options, more technology, and more incentive to distract us from the person who is dying.[4]

But Abishag, even though failed as a cure, stays on as a person.

ADONIJAH: "I WILL BE KING"

As the oldest of David's sons, Adonijah is in line to succeed him to the throne. But David is taking a long time dying, and Adonijah is impatient. As long as David is alive, he obstructs Adonijah's future. Adonijah wants to be king, has long counted on being king, is impatient to become king. David's dying gets the juices going in Adonijah—it won't be long now!

But David is taking so long to die that Adonijah finally runs completely out of patience. His father, after all, is no longer capable of functioning as king, the country needs leadership, and Adonijah, as eldest surviving son, is doing the only logical and responsible thing by taking charge. He has the support of two of the outstanding and prominent leaders in the kingdom, Abiathar the priest and Joab the general. He proclaims himself king.

His coronation is also a celebration. There's extravagant feasting, with everybody who's anybody invited. David's dying gives Adonijah room, finally, to be himself—to spread his wings, to fulfill his potential. As long as David is king, Adonijah *can't* be king. Year after year Adonijah has felt more and more crowded, restricted, limited. He can't wait to break free of the limitation.

This is the second time this has happened to David. First Absalom, now Adonijah. Both handsome, both ambitious, both pretty much stuck on themselves. And both treating their father as an obstruction to living out their personal destinies. Now it's Adonijah's turn: instead of honoring his father, he forgets about him and proceeds to live out his personal sovereignty as if David were already dead. Absalom tried to kill his father; Adonijah simply ignores him.

Every life is a limitation on my life. Those closest to me limit me most. Children are a limitation; spouses are a limitation; parents are a limitation. These limitations aren't minor inconveniences; they're major and unavoidable conditions in the all-demanding exercise of being human. Given our propensity for wanting to live not as humans but as gods and goddesses, it's quite inevitable that from time to time we fantasize an end to the limitations: death of the other as freedom for the sovereign self.

But it never works out that way: honoring the limits, giving dignity to the death, is what deepens life. Those who take a firm and prayerful stand against the removal of limits know what they're doing: ridding ourselves of inconvenient lives that seem to interfere with *our* living results not in more life for us, but less.[5]

Artists learn to love limits: a poet respects the fourteen-line limit on the sonnet as a form of freedom; a painter respects the limiting frame of the canvas as a check on endless subjectivism and so a freedom to deal with *this* piece of reality; a performing musician respects the limitations of the score as freedom to participate in another and usually larger world of music; a composing musician respects the limits of a key signature in order to be free to explore *that* tonality without interference from all the others.

And men and women learn to respect deaths, both their own and others', as limits, the boundaries of the human. It's *within* these boundaries, not by transgressing them, that we become human.

In treating David's imminent death as an opportunity for a larger life for himself, Adonijah precipitates his own death. In failing to honor David's death, Adonijah hastens his own. Shortly after Adonijah's coronation, David does die, but by then Solomon has been anointed and crowned king by David's orders, and Adonijah is exposed as an opportunistic usurper.

Significantly, the name Abishag here reenters the story. Adonijah, having been let off by Solomon for preempting the throne, is as grasping as ever and shows it by asking that Abishag be given to him as his wife. No one who reads this story imagines for a minute that Adonijah is in love with Abishag herself; he's infatuated with what she stands for. Abishag provides a powerful symbolic link with David—sexuality and royalty, *eros* and *thanatos*. Abishag is a way by which Adonijah might recover prestige among the people, maybe even a means for undermining the reign of Solomon. Solomon recognizes the request for the opportunism that it is and orders Adonijah's execution.

BATHSHEBA: "WHO SHALL SIT ON THE THRONE OF MY LORD THE KING?"

The third response to David's dying that strikes us as less than satisfactory is Bathsheba's. Bathsheba's response isn't wrong in its content as much as in its style and timing, for what Bathsheba does is quite necessary. Her task is to make sure that Solomon succeeds David as king (as, she reminds him, he has so solemnly promised her). The Davidic promise is repeated three times, first from the lips of Nathan, then Bathsheba, and finally David himself (1 Kings 1:13, 17, 30).

There's a strong narrative thread—some think it's the most prominent element in the story as a whole—worked in and out of this tale that focuses on the question, Who will succeed David to the throne? We're now ready for the answer: Solomon.

Bathsheba is only being responsible. What can be wrong with that? Well, nothing as far as *responsible* is concerned. It's the *only* that gives pause. David's dying precipitates Bathsheba into a flurry of legitimate but anxious activity to make sure that David's promise is kept and that his kingdom continues along "Davidic" lines.[6]

Again it's the citing of Abishag's name that alerts us. After Nathan has called Bathsheba's attention to the danger posed by Adonijah, the text tells us, "So Bathsheba went to the king in his room. The king was very old; Abishag the Shunammite was attending to the king" (1 Kings 1:15, NRSV).

David is dying: Abishag is with him, and Bathsheba isn't. Abishag is with him *because* he's dying. Bathsheba *isn't* with him because that's no longer where the action is, and she's a woman of action. And then Nathan lets her know that she needs to go into action with David or both she and Nathan will be out of action for good. The thing that brings Bathsheba to David's deathbed isn't his death as such but responsibilities connected with his death. David has been negligent in taking care of kingdom affairs; David hasn't made out his will. If David dies as is, things will be a mess.

Bathsheba's intervention, guided by Nathan, rouses David to action. He acts kingly once more. He takes care of his affairs, honors his old promise to Bathsheba, gives concise orders for the ceremony of anointing and crowning Solomon, charges Solomon with his responsibilities as *God's* king maintaining the continuities of *God's* revelation, instructs Solomon to take care of unfinished business regarding Joab, Abiathar, and Shimei, and—only then, with his responsibilities carried out—dies.

Responsible Bathsheba makes David responsible. Because of Bathsheba's concern and intervention, the Davidic kingdom continues without interruption into the Solomonic kingdom. Insofar as this is a political story of Solomon's succession to David's throne, it's quite satisfactory. Insofar as it's a theological story of God keeping covenant through the turbulent uncertainties of human sin and by means of sometimes sordid human motives, it's flourishingly brilliant. But as a *David* story—a narration of what we can expect as human beings made in the image of God, saved by the cross of Christ, blessed by the Holy Spirit—it's disappointing. We would have liked a better ending: Bathsheba in lament; Bathsheba in awe before the sacred mystery of death, reading David one of his own psalms.

And yet the plain fact is that many of us will die like this. Death brings out the worst in many people: we'll be treated as a problem to be fixed, or as an opportunity to be seized, or as a responsibility to be carried out and put right. Like David. The David story doesn't trade in illusion and doesn't sentimentalize. The Christian life isn't a romantic idyll, and those who say otherwise deceive us. What we need more than anything is a detailed acquaintance with and feel for the reality of a life that's truly and deeply human, a humanity in which death is both basic experience and pervasive metaphor. This David story as it's given to us does just that, preparing us to live the Jesus life that finally, but only finally, yields to resurrection.

JESUS' DEATH

Well, not quite the last word. Jesus gets that. Jesus praying on the cross, praying a David prayer: "'*Eloi, Eloi, lama sabachthani?*' which means, 'My God, my God, why hast thou forsaken me?'" (Mark 15:34). Jesus, the Son of David, utters his last prayer using the words of David.

Psalm 22 is the prayer. The psalm is in two parts: the first gives voice to the agonies of death; the second part gives the last word to life. Two parts but one psalm, one prayer, one coherent, integrated experience.

First, the detailed exposition of dying—the desperate feelings of loss, the violation of the body, the bewilderment that this is happening to *me,* the feeling of God's absence:

> *God, God . . . my God!*
> > *Why did you dump me*
> > *miles from nowhere?*
> *Doubled up with pain, I call to God*
> > *all the day long. No answer. Nothing.*
> *I keep at it all night, tossing and turning.*
>
> *And you! Are you indifferent, above it all,*
> > *leaning back on the cushions of Israel's praise?*
> *We know you were there for our parents:*
> > *they cried for your help and you gave it;*
> > *they trusted and lived a good life.*
>
> *And here I am, a nothing—an earthworm,*
> > *something to step on, to squash.*
> *Everyone pokes fun at me;*
> > *they make faces at me, they shake their heads:*
> *"Let's see how Yahweh handles this one;*
> > *since God likes him so much, let* him *help him!"*
> *And to think you were midwife at my birth,*
> > *setting me at my mother's breasts!*
> *When I left the womb you cradled me;*
> > *since the moment of birth you've been my God.*
> *Then you moved far away*
> > *and trouble moved in next-door.*
> *I need a neighbor.*
>
> *Herds of bulls come at me,*
> > *the raging bulls stampede,*
> *Horns lowered, nostrils flaring,*
> > *like a herd of buffalo on the move.*

I'm a bucket kicked over and spilled,
   every joint in my body has been pulled apart.
My heart is a blob
   of melted wax in my gut.
I'm dry as a bone,
   my tongue black and swollen.
They have laid me out for burial
   in the dirt.

Now packs of wild dogs come at me;
   thugs gang up on me.
They pin me down hand and foot,
   and lock me in a cage—a bag
Of bones in a cage, stared at
   by every passerby.
They take my wallet and the shirt off my back,
   and then throw dice for my clothes.

You, Yahweh—don't put off my rescue!
   Hurry and help me!
Don't let them cut my throat;
   don't let those mongrels devour me.
If you don't show up soon,
   I'm done for—gored by the bulls,
   meat for the lions.

(VV. 1–21)

This is death and dying in excruciating detail. There isn't a single euphemism. There's no avoidance, no averting of the head, no cover-up. This is the way David anticipated, but Jesus experienced, death. The four Gospel narratives all bring us into the presence of Jesus in the act of dying, making sure we realize that there's nothing we'll face in dying that he hasn't already entered into.

The second part of David's prayer is an exuberant call to praise God, a gathering of friends and family together to participate in and give witness to life:

Here's the story I'll tell my friends when they come to worship,
and punctuate it with Hallelujahs:
Shout Hallelujah, you God-worshipers;
give glory, you sons of Jacob;
adore him, you daughters of Israel.
He has never let you down,
never looked the other way
when you were being kicked around.
He has never wandered off to do his own thing;
he has been right there, listening.

Here in this great gathering for worship
I have discovered this praise-life.
And I'll do what I promised right here
in front of the God-worshipers.
Down-and-outers sit at Yahweh's table
and eat their fill.
Everyone on the hunt for God
is here, praising him.
"Live it up, from head to toe.
Don't ever quit!"

From the four corners of the earth
people are coming to their senses,
are running back to Yahweh.
Long-lost families
are falling on their faces before him.
Yahweh has taken charge;
from now on he has the last word.

All the power-mongers are before him
—worshiping!
All the poor and powerless, too
—worshiping!
Along with those who never got it together
—worshiping!

> *Our children and their children*
> *will get in on this*
> *As the word is passed along*
> *from parent to child.*
> *Babies not yet conceived*
> *will hear the good news—*
> *that God does what he says.*

(VV. 22–31)

This is an incredible witness to life. Can it have been prayed by the same person who gave voice to the death pangs? It can. It was. By David. By Jesus. But Jesus goes David one better: resurrection. A resurrection that we followers of Jesus experience in part *before* we die.[7] We don't have to wait until after we die for resurrection; resurrection is part of *this* life. "Practice resurrection," says poet Wendell Berry.[8] David did.

Jesus knew he was dying long before he actually died. He deliberately set out for Jerusalem knowing that death by crucifixion was being prepared for him. A slow death, full of pain—Psalm 22 pain. All the while he was doing that he exhibited in word and presence a wonderful vitality, beauty, and faith. There were celebrations with hosannas, conversations full of hope and promise, painful confrontations, tender acts of sacrificial love. The imminence of death didn't cancel out the revelation of God in Jesus but rather gave it added poignancy and power. And resurrection confirmed it.

SEEDS OF RESURRECTION

How is a transition like this accomplished? How does David move from cries of desperation to shouts of anticipation? How does Jesus move from crucifixion to resurrection?

There's nothing written in the text of Psalm 22 to account for this— no transitional sentence, no explanation, not even a footnote.

But men and women who pray after the manner of David and live in the name of Jesus find this kind of thing happening all the time: laments poured out and then, without transition, praises erupting. We find ourselves praying in a dark forest—days, weeks, months without a glimmer of light—and then we're out in the clear and the sun is shining. One day we don't have a clue to God or meaning or life, and then we do. We thought he was absent and then realize he's present. Because nothing was said, we thought nothing was done—but it was done silently, hiddenly. That's the way resurrection happens—and it happens a lot.

We get very few explanations in this business. What we do get is life: these silent and hidden pivots in our prayers and our lives are seeds of resurrection.

• • •

ALL THROUGH THE TELLING of David's dying and death, Abishag was silently and persistently present—a witness to the dignity of death. Her name was placed, unobtrusively and without comment, in the context of each attempt to deny or ignore or reduce the large, sacred, and human mystery of death. Abishag, without saying a word, got the last word.

In the story of Jesus' death, the apostles, with one exception (John), were conspicuously absent. But all four Gospel writers make a point of telling us that the women who had followed and served Jesus in his life were there—silently and prayerfully there at his death. And one of them was the first to witness the resurrection.

Notes

Chapter 1: Stories—David and Jesus

1. The Psalms provide the "inside" to the "outside" narrative of 1–2 Samuel. Not all the Psalms were written by David, but many were. Clearly, David prayed, and prayed in every conceivable circumstance. Following a long Jewish and Christian tradition, from time to time I insert a psalm into the story to give witness to this interior dimension. In commenting on Psalm 28, John Calvin wrote, "Let us therefore remember that David is like a mirror, in which God sets before us the continual course of his grace." *Commentary on the Psalms*, vol. 1 (Grand Rapids, MI: Eerdmans, 1949), 474.

2. The preponderance of Christian heresies around the person of Jesus Christ, whom our theologians designated "very God and very man," have involved the diminishing or denial of "very man." (Consider, for example, the Gnostic, Arian, and Apollinarian heresies).

3. From the Nicene Creed.

4. Austin Farrer, *The Triple Victory* (London: Faith Press, 1965), 24.

5. J.I.M. Stewart, ed., *Eight Modern Writers* (Oxford: Oxford University Press, 1963), 107.

6. R. P. Blackmur, *Henry Adams* (New York: Harcourt Brace Jovanovich, 1980), 73.

Chapter 2: Names—David and Samuel

1. The next three sons are named in 1 Chronicles 2:13–15 as Nethanel, Raddai, and Ozem; the seventh, Elihu, is named in 1 Chronicles 27:18. But I much prefer my mother's inventions.

2. Interestingly, though, while the work was menial, the image of *shepherd* was widespread in the ancient East as a symbol for political leadership, particularly kingly leadership. Apparently, it was one of those positions that from a distance it was easy to glamorize—like the cowboy of the North American West. See "Sheep, Shepherds" in *Anchor Bible Dictionary*, vol. 5 (New York: Doubleday, 1992), 1187.

3. Earlier patriarchal patterns are being repeated here—the younger being chosen over the older, reflecting the Lord's sovereign work over against the expectations and plans of people and tradition. In David's case the impact is even stronger, since he's chosen over not one older brother but seven.

4. Ruth 4:18–24 and Matt. 1:5–6.

5. There was, of course, among the Hebrews also an instituted priesthood in Aaron, the Levites, and (later) Zadok. But it is also clearly a *subordinate* priesthood—priests who served a priestly people.

6. "The statement, 'I am a mere layman and not a theologian,' is evidence not of humility but of indolence." Karl Barth, *Church Dogmatics*, IV/3, 871.

7. Eugen Rosenstock-Huessy is one of our most eloquent witnesses to this feature of speech. For instance, "Words classify, but names orient. Words generalize, but names personify. Words dismiss living subjects into the realm of objectivity. Names pick up the little baby or the flower or the sun, and incorporate them into one society of communication. Without names, communication would be impossible." *I Am an Impure Thinker* (Norwich, VT: Argo Books, 1970), 44.

CHAPTER 3: WORK—DAVID AND SAUL

1. See Robert Banks, *God the Worker* (Claremont, CA: Albatross Books, 1992).

2. See George Ernest Wright, *The God Who Acts* (London: SCM Press, 1963).

3. Charles Williams, *Shadows of Ecstasy* (Grand Rapids, MI: Eerdmans, 1965), 60–62.

4. In some ways pastors, priests, and missionaries have it easier in this regard, for they have social reinforcement in recognizing the God-called basis of their work. But the laity must never envy the clergy, because the difficulties that accompany the role-affirmation far exceed the benefits. I've written about these aspects of vocational spirituality in *Under the Unpredictable Plant* (Grand Rapids, MI: Eerdmans, 1992).

CHAPTER 4: IMAGINATION—DAVID AND GOLIATH

1. "Nearly ten feet tall" is the traditional designation. The reduction to seven results from a reading from the Dead Sea Scrolls (4QSam).

2. This assessment of their relationship is based on 16:14–23. The contrasting view in 17:55–58 is a puzzle. Since these verses aren't found in the Greek translation (the Septuagint), many scholars conclude that they weren't part of the original text but were added by a later writer. See Ralph W. Klein, *I Samuel,* vol. 10 of *Word Biblical Commentary* (Waco, TX: Word, 1983), 172–175.

3. Isaac Pennington, quoted in *Quaker Spirituality*, ed. Douglas Steere (New York: Paulist Press, 1984), 155.

4. David's running frames the concluding scene: "David ran quickly toward the battle line . . . " (v. 48); "then David ran and stood over the Philistine" (v. 51).

CHAPTER 5: FRIENDSHIP—DAVID AND JONATHAN

1. Douglas Steere, *Together in Solitude* (New York: Crossroad, 1982), 31ff.

2. William Butler Yeats, "Why Should Not Old Men Be Mad?" *The Poems of W. B. Yeats: A New Edition,* edited by Richard J. Finneran (New York: Simon & Schuster, 1940).

3. Walter Brueggemann, *I and II Samuel* (Louisville: John Knox Press, 1990), 145. Brueggemann further comments on the episode:

> It is helpful to compare this scene with 10:9–10. We do not have any access to the psychological phenomenon of these scenes, even though scholars continue to probe such matters. What is probably most important in these two episodes is their literary placement and the place they have in the larger narrative. What is obvious and surely intentional is that 10:9–13 is placed at the very beginning of Saul's career, when he has been anointed and authorized as king. The rush of the spirit so

evident then was taken affirmatively to assert that Saul is indeed energized and authorized by God's power, which is larger than himself.

Conversely, in chapter 19 Saul is presented as the would-be killer of God's chosen. The second episode with the spirit signals the end of Saul's career. That career will be awhile winding down, but the narrator wants us to see that Saul is, in fact, finished.

CHAPTER 6: SANCTUARY—DAVID AND DOEG

1. The best exposition of this subject from the side of human experience is Rudolph Otto, *The Idea of the Holy* (London: Oxford University Press, 1924).

2. *Holy the Firm* (New York: HarperCollins, 1977), 72–73. Facing the worst kind of pain and entertaining the most relentless and unanswerable questions, she exclaims,

> Hoopla! All that I see arches, and light arches around it. The air churns out forces and lashes the marveling land. A hundred times through the fields and along the deep roads I've cried Holy. I see a hundred insects moving across the air, rising and falling. Chipped notes of birdsong descend from the trees, tuneful and broken; the notes pile about me like leaves. Why do these molded clouds make themselves overhead innocently changing, trailing their flat blue shadows up and down everything, and passing, and gone? Ladies and gentlemen! You are given insects, and birdsong, and a replenishing series of clouds. The air is buoyant and wholly transparent, scoured by grasses. The earth stuck through it is noisome, lighted, and salt. Who shall ascend into the hill of the Lord? or who shall stand in his holy place? "Whom shall I send," heard the first Isaiah, "and who will go for us?" And poor Isaiah, who happened to be standing there—and there was no one else—burst out, "Here I am; send me."

3. P. Kyle McCarter, Jr., *I Samuel,* vol. 8 of *Anchor Bible* (Garden City, NY: Doubleday, 1980), 350.

4. John Calvin, *Commentary on the Psalms,* vol. 2 (Grand Rapids, MI: Eerdmans, 1949), 311.

CHAPTER 7: WILDERNESS—DAVID AT EN-GEDI

1. St. Anthony of Egypt is the most prominent name in early desert spirituality. His story was written by his friend Athanasius, a pastor and theologian, in the fourth century. A contemporary witness to the still-living tradition is offered by poet Kathleen Norris in her book *Dakota: A Spiritual Geography* (New York: Ticknor & Fields, 1993).

2. "What I want to speak for is not so much the wilderness uses, valuable as those are, but the wilderness *idea,* which is a resource in itself. Being an intangible and spiritual resource, it will seem mystical to the practical-minded—but then anything that cannot be moved by a bulldozer is likely to seem mystical to them." Wallace Stegner, *The Sound of Mountain Water* (Lincoln: University of Nebraska Press, 1980), 146.

3. Quoted by John McPhee, *Encounters with the Archdruid* (New York: Farrar, Straus, & Giroux, 1971), 84.

4. From "Inversnaid," by Gerard Manley Hopkins, in W. H. Gardner and N. H. Mackenzie, eds., *The Poems of Gerard Manley Hopkins,* fourth ed. (Oxford: Oxford University Press, 1970), 89.

5. Johannes Botterweck and Helmer Ringgren, eds., *Theological Dictionary of the Old Testament,* vol. 5 (Grand Rapids, MI: Eerdmans, 1986), 74–75.

6. Psalm 142 is also connected with David when he was in "the cave." There are two "cave" experiences in the David story: the first at Adullam (1 Sam. 22:1), the second here at En-gedi. Both caves provide interpretive stimulus to those of us who live Davidic lives and pray the Psalms.

CHAPTER 8: BEAUTY—DAVID AND ABIGAIL

1. In Eastern Orthodox spirituality the icon is a kind of painting, highly stylized, that's exclusively devoted to prayer and worship.

2. In 16:12 and 17:42 he's called *yaphah;* the same word is used here to describe Abigail.

3. "The Orthodox mind believes in a 'salvific beauty,' a beauty that radiates from the Godhead itself and draws us in with its grace." Anthony Ugolnik, *The Illuminating Icon* (Grand Rapids, MI: Eerdmans, 1989), 187.

4. Unless, of course, we cultivate a snobbish "aesthetic" detachment and join the modern and widespread anti-Christian heresy of "art for art's sake," which sacrilegiously violates what it pretends to admire.

5. Ugolnik, *The Illuminating Icon,* 188.

6. Caleb is an honored name in Israel (see especially Num. 13–14), but Nabal's character brings dishonor to it; the name is turned into a pun in 25:3: giving the sense in Hebrew as "a real Calebite dog." See Hertzberg, *I and II Samuel* (Philadelphia: Westminster Press, 1964), 199.

7. Psalm 37 also has a long history of being read in the context of this story.

CHAPTER 9: COMPANY—DAVID AT ZIKLAG

1. See *Anchor Bible Dictionary,* vol. 3, "Habiru/hapiru (New York: Doubleday, 1992), 6–10.

2. See W. G. Blaikie, *The First Book of Samuel* (London: Hodder & Stoughton, 1902), 402:

> It was to all appearance a time of spiritual declension; and as distrust ruled his heart, so dissimulation ruled his conduct. It could hardly have been other than a time of merely formal prayers and comfortless spiritual experience. If he would but have allowed himself to believe it, he was far happier in the cave of Adullam or the wilderness of Engedi, when the candle of the Lord shone upon his head, than he was afterwards amid the splendour of the palace of Achish, or the princely independence of Ziklag.

3. Brueggemann, *I and II Samuel,* 199.

4. See Hans Hertzberg, *I and II Samuel* (Philadelphia: Westminster Press, 1964), 224:

> Although the actual words do not say as much, we have here a section which is concerned with God's dealings with David. This chapter occupies a prominent place among the many indications of the way in which the Lord protected and guided the future king during his greatest time of need. Even the mistrust of the Philistines is worked into the plans of the God of Israel. "David's deliverance here is remarkable. He is protected from himself and from the unfaithfulness to his calling by the enemies of the Lord" (H. Asmussen).

5. I think it's an excellent exercise in biblical realism to mentally rename whatever church we attend "Ziklag Church." I encourage the exercise wherever I can get a hearing: Ziklag Anglican, Ziklag Methodist, Ziklag Presbyterian, Ziklag Roman Catholic.

6. In sixty-three years I've worshiped and worked in and sometimes for eleven Christian congregations. They've all fit the basic profile of Ziklag. I was pastor to one of these companies for thirty years and thought I could beat the odds and organize something more along the lines

of Eden, or better yet New Jerusalem. But sinners kept breaking and entering and insisting on baptism, defeating all my utopian fantasies.

7. From "Inversnaid," by Gerard Manley Hopkins, in W. H. Gardner and N. H. Mackenzie, eds., *The Poems of Gerard Manley Hopkins,* fourth ed. (Oxford: Oxford University Press, 1970), 90.

CHAPTER 10: GENEROSITY—DAVID AT THE BROOK BESOR

1. Quoted by Ralph Harper, *On Presence* (Philadelphia: Trinity Press International, 1991), 62.

2. Earlier topographers located the Brook Besor twenty-five miles from Ziklag. Recent site identifications put it at twelve to fifteen miles. See McCarter, *I Samuel,* 435.

3. But it wasn't as if they didn't have any responsible part in it. Guarding the supplies was an acknowledged part of military operations, noted earlier in the Goliath story (1 Sam. 17:22) and the Nabal incident (1 Sam. 25:13).

4. "Besor" probably means "good news" or "gospel." See Hertzberg, *I and II Samuel,* 227.

5. Baron Frederick von Hugel, *Letters to a Niece* (London: J. M. Dent & Sons, Ltd., 1928), 64.

6. Quoted in Monroe K. Spears' *The Poetry of W. H. Auden* (New York: Oxford University Press, 1968), 136.

7. Augustine, *The City of God* (Garden City, NY: Image Books, 1958), 78.

CHAPTER 11: GRIEF—DAVID IN LAMENT

1. Flannery O'Connor, *Mystery and Manners* (New York: Farrar, Straus, & Giroux, 1979), 34.

2. C. S. Lewis, *The Four Loves* (London: Geoffrey Bles, 1960), 91.

3. By using the adjective *spiritual,* Lewis, I think, is calling attention to the fact that friendship is the "least *natural* of loves; the least instinctive, organic, biological, gregarious and necessary" (Lewis, *The Four Loves,* 70). Furthermore: "Friendship is unnecessary, like philosophy, like art, like the universe itself (for God did not need to create). It has no survival value; rather it is one of those things which give value to survival" (84).

4. Gerald May is a perceptive guide in understanding the spiritual dimensions of this culturally sanctioned sin. See *Addiction and Grace* (San Francisco: HarperCollins, 1990).

5. Two contemporary Davidic lamentations that kept their authors (and can help keep us) *in* the story are Nicholas Woltersdorf, *Lament for a Son* (Grand Rapids, MI: William B. Eerdmann, 1987), and Luci Shaw, *God in the Dark* (Grand Rapids, MI: Zondervan, 1989).

CHAPTER 12: BONEHEADS—DAVID AND THE SONS OF ZERUIAH

1. T. S. Eliot, "Murder in the Cathedral," *The Complete Poems and Plays* (New York: Harcourt Brace & Company, 1935), 196.

CHAPTER 13: GROWTH—DAVID AND JERUSALEM

1. See P. Kyle McCarter, Jr., *II Samuel,* vol. 9 of *Anchor Bible* (Garden City, NY: Doubleday, 1984), 138.

2. An alternate and influential contemporary exegetical solution to this difficult passage is that David doesn't want to end up with a hospital on his hands, a city of wounded wretches. McCarter paraphrases David's words: "Whoever strikes down a Jebusite must deal a fatal blow, for otherwise the city will be filled with mutilated men whom we have wounded but not slain. . . . " He understands the remark as reflecting "religious scruples against the mutilation

of living human beings, a violation of the sanctity of the body to which David finds killing preferable." See McCarter, *II Samuel*, 137–140.

3. Thomas Merton is one of the most famous converts to the Christian faith in the twentieth century. It's hard to imagine a more radical change of life: from a dissolute, gregarious, avant garde New York intellectual to a Trappist monk in a Kentucky monastery. His former friends couldn't imagine what he must have become, but they speculated. After thirteen years Mark van Doren, his literature professor, visited and then reported back to the "world": "[O]f course he looked a little older; but as we sat and talked I could see no important difference in him, and once I interrupted a reminiscence of his by laughing. 'Tom,' I said, 'you haven't changed at all.' 'Why would I? Here,' he said, 'our duty is to be more ourselves, not less.' It was a searching remark and I stood happily corrected." Monica Furlong, *Merton: A Biography* (San Francisco: HarperCollins, 1980), 225.

CHAPTER 14: RELIGION—DAVID AND UZZAH

1. The Psalms of Ascent, Psalms 120 through 134, use the imagery of pilgrim ascent to Jerusalem worship to describe the life of faith. I've written an exposition of these psalms as a manual for Christian discipleship in *A Long Obedience in the Same Direction* (Downers Grove, IL: InterVarsity, 1980).

2. The exact dimensions: two and a half cubits in length (about forty-five inches), a cubit and a half in breadth and height (about twenty-seven inches). See Exodus 25:10.

3. The relevant texts are Deuteronomy 10:8; Exodus 25:13–14 and 37:4–5; and 1 Chronicles 15:12–15.

4. Alexander Whyte, *Bible Characters* (Edinburgh: Oliphant, Anderson & Ferrier, 1900), 172.

5. See Hans Urs von Balthesar, *The Glory of the Lord*, vol. 2 (San Francisco: Ignatius Press, 1984), 75.

CHAPTER 15: SOVEREIGN GRACE—DAVID AND NATHAN

1. There's a later echo of this divine no that opens up a gospel yes in Paul's plan for missionary work in Bythinia, which was replaced by the invitation to enter Europe. See Acts 16:6–10.

2. Martin Buber's seminal book *I and Thou* demonstrates the vast implications that this seemingly small item of grammar has for the way we understand God and ourselves, for the way we live our lives. *I and Thou*, trans. Walter Kauffman (New York: Scribner, 1970).

3. Walter Brueggemann, *I and II Samuel* (Louisville: John Knox Press, 1990), 253.

CHAPTER 16: LOVE—DAVID AND MEPHIBOSHETH

1. His birth name was probably Meribaal (see 1 Chron. 9:40). Mephibosheth may well have been a name others gave him, calling attention to his victimized life, and the nickname stuck. But this is conjecture; the difficulties of determining the actual name and its meanings are laid out in careful detail by McCarter, *II Samuel*, 124–125.

2. Even though abundantly reported, this isn't always readily apparent, and so I find it useful to surround myself with corroborating voices. Here's one of which I'm particularly fond:

> Few things are more disconcerting than the oft-recurring phenomenon of high ideals and fine and subtle speculations upon the nature of God and of the spiritual life—much devotion too, and even austerity—in combination with an almost total insensibility to the duty of charity to others. In such persons one is sometimes

bewildered to find a sort of contempt for this realized charity, as if it were an inferior, elementary, unintelligent kind of thing. Or perhaps, by a remarkable obliquity of judgment, they will consider that their superior perceptions somehow absolve them from deference to this Commandment, or at least from anything so coarse as putting it into vulgar practice. But though one may be a competent art critic without having ever handled a brush or a chisel, and may legitimately pass judgment upon a book which one could not have written oneself, in the life of the soul there are no such privileges: there is no knowledge at all unless it is also and equally action, and if it is not that, then it is worse than ignorance.

See John Baillis, *A Diary of Ressling* (New York: Charles Scribner's Sons, 1955), Day 9.

3. "Mephibosheth's response is crafted in a peculiarly delicate way. It could be that he is genuine in his allegiance to David, or it could be that he is only expedient. The words themselves do not give us certainty on the matter. The narrative wants us to experience the uncertainty that David has to adjudicate." Brueggemann, *I and II Samuel,* 327.

CHAPTER 17: SIN—DAVID AND BATHSHEBA

1. I owe these observations on the narrative use of *send* in this passage to Old Testament scholar Walter E. Brown in a private communication (December 10, 1995).

2. Traditionally, there are seven psalms designated "penitential"—prayers particularly useful for "praying our sin" (Psalms 6, 32, 38, 51, 102, 130, 143). When Augustine was dying and confined to his bed, he had the seven "sin" psalms inscribed on the ceiling of his room so that he could have them before him as his "last words." This isn't morbid, as some have supposed, but an exercise of lively joy in what God does best: graciously forgive sins, gloriously save sinners.

3. Because English translations vary in how they render these words, I'm making my count from the Hebrew text.

4. From "God's Grandeur," by Gerard Manley Hopkins, in W. H. Gardner and N. H. Mackenzie, eds., *The Poems of Gerard Manley Hopkins,* fourth ed. (Oxford: Oxford University Press, 1970), 61.

CHAPTER 18: SUFFERING—DAVID AND ABSALOM

1. John Henry Newman, "Lead, Kindly Light," *Hymnbook* (Philadelphia: United Presbyterian Church, 1955), no. 331.

2. I've sometimes fantasized a collection of *Best Iron Age Sermons,* in which sermons by Nathan and Shimei appear side by side.

3. Ahithophel was also the grandfather of Bathsheba. Old resentments against David's treatment of his granddaughter may very well have contributed to the defection.

CHAPTER 19: THEOLOGY—DAVID AND GOD

1. Psalm 18 and 2 Samuel 22 are virtually the same. There are a few instances when the wording varies slightly, there are some minor variations in spelling, and the verse numbering differs because of an introductory sentence in Samuel. Where the texts diverge, I've followed the Samuel reading; I've also followed that source's verse numbering.

2. Irenaeus was a pastor in Lyons, France, in the late second century. The quoted sentence comes from *Against Heresies.* See Adolph Hamask, *History of Dogma,* vol. 2 (New York: Dover Publications, 1961), 269.

3. Most men and women in North America today are equally uneasy with poetry and prayer. Insofar as we let the culture depersonalize us—turn us into nonrelational technicians and consumers—we lose our capacity for intimacy both in language (poetry) and before God (prayer). The recovery of either prayer or poetry doesn't guarantee the recovery of the other, but it certainly encourages it.

4. Charles Williams, *Descent of the Dove* (Grand Rapids, MI: William B. Eerdmans, 1939).

CHAPTER 20: DEATH—DAVID AND ABISHAG

1. Poet Galway Kinnell comments, "Many think we should forget about death. Much of contemporary culture is devoted to helping us do this. But I like what Hegel says: 'the life of the spirit is not frightened at death and does not keep itself pure of it. It lives with death and maintains itself in it.'" *Walking Down the Stairs* (Ann Arbor: University of Michigan Press, 1978), 24.

2. The most powerful and complex contemporary rendition of this way of thinking is found in T. S. Eliot's long poem "The Waste Land" (1922), in which he wove the threads of spiritual, cultural, and sexual sterility into a tapestry that revealed a dying civilization. His later poems, especially "Four Quartets," became for our century perhaps what Abishag was for David—a witness through beauty to life. A recovery of potency, but not through brandishing power. See T. S. Eliot, *The Complete Poems and Plays* (New York: Harcourt, Brace, 1958).

3. This village turns up later as the home of the woman whose son Elisha restored to life (2 Kings 4:12ff), and it's very close to the village of Nain, where Jesus restored the widow's son to life (Luke 7:11); both stories combine the elements of youth and death.

4. These four verses of text may seem a meager soapbox from which to speak, but there's so much of this kind of stuff going under the cover of "science" and "compassion" that nearly any text serves as a pretext. Ernest Becker's *The Denial of Death* (New York: The Free Press, 1973) is a brilliant and thoroughgoing analysis and exposition of the ways in which the sacrilege and trivialization of death occur in our culture.

5. Abortion at one end of the life spectrum, euthanasia at the other, and murder anywhere in between are the commonest attempts at this "removal of limitations," but there seem to be plenty of other ways to accomplish the same thing through both subtle and blatant species of abandonment, abuse, desertion, and avoidance.

6. We're given clear indications through the narrative that under Adonijah the kingdom would have been quite a different one, even as Absalom's would have been: no longer would there have been any prayers or hymns saying, "God is king!" All theology would have given way to the royal ego.

7. St. Paul, without diminishing in any way the significance of the final resurrection of the Christian, asserts that resurrection is at the core of our present living. For instance, "If the Spirit of him who raised Jesus from the dead dwells in you, he who raised Christ from the dead will give life to your mortal bodies also through his Spirit that dwells in you" (Rom. 8:11).

8. Wendell Berry, "Manifesto: The Mad Farmer Liberation Front," in *The Collected Poems* (San Francisco: North Point Press, 1985), 152.

Steps to Peace with God

Step 1   God's Purpose: Peace and Life

God loves you and wants you to experience peace and life—abundant and eternal.

The Bible Says . . .

". . . we have peace with God through our Lord Jesus Christ." Romans 5:1

"For God so loved the world that He gave His only begotten Son, that whoever believes in Him should not perish but have everlasting life." John 3:16

". . . I have come that they may have life, and that they may have it more abundantly." John 10:10b

Since God planned for us to have peace and the abundant life right now, why are most people not having this experience?

Step 2   Our Problem: Separation

God created us in His own image to have an abundant life. He did not make us as robots to automatically love and obey Him, but gave us a will and a freedom of choice.

We chose to disobey God and go our own willful way. We still make this choice today. This results in separation from God.

Our choice results in separation from God.

The Bible Says . . .

"For all have sinned and fall short of the glory of God." Romans 3:23

"For the wages of sin is death, but the gift of God is eternal life in Christ Jesus our Lord." Romans 6:23

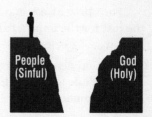

Our Attempts

There is only one remedy for this problem of separation.

Through the ages, individuals have tried in many ways to bridge this gap . . . without success . . .

The Bible Says . . .

"There is a way that seems right to man, but in the end it leads to death." Proverbs 14:12

"But your iniquities have separated you from God; and your sins have hidden His face from you, so that He will not hear." Isaiah 59:2

Step 3 God's Remedy: The Cross

Jesus Christ is the only answer to this problem. He died on the Cross and rose from the grave, paying the penalty for our sin and bridging the gap between God and people.

The Bible Says . . .

". . . God is on one side and all the people on the other side, and Christ Jesus, Himself man, is between them to bring them together . . ." 1 Timothy 2:5

"For Christ also has suffered once for sins, the just for the unjust, that He might bring us to God . . ." 1 Peter 3:18a

"But God demonstrates His own love for us in this: While we were still sinners, Christ died for us." Romans 5:8

God has provided the only way . . . we must make the choice . . .

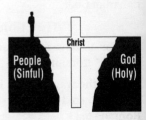

Step 4 | Our Response: Receive Christ

We must trust Jesus Christ and receive Him by personal invitation.

The Bible Says . . .

"Behold, I stand at the door and knock. If anyone hears My voice and opens the door, I will come in to him and dine with him, and he with Me." Revelation 3:20

Are you here . . . or here?

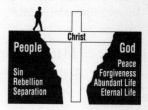

"But as many as received Him, to them He gave the right to become children of God, even to those who believe in His name." John 1:12

". . . if you confess with your mouth the Lord Jesus and believe in your heart that God has raised Him from the dead, you will be saved." Romans 10:9

Is there any good reason why you cannot receive Jesus Christ right now?

How to receive Christ:

1. Admit your need (I am a sinner).
2. Be willing to turn from your sins (repent).
3. Believe that Jesus Christ died for you on the Cross and rose from the grave.
4. Through prayer, invite Jesus Christ to come in and control your life through the Holy Spirit. (Receive Him as Lord and Savior.)

What to Pray:

Dear Lord Jesus,

I know that I am a sinner and need Your forgiveness. I believe that You died for my sins. I want to turn from my sins. I now invite You to come into my heart and life. I want to trust and follow You as Lord and Savior.

In Jesus' name. Amen.

_____   _____
Date   Signature

God's Assurance:
His Word

If you prayed this prayer,
The Bible Says...

"For 'whoever calls upon the name of the Lord will be saved.'"
Romans 10:13

Did you sincerely ask Jesus Christ to come into your life? Where is He right now? What has He given you?

"For it is by grace you have been saved, through faith—and this is not from yourselves, it is the gift of God—not by works, so that no one can boast." Ephesians 2:8,9

The
Bible Says...

**"He who has the Son has life; he who does not have the Son of God does not have life. These things I have written to you who believe in the name of the Son of God, that you may know that you have eternal life, and that you may continue to believe in the name of the Son of God."
1 John 5:12–13, NKJV**

Receiving Christ, we are born into God's family through the supernatural work of the Holy Spirit who indwells every believer...this is called regeneration or the "new birth."

This is just the beginning of a wonderful new life in Christ. To deepen this relationship you should:

1. Read your Bible every day to know Christ better.
2. Talk to God in prayer every day.
3. Tell others about Christ.
4. Worship, fellowship, and serve with other Christians in a church where Christ is preached.
5. As Christ's representative in a needy world, demonstrate your new life by your love and concern for others.

God bless you as you do.

Billy Graham

If you want further help in the decision you have made, write to:
Billy Graham Evangelistic Association P.O. Box 779, Minneapolis, Minnesota 55440-0779